NT Server 4
The Cram Sheet

This Cram Sheet contains the distilled, key facts about Windows NT Server 4. Review this information last thing before you enter the test room, paying special attention to those areas where you feel you need the most review. You can transfer any of these facts from your head onto a blank piece of paper before beginning the exam.

INSTALLATION

1. Know these WINNT and WINNT32 switches:

   - **/O** Creates boot floppies after install with /X or /B switches. Only builds boot floppies.

   - **/OX** Creates boot floppies for CD-ROM or floppy-based installation.

   - **/X** Installs NT without creating the Setup boot floppies.

   - **/B** Installs NT without making or using Setup boot floppies.

2. When upgrading an existing version of NT, the following information stays intact:

   - Any edits made to the Registry using Registry Editor

   - Custom program groups, desktop layout, setting, and Control Panel preferences

   - Local security accounts (users and groups)

   - Network adapter, protocol, service configurations, and addresses (including Mac and RAS)

   - Preferences for Accessories and Administrative Tools

3. You cannot change server roles between member server and domain controller (PDC or BDC), or vice versa, without reinstalling NT.

DISK MANAGEMENT

4. Network Client Administrator creates installation and startup disks for these operating systems:

   - Network Client 3.0 for MS-DOS
   - LAN Manager 2.2c for MS-DOS
   - LAN Manager 2.2c for OS/2
   - Windows for Workgroups 3.11

5. Review Disk Administrator menus and options (Table 4.1, page 79).

6. Only primary partitions can be active: Select Mark Active from the Partition menu in Disk Administrator.

FILE SYSTEMS AND FAULT TOLERANCE

7. Vital statistics for FAT and NTFS:

	FAT	NTFS
Maximum volume size	2 GB	16 EB
Maximum file size	2 GB	16 EB
File-level security	No	Yes
Long file name support	No	Yes
Self-repairing	No	Yes
Transaction logging capabilities	No	Yes
File-level compression	No	Yes

PRINTING

31. DLC or LPR must be installed to enable communication with network-attached printers.

32. To fix a stalled print spooler, select Services in Control Panel, stop Spooler Service, then restart it.

33. For a printer pool, all devices must connect to same print server and all printers should be identical.

34. Only Windows 95 and NT clients can use print drivers on NT print server.

NETWARE

35. NWLink default frame type (auto) detection usually works OK, but some Ethernet adapters won't work with this setting. To communicate with older NetWare versions, manually enter all frame types.

36. Always consider frame type mismatch when NT and NetWare (v3.12 and older) can't interact.

37. To give NetWare clients NT access, install FPNW and NWLink. NWLink works without NetWare, too.

38. GSNW lets MS Network clients (Windows 3.x, 95, NT Workstation/Server) access NetWare resources.

39. Use the NWCONV.EXE utility to migrate NetWare users, groups, and resources to Windows NT.

40. WINS maps computer names to IP addresses and reduces broadcast traffic on network.

41. Important RAS facts:

- RAS supports PPP dialup clients only (not SLIP).
- RAS supports up to 256 incoming connections.
- NetBIOS gateway on server sustains standard NT network operations for PPP-attached clients.
- RAS supports IP and IPX routing.
- RAS supports PPTP and Multilink PPP.
- RAS supports NetBIOS, NetBEUI gateway, and Windows Sockets applications.

42. RAS connection security settings are managed using the Security tab of the phonebook entry for outbound links and the Network Protocol Configuration dialog box for inbound links.

43. Put LMHOSTS files on RAS clients. Entries use #PRE tag to cache IP addresses locally, which speeds access.

44. RAS maintains a list of WAN resources. When resources are referenced, RAS attempts to AutoDial to regain the WAN connection.

45. Performance Monitor displays server characteristics. All data is viewable in Chart, Alert, and Report views.

46. Define administrative alerts by selecting Alert from the Options menu in Performance Monitor.

47. Look at Memory: Pages/Second to decide whether more RAM is needed.

48. The Performance Monitor Log option collects data to file to view later.

**Certification
Insider** Press

Resides in the root directory of the system partition. (Required for NT boot floppy.)

- **BOOTSECT.DOS** MS-DOS boot sector file: Used if NTLDR permits boot to some other Microsoft OS like DOS or Windows 95. Resides in the root directory of system partition. (Not required.)

- **NTDETECT.COM** PC hardware detection: Reads device and config info before Windows NT boots. Resides in the root directory of system partition. (Required for NT boot floppy.)

- **NTLDR** OS loader program: Loads Windows NT or other designated OS. Relinquishes control once loading completes. Resides in the root directory of a system partition. (Required for NT boot floppy.)

- **NTOSKRNL.EXE** Executable file for Windows NT OS: Includes all basic capabilities and items necessary to establish runtime environment. Resides in \Winnt_root\system32 on boot partition.

- **OSLOADER.EXE** RISC OS loader: Provides services and info equal to NTDETECT.COM, BOOTSECT.DOS, NTDETECT.COM, and NTLDR on PCs. Resides in the RISC boot PROM area.

- **NTBOOTDD.SYS** Used when system or boot SCSI drive has BIOS disabled. Replaces BIOS functions with software driver. Resides in the root directory of system partition.

23. ARC name information:

- **scsi(*) or multi(*)** Most ARC names begin with multi(*); scsi(*) appears only when SCSI has BIOS disabled. Multi(*) applies to IDE, EIDE, ESDI, and SCSI (where BIOS enabled). (*) indicates the address of the hardware adapter. Numbers start at zero, with controller seated closest to slot 0 in PC.

- **disk(*)** Applies only when scsi(*) keyword appears. Then, the value of (*) indicates SCSI bus ID, starting with zero, for drive where files reside. If multi(*) appears, disk(*) is always disk(0).

- **rdisk(*)** Applies only when multi(*) keyword appears. It indicates SCSI logical unit number (LUN) for the drive. Numbering begins with zero, so the first drive in the chain is named rdisk(0), the second is named rdisk(1), and so on.

- **partition(*)** Indicates the disk partition that contains designated files. Unlike other ARC numbering, partition numbers start at one, so the first partition is partition(1), the second partition(2), and so on.

- **\path** Indicates the directory on the partition for OS files. Default path for Windows NT is \winnt.

24. The ERD process often corrects boot sector problems. Otherwise, replace NTLDR or repair NTOSKRNL.

DOMAIN CONTROLLERS, TRUSTS, LOGINS, PROFILES, POLICIES

25. To promote BDC to PDC:

Launch Server Manager and select Promote To Primary Domain Controller from the Computer menu. Finally, confirm the promotion.

26. To allow workstations to log onto a domain:

(1) Add the computer names of all domain workstations using Server Manager.

(2) Add user accounts using User Manager for Domains.

(3) Configure each workstation to use the new domain within the Network applet.

27. Trusts between domains are one-way only. A two-way trust = two one-way trusts between domains.

28. User profiles are located in <WINNT Root>\Profiles\<Username> directories.

29. The default export directory for logon scripts on domain controllers is Winnt\System32\Repl\Export\Scripts.

30. To manage Windows NT Server shares remotely, use Server Manager, not Windows NT Explorer.

8. Use FAT for 50 MB partitions or smaller and NTFS for partitions 400 MB or larger.

9. Rules for Permissions on NTFS Move and Copy operations:

- If you move files within the same NTFS partition, they *retain* original permissions.
- If you create, copy, or move files from one NTFS partition to another, they *inherit* parent folder permissions.
- All NTFS permissions disappear when files are moved or copied from NTFS to FAT.

10. Convert FAT partitions into NTFS using CONVERT.EXE; HPFS is not supported in Windows NT 4.

11. NTBACKUP features and functions:

- Do not back up temp files.
- Back up the Registry on PDC and all BDCs.
- NTBACKUP cannot back up the Registry across the network.

12. About disk striping with parity:

- All partitions in set must be equal sizes (or close)
- Partitions must be on different physical disks
- Can be implemented with NTFS or FAT
- 3 drives minimum; 32 drives maximum
- Slower than striping without parity, faster than mirroring

13. If one drive in a set fails, missing data can be rebuilt from remaining devices and parity info.

14. If you lose a member of a volume set or stripe set without parity, everything is lost.

15. RAID levels and details:

Type	Fault	Speed Tolerant?	Includes
RAID 0	No	Fastest	Disk striping without parity, volume sets
RAID 1	Yes	Slowest RAID	Disk mirroring (slower), disk duplexing (faster)
RAID 5	Yes	Intermediate	Disk striping with parity

16. Neither boot nor system partitions can reside on a volume set or disk stripe set, even with parity.

USERS AND GROUPS

17. There are two types of groups: local and global. Local groups are only available on local domains; global groups are available across domains. Local groups can contain users and global groups, global groups contain users only. You cannot place groups within global groups, nor can you place local groups within other local groups.

18. For group permissions, the least restrictive right takes precedence, except that No Access always wins. When combining NTFS and share permissions, the least restrictive wins for each kind (except No Access). When combining resulting NTFS and share permissions, the most restrictive wins.

19. You can perform the following in User Manager For Domains:

- Produce, change, duplicate, and remove user and group accounts
- Enable account policies (assign defaults for passwords, account lockouts, disconnect status, etc.)
- Create user rights and audit policies
- Establish trust relationships

BOOT FACTS

20. Boot and system partitions can reside on the primary disk in a disk mirror or duplex set. If the primary fails, you must hand-edit the BOOT.INI file on the boot drive to point to the ARC name for the remaining mirror or duplex drive instead.

21. Boot files—NTLDR, BOOT.INI, NTDETECT.COM, etc.—reside on the system partition. Windows NT OS files—including NTOSKRNL.EXE—reside on the boot partition. BACKWARDS!

22. The most important Windows NT boot process components:

- **BOOT.INI** Boot initialization file: Describes Windows NT boot defaults, plus OS location, settings, menu selections.

Are You Certifiable?

That's the question that's probably on your mind. The answer is: You bet! But if you've tried and failed or you've been frustrated by the complexity of the MCSE program and the maze of study materials available, you've come to the right place. We've created our new publishing and training program, *Certification Insider Press*, to help you accomplish one important goal: to ace an MCSE exam without having to spend the rest of your life studying for it.

The book you have in your hands is part of our *Exam Cram* series. Each book is especially designed not only to help you study for an exam but also to help you understand what the exam is all about. Inside these covers you'll find hundreds of test-taking tips, insights, and strategies that simply cannot be found anyplace else. In creating our guides, we've assembled the very best team of certified trainers, MCSE professionals, and networking course developers.

Our commitment is to ensure that the *Exam Cram* guides offer proven training and active-learning techniques not found in other study guides. We provide unique study tips and techniques, memory joggers, custom quizzes, insights about trick questions, a sample test, and much more. In a nutshell, each *Exam Cram* guide is closely organized like the exam it is tied to.

To help us continue to provide the very best certification study materials, we'd like to hear from you. Write or email us (craminfo@coriolis.com) and let us know how our *Exam Cram* guides have helped you study, or tell us about new features you'd like us to add. If you send us a story about how an *Exam Cram* guide has helped you ace an exam and we use it in one of our guides, we'll send you an official *Exam Cram* shirt for your efforts.

Good luck with your certification exam, and thanks for allowing us to help you achieve your goals.

Keith Weiskamp
Publisher, Certification Insider Press

NT Server 4

Ed Tittel
Kurt Hudson
J. Michael Stewart

Certification
Insider™ Press

an International Thomson Publishing company

Albany, NY • Belmont, CA • Bonn • Boston • Cincinnati • Detroit • Johannesburg • London
Madrid • Melbourne • Mexico City • New York • Paris • Singapore • Tokyo • Toronto • Washington

MCSE NT Server 4 Exam Cram

Copyright © The Coriolis Group, 1998

Limits of Liability and Disclaimer of Warranty

Trademarks

The Coriolis Group, Inc.
An International Thomson Publishing Company
14455 N. Hayden Road, Suite 220
Scottsdale, Arizona 85260

602/483-0192
FAX 602/483-0193
http://www.coriolis.com

Printed in the United States of America
ISBN: 1-57610-190-8
10 9 8

Publisher
Keith Weiskamp

Project Editor
Paula Kmetz

Production Coordinator
Michael Peel

Cover Design
Anthony Stock

Interior Design
Jimmie Young
April Nielsen

(From L. to R., Ed Tittel, J. Michael Stewart, Kurt Hudson)

About The Authors

Ed Tittel

Ed Tittel recently worked as an instructor and course developer for American Research Group, where he developed and taught from a set of materials on Windows NT 4, both Workstation and Server. Ed is also a regular contributor to *Windows NT* magazine and an instructor for Softbank Forums at its Interop and NT Intranet tradeshows. Prior to going out on his own in 1994, Ed worked at Novell for six years, starting as a field engineer and departing as the director of technical marketing.

Ed has written over 40 computer books, including *HTML for Dummies* (with Stephen N. James, IDG Books Worldwide, 3rd ed., 1997); *Networking Windows NT 4.0 for Dummies* (with Mary Madden and Dave Smith, IDG Books Worldwide, 1996); and a variety of titles on Windows NT, NetWare, networking, and Web-related topics.

Ed has written over 200 articles for publications such as *Byte, InfoWorld, LAN Magazine, LAN Times, The NetWare Advisor, PC Magazine*, and *WindowsUser*. At present, Ed also writes a biweekly column for *Interop Online*. You can reach Ed by email at etittel@lanw.com or on the Web at http://www.lanw.com/etbio.htm.

Kurt Hudson

Kurt Hudson is a technical author, trainer, and consultant in the field of networking and computer-related technologies. For the past six years, he has focused his energy on learning and teaching technical skills. He has written several training manuals and books for government and private industry on topics ranging from inventory control to network administration.

As a former trainer for the U.S. Air Force, Kurt worked on high-security government projects employing technologies most people see only in the cinema. During his six-year engagement with the military, he earned three medals for improving systems efficiency, training excellence, and increasing national security. After departing the U.S. Air Force, he worked for a variety of private corporations, including Unisys and Productivity Point International, where he continued to learn and teach technical topics.

Since achieving Microsoft Certified Systems Engineer (MCSE) and Microsoft Certified Trainer (MCT) ratings, he has been writing books and conducting training sessions that have helped many individuals succeed in their pursuit of professional certification. You can reach Kurt on the Internet at kurt@hudlogic.com or on the Web at www.hudlogic.com.

James Michael Stewart

James Michael Stewart is a full-time writer focusing on Windows NT and Internet topics. In addition to working on the *Exam Cram* series, he has recently co-authored the *Intranet Bible* (IDG Books Worldwide, 1997) and the *Hip Pocket Guide to HTML 3.2* (IDG Books Worldwide, 1997). He also contributed to *Windows NT Networking for Dummies* (IDG Books Worldwide, 1997), *Building Windows NT Web Servers* (IDG Books Worldwide, 1997), and *Windows NT, Step by Step* (Microsoft Press, 1995).

Michael has written articles for numerous print and online publications, including C|Net, *InfoWorld*, *Windows NT* magazine, and *Datamation*. He is also the moderator for a Softbank online forum focusing on NT, located at http://forums.sbexpos.com/forums-interop/get/HOS_3.html and a former leader of an NT study group at the Central Texas LAN Association. He is currently an MCP for Windows NT Server 4, Workstation, and Windows 95.

Michael graduated in 1992 from the University of Texas at Austin with a bachelor's degree in Philosophy. Despite his degree, his computer knowledge is self-acquired, based on almost 14 years of hands-on experience. Michael has been active on the Internet for quite some time, where most people know him by his *nom de wire*, McIntyre. You can reach Michael by email at michael@lanw.com or through his Web pages at http://www.lanw.com/jmsbio.htm or http://www.impactonline.com/.

Acknowledgments

Ed Tittel

To begin with, I'd like to thank Keith Weiskamp at the Coriolis Group for understanding, and then championing, our idea for the *Exam Cram* series. I'd also like to thank the whole Coriolis team who helped turn the idea into a workable proposition, including Sharijo Hehr, Lynn Guy, Josh Mills, Brad Grannis, and many others. Finally, I want to thank Paula Kmetz and Jeff Kellum for working out a design and a philosophy for these books that makes as much sense to its authors as we want it to make to our readers.

Closer to home, the whole LANWrights team pitched in and made good on some truly savage deadlines. Starting with my co-authors, Kurt Hudson and James Michael Stewart, the work never stopped. But we couldn't have made this book happen without the stalwart efforts of Dawn Rader, who, as a part-time contributor, and full-time editor and project manager, coordinated all the many bits and pieces that must go into a book. Likewise, Mary Burmeister, our Jill of all trades, and Natanya Pitts, Webmistress and HTML Goddess without compare, produced screen shots, graphics, tables, and the Glossary. Thanks a million to each and every one of you.

Thanks most of all to my dear, departed Labrador retriever, Dusty. You gave me the best ten years of my life; I'd gladly have given you some of mine to have kept you around longer. Rest in peace, old friend...

Kurt Hudson

I want to first thank all of the employees at LANWrights (including Ed and Michael) for their help, encouragement, and hard work. I also want to thank Ed Tittel and the people at Coriolis for sharing my vision of producing a line of training materials for the general public. Thanks to the Marcinkiewicz and Smit families for offering their unfailing support all these years. I must also give a heartfelt thanks to my wonderful wife, Julie, who not only supports me (and tolerates my irregular hours), but also helps me by offering opinions and suggestions.

James Michael Stewart

Thanks to my boss and co-author, Ed Tittel, for including me in this book series. You seem to have a knack for finding great projects where I can influence the world, warped though I am. Thanks to the real trooper on this book, Dawn Rader—who not only wrote numerous chapters, but had the unending pleasure of editing the rantings of multiple authors. Hats off to Mary Burmeister, the latest office accessory: Your accounting and project management wizardry is astounding. Love to my parents, Dave and Sue, whose door is always open, phone is always answered, fridge is always full, and pool is always waiting. To Dave and Laura Nighorn: Whether darts or bikes or movies, we are going to have fun if it kills us! To Mark Gibson: I always have been and always shall be your friend. Please get your butt back to Austin—FAST! To Herbert: May your nine lives never end. And finally, as always, to Elvis: The jungle room, what were you thinking?!?!

Contents

Introduction

Welcome to *Windows NT Server 4 Exam Cram*! This book aims to help you get ready to take—and pass—the Microsoft certification test numbered "Exam 70-067," entitled "Implementing And Supporting Microsoft Windows NT Server 4." This introduction explains Microsoft's certification programs in general and talks about how the *Exam Cram* series can help you prepare for Microsoft's certification exams.

Exam Cram books help you understand and appreciate the subjects and materials you need to pass Microsoft certification exams. *Exam Cram* books are aimed strictly at test preparation and review. They do not teach you everything you need to know about a topic. Instead, we (the authors) present and dissect the questions and problems that we've found that you're likely to encounter on a test. We've worked from Microsoft's own training materials, preparation guides, and tests, and from a battery of third-party test preparation tools. Our aim is to bring together as much information as possible about Microsoft certification exams.

Nevertheless, to completely prepare yourself for any Microsoft test, we recommend that you begin your studies with some classroom training, or that your pick up and read one of the many study guides available from Microsoft and third-party vendors. We also strongly recommend that you install, configure, and fool around with the software or environment that you'll be tested on, because nothing beats hands-on experience and familiarity when it comes to understanding the questions you're likely to encounter on a certification test. Book learning is essential, but hands-on experience is the best teacher of all!

The Microsoft Certified Professional (MCP) Program

The MCP Program currently includes four separate tracks, each of which boasts its own special acronym (as a would-be certificant, you need to have a high tolerance for alphabet soup of all kinds):

➤ **MCPS (Microsoft Certified Product Specialist)** This is the least prestigious of all the certification tracks from Microsoft. Attaining MCPS status requires an individual to pass at least one core operating system exam. Passing any of the major Microsoft operating system exams—including those for Windows 95, Windows NT Workstation, or Windows NT Server—qualifies an individual for MCPS credentials. Individuals can demonstrate proficiency with additional Microsoft products by passing additional certification exams.

➤ **MCSD (Microsoft Certified Solution Developer)** This track is aimed primarily at developers. This credential indicates that individuals who pass it are able to design and implement custom business solutions around particular Microsoft development tools, technologies, and operating systems. To obtain an MCSD, an individual must demonstrate the ability to analyze and interpret user requirements; select and integrate products, platforms, tools, and technologies; design and implement code and customize applications; and perform necessary software tests and quality assurance operations.

To become an MCSD, an individual must pass a total of four exams: two core exams plus two elective exams. The two core exams are the Microsoft Windows Operating Systems And Services Architecture I and II (WOSSA I and WOSSA II, numbered 70-150 and 70-151). Elective exams cover specific Microsoft applications and languages, including Visual Basic, C++, the Microsoft Foundation Classes, Access, SQL Server, Excel, and more.

➤ **MCT (Microsoft Certified Trainer)** Microsoft Certified Trainers are individuals who are deemed capable of delivering elements of the official Microsoft training curriculum, based on technical knowledge and instructional ability. Thus, it is necessary for an individual seeking MCT credentials (which are granted on a course-by-course basis) to pass the related certification exam for a course and successfully complete the official Microsoft training in the subject area, as well as demonstrate an ability to teach.

This latter criterion may be satisfied by proving that one has already attained training certification from Novell, Banyan, Lotus, the Santa Cruz Operation, or Cisco, or by taking a Microsoft-sanctioned workshop on instruction. Microsoft makes it clear that MCTs are an important cog in the Microsoft training channels. Instructors must be MCTs to teach in any of Microsoft's official training channels, including its affiliated Authorized Technical Education Centers (ATECs), Authorized Academic Training Programs (AATPs), and the Microsoft Online Institute (MOLI).

➤ **MCSE (Microsoft Certified Systems Engineer)** Anyone who possesses a current MCSE is warranted to possess a high level of expertise with Windows NT (either version 3.51 or 4) and other Microsoft operating systems and products. This credential is designed to prepare individuals to plan, implement, maintain, and support information systems and networks built around Microsoft Windows NT and its BackOffice family of products.

To obtain an MCSE, an individual must pass four core operating system exams plus two elective exams. The operating system exams require individuals to demonstrate competence with desktop and server operating systems and with networking components.

At least two Windows NT-related exams must be passed to obtain an MCSE: Implementing And Supporting Windows NT Server (version 3.51 or 4) and Implementing And Supporting Windows NT Server In The Enterprise (version 3.51 or 4). These tests are intended to indicate an individual's knowledge of Windows NT in smaller, simpler networks and in larger, more complex, and heterogeneous networks, respectively.

Two more tests must be passed. These tests are networking and desktop operating system related. At present, the networking requirement can only be satisfied by passing the Networking Essentials test. The desktop operating system test can be satisfied by passing a Windows 3.1, Windows for Workgroups 3.11, Windows NT Workstation (the version must match whichever core curriculum is pursued), or Windows 95 test.

The two remaining exams are elective exams. The elective exams can be in any number of subject or product areas, primarily BackOffice components. These include tests on SQL Server, SNA Server, Exchange, Systems Management Server, and the like. But it is also possible to test out on electives by taking advanced networking topics like Internetworking with Microsoft TCP/IP (here again, the version of Windows NT involved must match the version for the core requirements taken).

Whatever mix of tests is completed toward MCSE certification, individuals must pass six tests to meet the MCSE requirements. It's not uncommon for the entire process to take a year or so, and many individuals find that they must take a test more than once to pass. Our primary goal with the *Exam Cram* series is to make it possible, given proper study and preparation, to pass all of the MCSE tests on the first try.

Finally, certification is an ongoing activity. Once a Microsoft product becomes obsolete, MCSEs (and other MCPs) typically have a 12 to 18 month time frame in which they can become recertified on current product versions (if individuals do not get recertified within the specified time period, their certification is no longer valid). Because technology keeps changing and new products continually supplant old ones, this should come as no surprise.

The best place to keep tabs on the MCP Program and its various certifications is on the Microsoft Web site. The current root URL for the MCP program is entitled "Certification Online" at www.microsoft.com/Train_Cert/ mcp/default.htm. Microsoft's Web site changes frequently, so if this URL doesn't work, try using the Search tool on Microsoft's site with either "MCP" or the quoted phrase "Microsoft Certified Professional Program" as the search string. This will help you find the latest and most accurate information about the company's certification programs. You can also obtain a special CD that contains a copy of the Microsoft Education And Certification Roadmap. The Roadmap covers much of the same information as the Web site, and it is updated quarterly. To obtain your copy of the CD, call Microsoft at 1-800-636-7544, Monday through Friday, 6:30 AM through 7:30 PM Pacific Time.

Taking A Certification Exam

Alas, testing is not free. You'll be charged $100 for each test you take, whether you pass or fail. In the United States and Canada, tests are administered by Sylvan Prometric. Sylvan Prometric can be reached at 1-800-755-3926 or 1-800-755-EXAM, any time from 7:00 AM to 6:00 PM, Central Time, Monday through Friday. If this number doesn't work, try (612) 896-7000 or (612) 820-5707.

To schedule an exam, call at least one day in advance. To cancel or reschedule an exam, you must call at least 12 hours before the scheduled test time (or you may be charged regardless). When calling Sylvan Prometric, please have the following information ready for the telesales staffer who handles your call:

➤ Your name, organization, and mailing address.

➤ Your Microsoft Test ID. (For most U.S. citizens, this is your social security number. Citizens of other nations can use their taxpayer IDs or make other arrangements with the order taker.)

➤ The name and number of the exam you wish to take. (For this book, the exam number is 70-067, and the exam name is "Implementing And Supporting Windows NT Server 4.")

➤ A method of payment must be arranged. (The most convenient approach is to supply a valid credit card number with sufficient available credit. Otherwise, payments by check, money order, or purchase order must be received before a test can be scheduled. If the latter methods are required, ask your order taker for more details.)

When you show up to take a test, try to arrive at least 15 minutes before the scheduled time slot. You must bring and supply two forms of identification, one of which one must be a photo ID.

All exams are completely closed-book. In fact, you will not be permitted to take anything with you into the testing area, but you will be furnished with a blank sheet of paper and a pen. We suggest that you immediately write down the most critical information about the test you're taking on the sheet of paper. *Exam Cram* books provide a brief reference—The Cram Sheet, located inside the front cover—that lists the essential information from the book in distilled form. You will have some time to compose yourself, to record this information, and even to take a sample orientation exam before you must begin the real thing. We suggest you take the orientation test before taking your first exam; because they're all more or less identical in layout, behavior, and controls, you probably won't need to do this more than once.

When you complete a Microsoft certification exam, the software will tell you whether you've passed or failed. All tests are scored on a basis of 1,000 points, and results are broken into several topical areas. Even if you fail, we suggest you ask for—and keep—the detailed report that the test administrator should print for you. You can use the report to help you prepare for another go-round, if needed. If you need to retake an exam, you'll have to call Sylvan Prometric, schedule a new test date, and pay another $100.

Tracking MCP Status

As soon as you pass any Microsoft operating system exam, you'll attain Product Specialist (MCPS) status. Microsoft also generates transcripts that indicate the exams you have passed and your corresponding test scores. You can order a transcript by email at any time by sending an email addressed to mcp@msprograms.com. You can also obtain a copy of your transcript by downloading the latest version of the MCT Guide from the Web site and consulting the section entitled "Key Contacts" for a list of telephone numbers and related contacts.

Once you pass the necessary set of six exams, you'll be certified as an MCSE. Official certification normally takes anywhere from four to six weeks, so don't expect to get your credentials overnight. When the package arrives, it will include a Welcome Kit that contains a number of elements, including:

➤ An MCSE certificate, suitable for framing, along with an MCSE Professional Program membership card and lapel pin.

➤ A license to use the MCP logo, thereby allowing you to use the logo in advertisements, promotions, and documents, and on letterhead, business cards, and so on. Along with the license comes an MCP logo sheet, which includes camera-ready artwork. (Note: before using any of the artwork, individuals must sign and return a licensing agreement that indicates they'll abide by its terms and conditions.)

➤ A one-year subscription to TechNet, a collection of CDs that includes software, documentation, service packs, databases, and more technical information than you can possibly ever read. In our minds, this is the best and most tangible benefit of attaining MCSE status.

➤ A subscription to *Microsoft Certified Professional* magazine, which provides ongoing data about testing and certification activities, requirements, and changes to the program.

➤ A one-year subscription to the Microsoft Beta Evaluation program. This subscription will get you all beta products from Microsoft for the next year. (This does not include developer products. You must join the MSDN program or become an MCSD to qualify for developer beta products.)

Many people believe that the benefits of MCSE certification go well beyond the perks that Microsoft provides to newly anointed members of this elite group. We're starting to see more job listings that request or require applicants to have an MCSE, and many individuals who complete the program can qualify for increases in pay or responsibility. As an official recognition of hard work and broad knowledge, MCSE certification is indeed a badge of honor in many IT organizations.

How To Prepare For An Exam

At a minimum, preparing for a Windows NT Server-related test requires that you obtain and study the following materials:

➤ The Microsoft Windows NT Server manuals (or online documentation and help files, which ship on the CD with the product and also appear on the TechNet CDs).

➤ The *Microsoft Windows NT Server Resource Kit* (for Microsoft NT Server Version 4), published by Microsoft Press, Redmond, WA, 1996. ISBN: 1-57231-343-9. Even though it costs a whopping $149.95 (list price), it's worth every penny—not just for the documentation, but also for the utilities and other software included (which add considerably to the base functionality of Windows NT Server 4). Two supplements for this Resource Kit are currently available: Supplement One (ISBN: 1-57231-559-8), which is a book/disk that includes new information and utilities for IIS, capacity planning, viewing network connections, and more; and Supplement Two (ISBN: 1-57231-626-8), which includes a new Registry editing tool, a service monitor, a domain management utility, and information about PPTP.

➤ The exam prep materials, practice tests, and self-assessment exams on the Microsoft Training And Certification Download page (www.microsoft.com/Train_Cert/download/downld.htm). Find the materials, download them, and use them!

➤ This *Exam Cram* book! It's the first and last thing you should read before taking the exam.

In addition, you'll probably find any or all of the following materials useful in your quest for Windows NT Server expertise:

➤ **Microsoft Training Kits** Although there's no training kit currently available from Microsoft Press for Windows NT Server 4, many other topics have such kits. It's worthwhile to check to see if Microsoft has come out with anything by the time you need the information.

➤ **Study Guides** I recommend Exam Preps from The Coriolis Group's Certification Insider Press. These comprehensive study guides feature highly interactive, real-world exercises and projects to reinforce important topical discussions. The companion CD-ROM includes two complete interactive practice exams.

Watch for new titles coming soon!

➤ **Classroom Training** ATECs, AATPs, MOLI, and unlicensed third-party training companies (like Wave Technologies, American Research Group, Learning Tree, Data-Tech, and others) all offer classroom training on Windows NT Server 4. These companies aim to help prepare network administrators to run Windows NT installations and pass the MCSE tests. While such training runs upwards of $350 per day in class, most of the individuals lucky enough to partake (including your humble authors, who've even taught such courses) find them to be quite worthwhile.

➤ **Other Publications** You'll find direct references to other publications and resources in this book, but there's no shortage of materials available about Windows NT. To help you sift through some of the publications out there, we end each chapter with a "Need To Know More?" section that provides pointers to more complete and exhaustive resources covering the chapter's information. This should give you an idea of where we think you should look for further discussion.

➤ **The TechNet CD** TechNet is a monthly CD subscription available from Microsoft. TechNet includes all the Windows NT BackOffice Resource Kits and their product documentation. In addition, TechNet provides the contents of the Microsoft Knowledge Base and many kinds of software, white papers, training materials, and other good stuff. TechNet also contains all service packs, interim release patches, and supplemental driver software released since the last major version for most Microsoft programs and all Microsoft operating systems. A one-year subscription costs $299—worth every penny, even if only for the download time it saves.

By far, this set of required and recommend materials represents a nonpareil collection of sources and resources for Windows NT Server topics and software. We anticipate that you'll find this book belongs in this company. In the section that follows, we explain how this book works, and we give you some good reasons why this book counts as a member of the required and recommended materials list.

About This Book

Each topical *Exam Cram* chapter follows a regular structure, along with graphical cues about especially important or useful material. Here's the structure of a typical chapter:

► **Opening Hotlists** Each chapter begins with lists of the terms, tools, and techniques that you must learn and understand before you can be fully conversant with the chapter's subject matter. We follow the hotlists with one or two introductory paragraphs to set the stage for the rest of the chapter. Here, you'll find an estimate of the number of questions related to the chapter's topic likely to appear on any given certification test.

► **Topical Coverage** After the opening hotlists, each chapter covers a series of at least four topics related to the chapter's subject title. Throughout this section, we highlight material most likely to appear on a test using a special Exam Alert layout, like this:

This is what an Exam Alert looks like. Normally, an Exam Alert stresses concepts, terms, software, or activities that will most probably appear in one or more certification test questions. For that reason, we think any information found offset in Exam Alert format is worthy of unusual attentiveness on your part. Indeed, most of the facts appearing in The Cram Sheet (inside the front cover of this book) appear as Exam Alerts within the text.

Occasionally, you'll see tables called "Vital Statistics." The contents of vital statistics tables are worthy of an extra once-over. These tables contain informational tidbits that might well show up in a test question.

Even if material isn't flagged as an Exam Alert or included in a vital statistics table, *all* the contents of this book are at least tangential to something test-related. To focus on quick test preparation, this book is lean; you'll find that what appears in the meat of each chapter is critical knowledge.

We have also provided tips that will help build a better foundation of NT-based knowledge. Although the information may not be on the exam, it is highly relevant and will help you become a better test taker.

This is how tips are formatted. Keep your eyes open for these, and you'll become a Server test guru in no time!

➤ **Exam Prep Questions** This section presents a series of mock test questions and explanations of both correct and incorrect answers. We also try to point out especially tricky questions by using a special icon, like this:

Ordinarily, this icon flags the presence of an especially devious question, if not an outright trick question. Trick questions are calculated to "trap" you if you don't read them more than once, and carefully, at that. Although they're not ubiquitous, such questions make regular appearances in the Microsoft exams. That's why we say exam questions are as much about reading comprehension as they are about knowing Windows NT Server material inside out and backwards.

➤ **Details And Resources** Every chapter ends with a section entitled "Need To Know More?". This section provides direct pointers to Microsoft and third-party resources that offer further details on the chapter's subject. In addition, this section tries to rate the quality and thoroughness of the topic's coverage by each resource. If you find a resource you like in this collection, use it, but don't feel compelled to use all the resources. On the other hand, we only recommend resources we use on a regular basis, so none of our recommendations will be a waste of your time or money.

The bulk of the book follows this chapter structure slavishly. But, there are a few other elements that we'd like to point out: the answer key to the sample test that appears in Chapter 14, and a reasonably exhaustive glossary of Windows NT and Microsoft terminology. Finally, look for The Cram Sheet, which appears inside the front cover of this *Exam Cram* book. It is a very valuable tool that represents a condensed and compiled collection of facts, figures, and tips that we think you should memorize before taking the test. Because you can dump this information out of your head onto a piece of paper before answering any exam questions, you can master this information by brute force—you only need to remember it long enough to write it down when you walk into the test room. You might even want to look at it in the car or in the lobby of the testing center just before you walk in to take the test.

How To Use This Book

If you're prepping for a first-time test, we've structured the topics in this book to build on one another. Therefore, some topics in later chapters make more sense after you've read earlier chapters. That's why we suggest you read this book from front to back for your initial test preparation. If you need to brush up on a topic or you have to bone up for a second try, use the index or table of contents to go straight to the topics and questions that you need to study. Beyond the tests, we think you'll find this book useful as a tightly focused reference to some of the most important aspects of Windows NT. (For us, several chapters have already come in handy while working with our own in-house Windows NT network.)

We've tried to create a tool that you can use to prepare for—and pass— Microsoft Certification Exam 70-067, "Implementing And Supporting Microsoft Windows NT Server 4." Please share your feedback on the book with us, especially if you have ideas on how we can improve it for future test-takers. You can reach us through email at etittel@lanw.com (Ed Tittel), kurt@hudlogic.com (Kurt Hudson), and michael@lanw.com (James Michael Stewart). Please remember to include the title of the book in your message; otherwise, we'll be forced to guess which book you're making a suggestion about. And we don't like to guess—we want to KNOW!

For up-to-date information on certification, online discussion forums, sample tests, content updates, and more, visit the Certification Insider Press site at www.examcram.com and the authors' site at www.lanw.com/examcram.

Microsoft Certification Tests

1

Terms and concepts you'll need to understand:

√ Radio button

√ Checkbox

√ Exhibit

√ Multiple-choice question formats

√ Careful reading

√ Process of elimination

Techniques you'll need to master:

√ Preparing to take a certification exam

√ Practicing—to make perfect

√ Making the best use of the testing software

√ Budgeting your time

√ Saving the hardest questions until last

√ Guessing (as a last resort)

As experiences go, test-taking is not something that most people anticipate eagerly, no matter how well they're prepared. In most cases, familiarity helps ameliorate test anxiety. In plain English, this means you probably won't be as nervous when you take your fourth or fifth Microsoft certification exam as you will be when you take your first one.

But no matter whether it's your first test or your tenth, understanding the exam-taking particulars (how much time to spend on questions, the setting you'll be in, and so on) and the testing software will help you concentrate on the material rather than on the environment. Likewise, mastering a few basic test-taking skills should help you recognize—and perhaps even outfox—some of the tricks and gotchas you're bound to find in some of the Microsoft test questions.

In this chapter, we'll explain the testing environment and software, and describe some proven test-taking strategies that you should be able to use to your advantage. We've compiled this information based on the 40-plus Microsoft certification exams the authors have taken themselves, and we've also drawn on the advice of our friends and colleagues, some of whom have taken more than 30 tests each!

The Testing Situation

When you arrive at the Sylvan Prometric Testing Center where you scheduled your test, you'll need to sign in with a test coordinator. He or she will ask you to produce two forms of identification, one of which must be a photo ID. Once you've signed in and your time slot arrives, you'll be asked to deposit any books, bags, or other items you brought with you, and you'll be escorted into a closed room. Typically, that room will be furnished with anywhere from one to half a dozen computers, and each workstation is separated from the others by dividers designed to keep you from seeing what's happening on someone else's computer.

You'll be furnished with a pen or pencil and a blank sheet of paper, or in some cases, an erasable plastic sheet and an erasable felt-tip pen. You're allowed to write down any information you want on this palimpsest, and you can write stuff on both sides of the page. We suggest that you memorize as much as possible of the material that appears on The Cram Sheet (inside the front cover of this book), and then write that information down on the blank sheet as soon as you sit down in front of the test machine. You can refer to it anytime you like during the test, but you'll have to surrender the sheet when you leave the room.

Most test rooms feature a wall with a large picture window. This is to permit the test coordinator to monitor the room, to prevent test-takers from talking to one another, and to observe anything out of the ordinary that might go on. The test coordinator will have preloaded the Microsoft certification test you've signed up for—for this book, that's Exam 70-067—and you'll be permitted to start as soon as you're seated in front of the machine.

All Microsoft certification exams permit you to take up to a certain maximum amount of time to complete the test (the test itself will tell you, and maintains an ongoing on-screen counter/clock so you can check the time remaining anytime you like). Exam 70-067 consists of between 50 and 65 questions, randomly selected from a pool of questions. You're permitted to take up to 90 minutes to complete the exam.

All Microsoft certification exams are computer generated and use a multiple-choice format. Although this may sound quite simple, the questions are constructed not just to check your mastery of basic facts and figures about Windows NT Server; they also require you to evaluate one or more sets of circumstances or requirements. Often, you'll be asked to give more than one answer to a question; likewise, you may be asked to select the best or most effective solution to a problem from a range of choices, all of which technically are correct. It's quite an adventure, and involves real thinking, but this book will show you what to expect, and how to deal with the problems, puzzles, and predicaments you're likely to find on the test.

Test Layout And Design

Typical test questions are depicted on the pages that follow. The first is a multiple-choice question, taken from Chapter 5 of this book, that requires you to select a single correct answer. We've reproduced the entire text of this question and its own exposition from Chapter 5, and follow with some further explanation and discussion.

Question 1

What is the difference between local and global groups?

○   a. It is possible for local groups to contain global groups, but global groups cannot contain local groups.

○   b. Only user accounts from the local domain can be contained within a local group, whereas user accounts from both the local and trusted domains can be contained in global groups.

○   c. It is not possible to create a local group on the domain controllers, whereas global groups are created only on the domain controllers.

○   d. Local groups can contain only global groups, and global groups can contain only user accounts.

The correct answer is a. Global groups help organize domain users into logical units, whereas local groups provide users with permissions or rights to domain resources. The domain controllers of the domain are the only ones that can create global groups, while local groups can be created on any workstation or server within the domain. Global groups are limited to containing only user accounts for the domain.

The sample question above corresponds closely to those you'll see on Microsoft certification tests. To select the correct answer, position the cursor over the radio button next to answer a, and click the mouse to select that particular choice. In this case, knowing which answer to pick depends on understanding the differences between local and global groups, particularly with reference to the contents of each type of group.

Next, we'll examine a question that requires choosing multiple answers. This type of question provides checkboxes, rather than the radio buttons, for marking all appropriate selections.

Question 2

Which of the following types of computers can be configured to export files during replication? [Check all correct answers]

❏ a. Windows NT servers that are configured as domain controllers

❏ b. Windows NT member servers

❏ c. Windows NT workstations

❏ d. Windows 95 clients

Only those computers running Windows NT Server (member servers and primary and backup domain controllers) can export files during replication; therefore, choices a and b are correct.

For this type of question, one or more answers must be selected to answer the question correctly. As far as we can tell (and Microsoft won't comment), such questions are scored as wrong unless all the required selections are chosen. In other words, a partially correct answer does not result in partial credit when the test is scored. For Question 2, you'd have to position the cursor over the checkboxes next to items a and b and check both of them to obtain credit for a correct answer. Knowing that only machines that run Windows NT Server can act as export servers for the Windows NT Replication Service is the critical ingredient to answering this question correctly.

Although there are many forms in which these two basic types of questions can appear, they constitute the foundation upon which all the Microsoft certification exam questions rest. More complex questions may include so-called "exhibits," which are usually screen shots of some Windows NT utility or another. For some of these questions, you will be asked to make a selection by clicking a checkbox or radio button on the screen itself; for others, you'll be expected to use the information displayed therein to guide your answer to the question. Familiarity with the underlying utility is the key to the correct answer.

Other questions involving exhibits may use charts or network diagrams to help document a workplace scenario that you'll be asked to troubleshoot or configure. Careful attention to such exhibits is the key to success—be prepared to toggle between the picture and the question as you work. Often, both are complex enough that you may not be able to remember all of either one.

Using Microsoft's Test Software Effectively

A well-known principle when taking tests is to read over the entire test from start to finish first, but to answer only those questions that you feel absolutely sure of on the first pass. On subsequent passes, you can dive into more complex questions more deeply, knowing how many such questions you have to deal with.

Fortunately, Microsoft test software makes this approach easy to implement. At the bottom of each question, you'll find a checkbox that permits you to mark that question for a later visit. As you read each question, if you answer only those you're sure of, and mark for review those that you're not, you can keep going through a decreasing list of open questions as you knock the trickier ones off in order.

 There's at least one potential benefit to reading the test over completely before answering the trickier questions: Sometimes, you find information in later questions that shed more light on earlier ones. Other times, information you read on later questions may jog your memory about Windows NT facts, figures, or behavior that also will help with earlier questions. Either way, you'll come out ahead if you defer those questions about which you're not absolutely sure of the answer(s).

Keep working on the questions until you are absolutely sure of all your answers or until you know you'll run out of time. If there are still unanswered questions, you'll want to zip through them and guess. No answer guarantees no credit for a question and a guess has at least a chance of being correct. This strategy only works because Microsoft doesn't penalize for incorrect answers (that is, it treats incorrect answers and no answers as equally wrong).

> At the very end of your test period, you're better off guessing than leaving questions blank or unanswered.

Taking Testing Seriously

The most important advice we can give you about taking any Microsoft test is: Read each question *carefully*. Some questions are deliberately ambiguous; some use double negatives; others use terminology in incredibly precise ways. We've taken numerous practice tests and real tests, and in nearly every test we've missed at least one question because we didn't read it closely or enough.

Here are some suggestions on how to deal with the tendency to jump to an answer too quickly:

> ➤ Make sure you read every word in the question. If you find yourself jumping ahead impatiently, go back and start over.

> ➤ As you read, try to restate the question in your own terms. If you can do this, you should be able to pick the correct answer(s) much more easily.

> ➤ When returning to a question after your initial read-through, reread every word again—otherwise, the mind falls quickly into a rut. Some times, seeing a question afresh after turning your attention elsewhere lets you see something you missed before, but the strong tendency is to see what you've seen before. Try to avoid that tendency at all costs.

> ➤ If you return to a question more than twice, try to articulate to yourself what you don't understand about the question, why the answers don't appear to make sense, or what appears to be missing. If you chew on the subject for a while, your subconscious may provide the details that are lacking, or you may notice a "trick" that will point to the answer.

Above all, try to deal with each question by thinking through what you know about the NT utilities, characteristics, behaviors, facts, and figures involved. By reviewing what you know (and what you've written down on your information sheet), you will often recall or understand things sufficiently to determine the answer to the question.

Question-Handling Strategies

Based on the tests we've taken, a couple of interesting trends in the answers have become apparent. For those questions that take only a single answer, usually two or three of the answers will be obviously incorrect, and two of the answers will be plausible. But, of course, only one can be correct. Unless the answer leaps out at you (and if it does, reread the question to look for a trick; sometimes those are the ones you're most likely to get wrong), begin the process of answering by eliminating those answers that are most obviously wrong.

Things to look for in the "obviously wrong" category include spurious menu choices or utility names, nonexistent software options, and terminology you've never seen before. If you've done your homework for a test, no valid information should be completely new to you. In that case, unfamiliar or bizarre terminology probably indicates a totally bogus answer. As long as you're sure what's right, it's easy to eliminate what's wrong.

Numerous questions assume that the default behavior of a particular utility is in effect. It's essential, therefore, to understand that the default behavior for Windows NT security is to grant Full Control rights to the local group named Everyone, when dealing with matters of access and rights. The same is true for many other aspects of the system. If you know the defaults, and understand what they mean, this knowledge will help you cut through many Gordian knots.

Likewise, when dealing with questions that require multiple answers—such as one that asks what *must be* installed on Windows NT Server for Gateway Services for NetWare (GSNW) to work—it's vital to remember that GSNW automatically installs NWLink as part of its own installation if that protocol isn't already present on the Windows NT Server in question. In English, this means that it's not necessary to install the protocol separately, because GSNW does it for you if NWLink's not already available. Certainly, NWLink is absolutely required for GSNW to work, but it's not necessary that it be installed before installing GSNW. This, too, qualifies as an example of why "careful reading" is so important.

As you work your way through the test, another counter that Microsoft thankfully provides will come in handy—the number of questions completed and questions outstanding. Budget your time by making sure that you've completed one-fourth of the questions one-quarter of the way through the test period (or between 13 and 17 questions in the first 22 or 23 minutes). Check again, three-quarters of the way through (between 39 and 51 questions in the first 66 to 69 minutes).

If you're not through when 85 minutes have elapsed, use the last five minutes to guess your way through the remaining questions. Remember, guesses are potentially more valuable than blank answers, because blanks are always wrong, but a guess may turn out to be right. If you haven't a clue with any of the remaining questions, pick answers at random, or choose all a's, b's, and so on. The important thing is to submit a test for scoring that has some answer for every question.

Mastering The Inner Game

In the final analysis, knowledge breeds confidence, and confidence breeds success. If you study the materials in this book carefully, and review all of the Exam Prep questions at the end of each chapter, you should be aware of those areas where additional learning and study are required.

Next, follow up by reading some or all of the materials recommended in the Need To Know More? section at the end of each chapter. The idea is to become familiar enough with the concepts and situations that you find in the sample questions to be able to reason your way through similar situations on a real test. If you know the material, you have every right to be confident that you can pass the test.

Once you've worked your way through the book, take the practice test in Chapter 14. This will provide a reality check, and will help you identify areas you need to study further. Make sure you follow up and review materials related to the questions you miss before scheduling a real test. Only when you've covered all the ground, and feel comfortable with the whole scope of the practice test, should you take a real test.

If you take our practice test and don't score at least 75 percent correct, you'll want to practice further. At a minimum, download the Personal Exam Prep (PEP) tests and the self-assessment tests from the Microsoft Certification and Training Web site's download page (its location appears in the next section). If you're more ambitious, or better funded, you might want to purchase a practice test from one of the third-party vendors that offers them. We've had good luck with tests from Transcender Corporation and from Self Test Software (the vendors who supply the PEP tests). See the final section in this chapter for contact information.

Armed with the information in this book, and with the determination to augment your knowledge, you should be able to pass the certification exam. But if you don't work at it, you'll spend the test fee more than once before you finally do pass. If you prepare seriously, the execution should go flawlessly. Good luck!

Details And Resources

By far, the best source of information about Microsoft certification tests comes from Microsoft itself. Because its products and technologies—and the tests that go with them—change frequently, the best place to go for exam-related information is online.

If you haven't already visited the Microsoft Training and Certification pages, do so right now. As we're writing this chapter, the Training and Certification home page resides at http://www.microsoft.com/Train_Cert/default.htm (see Figure 1.1). *Note:* It may not be there by the time you read this, or it may have been replaced by something new and different, because things change regularly on the Microsoft site. Should this happen, please read the sidebar entitled "Coping With Change On The Web."

The menu options in the left-hand column of the home page point to the most important sources of information in the Training and Certification pages. Here's what to check out:

> **Train_Cert Summaries/By Product and Technology** Use this to jump to product-based summaries of all classroom education, training materials, study guides, and other information for specific products.

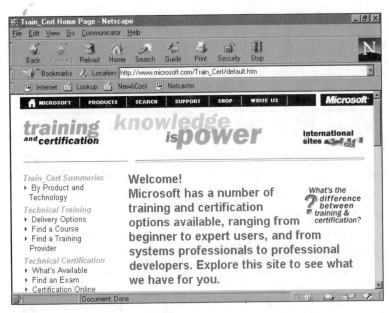

Figure 1.1 The Training and Certification home page should be your starting point for further investigation of the most current exam and preparation information.

Under the heading of Microsoft Windows/Windows NT Server, you'll find an entire page of information about Windows NT Server training and certification. This tells you a lot about your training and preparation options, and mentions all the tests that relate to Windows NT Server.

➤ **Technical Certification/Find an Exam** Pulls up a search tool that lets you list all Microsoft exams, and locate all exams pertinent to any Microsoft certification (MCPS, MCSE, MCT, and so on), or those exams that cover a particular product. This tool is quite useful not only to examine the options, but also to obtain specific test preparation information, because each exam has its own associated preparation guide. For this test, be sure to grab the one for 70-067.

➤ **Site Tools/Downloads** Here, you'll find a list of the files and practice tests that Microsoft makes available to the public. These include several items worth downloading, especially the Certification Update, the Personal Exam Prep (PEP) tests, various Assessment Exams, and a general Exam Study Guide. Try to make time to peruse these materials before taking your first test.

Of course, these are just the high points of what's available in the Microsoft Training And Certification pages. As you browse through them—and we strongly recommend that you do—you'll probably find other things we didn't mention here that are every bit as interesting and compelling.

Coping With Change On The Web

Sooner or later, all the specifics we've shared with you about the Microsoft Training And Certification pages, and all the other Web-based resources we mention throughout the rest of this book, will go stale or be replaced by newer information. In some cases, the URLs you find here may lead you to their replacements; in other cases, the URLs will go nowhere, leaving you with the dread "404 File not found" error message.

When that happens, please don't give up! There's always a way to find what you want on the Web, if you're willing to invest some time and energy. To begin with, most large or complex Web sites—and Microsoft's qualifies on both counts—offer a search engine. Looking back at Figure 1.1, you'll see that a Search button appears along the top edge of the page. As long as you can get to the site itself (and we're pretty sure that it will stay at www.microsoft.com for a long while yet), you can use this tool to help you find what you need.

The more particular or focused you can make a search request, the more likely it is that the results will include information you can use. For instance, you can search the string "training and certification" to produce lots of data about the subject in general, but if you're looking for the preparation guide for Exam 70-067, Implementing and Supporting Microsoft Windows NT Server 4, you'll be more likely to get there quickly if you use a search string such as:

Exam 70-067 AND preparation guide

Likewise, if you want to find the Training and Certification downloads, try a search string such as:

```
training and certification AND download page
```

Finally, do not be afraid to use general search tools such as www.search.com, www.altavista.com, or www.excite.com to search for related information. Even though Microsoft offers the best information about its certification exams online, there are plenty of third-party sources of information, training, and assistance in this area that do not have to follow a party line like Microsoft does. The bottom line is: If you can't find something where the book says it lives, start looking around. If worst comes to worst, you can always email us! We just might have a clue.

Third-Party Test Providers

Transcender Corporation is located at 242 Louise Avenue, Nashville, TN, 37203-1812. You can reach the company by phone at (615) 726-8779, or by fax at (615) 320-6594. Trancender's URL is http://www.transcender .com; you can download an order form for the materials online, but it must be mailed or faxed to Transcender for purchase. We've found these practice tests, which cost between $89 and $179 if purchased individually (with discounts available for packages containing multiple tests), to be pricey but useful.

Self Test Software is located at 4651 Woodstock Road, Suite 203-384, Roswell, GA, 30075. The company can be reached by phone at (770) 641-9719 or (800) 200-6446, and by fax at (770) 641-1489. Visit the Web site at http://www.stsware.com; you can even order the wares online. STS's tests are cheaper than Transcender's—$69 when purchased individually, $59 each when two or more are purchased simultaneously—but otherwise quite comparable, which makes them a good value.

Installing Windows NT Server

Terms you'll need to understand:

√ Hardware Compatibility List (HCL)

√ NT Hardware Qualifier (NTHQ)

√ File systems

√ Licensing

√ Primary Domain Controller (PDC)

√ Backup Domain Controller (BDC)

√ Member server

√ Emergency Repair Disk (ERD)

√ NetBIOS names

√ Network names

√ Network clients

√ FDISK

√ Network share

Techniques you'll need to master:

√ Installation and configuration of NT Server

√ Creating an ERD

√ Troubleshooting an NT installation

15

As network operating systems go, Windows NT usually is a breeze to install, especially for those who know what they're doing. But before a successful installation is possible, it's necessary to understand Windows NT's requirements and to learn how to evaluate your target systems for suitability. After the preliminaries are dispensed with, you'll then need to decide exactly how you want to install Windows NT. And because you never can be sure that everything will work the first time, it's a good idea to understand some common causes of potential difficulty and their well-known workarounds or outright solutions.

Because we intend our materials to help you prepare for exam questions related to planning for and installing Windows NT Server on a computer, we don't cover the installation process itself in great detail, other than to illuminate those aspects of the process that are likely to elicit attention on a test. If you're concerned about understanding the process in depth, or want to pursue more details than we cover here, we suggest that you consult the "Need To Know More?" section at the end of this chapter—the materials listed there should tell you everything you'd ever possibly want to know about the minutiae of Windows NT Server installation!

Planning The Configuration

Before you install Windows NT, it's a good idea to analyze and understand how you want to use your Windows NT Server in some detail. This will help you select new hardware or decide if the hardware you've got is suitable for use with Windows NT Server. Table 2.1 lists "bare minimum" and "recommended" machine configuration data for Windows NT Server.

Minimum Requirements Vs. Recommendations

When it comes to the minimum requirements in Table 2.1, there's no getting around them. For instance, we've tried installing Windows NT Server on a PC with only 12 MB of RAM: Unfortunately, everything goes quite well until the install program tries to load the Windows NT kernel, and then quits after issuing an error message that reads "insufficient RAM to run Windows NT Server." Thus, the minimum requirements represent hard

Table 2.1   The minimum and recommended requirements for running Windows NT Server.

Item	Minimum	Recommended	Discussion
CPU	Intel 486	Pentium or better	Windows NT Server works with non-Intel processors (e.g., MIPS R4x00, DEC Alpha AXP, IBM PPC), and supports up to four CPUs in the standard edition.
Display	VGA	VGA or better	Unless someone plans to work at the server console, plain vanilla VGA is all you'll need.
Hard Disk	124 MB free	200+ MB free	The more components (or BackOffice elements) you install on your server, the more disk space you'll need; if you install straight from a CD, you need only 10 MB of disk space for boot and temp files.
Floppy Disk	3.5" or 5.25"	3.5" or 5.25"	Floppies may be used during installation for setup disks.
CD-ROM	none	8X or better	Because NT ships on a CD, either direct- or network-based access to a CD-ROM is required.
Network Adapter	one	one or more	Without network access, networking features are disabled and cannot be configured.

(continued)

Table 2.1	**The minimum and recommended requirements for running Windows NT Server (*continued*).**		
Item	**Minimum**	**Recommended**	**Discussion**
Memory	16 MB	64 MB or more	Testing has proved that "more is better" for NT Server RAM. Be sure to fully load the motherboard with L2 Cache memory as well. In general, put as much memory into an NT Server as you can afford.
Pointing Device	mouse, etc.	mouse, etc.	A pointing device makes working with the GUI portion of the install program (and most of NT's utilities) much easier.

and fast limitations on the software. The recommended values are another story—they can be approached with a healthy skepticism, but should still be taken seriously. Windows NT runs much better if it has lots of system resources to work with, and a server is not a machine you'd want to shortchange on such resources anyway. As with most things, it's better to have the resources and not need them than to need them and not have them.

Assessing Hardware Compatibility

When it comes to setting up or buying a computer that will run Windows NT Server, "more is better" is an unwritten rule that's worth heeding for everything from CPU (or even, the number of CPUs in the machine), to memory, disk space, and more. If you're buying a new machine, be sure to ask the vendor if the equipment is fully Windows NT compatible. Any answer other than a resounding "Yes" probably means that you should find another vendor.

Whether you're buying a new machine or reusing one you already own, Microsoft provides an invaluable tool that can save hours of frustration and unnecessary expense when installing Windows NT Server. On the Windows NT distribution medium—that is, the CD labeled "Windows NT Server 4"—you'll find a file named MAKEDISK.BAT in the \Support\Hqtool directory. This utility will create a bootable DOS floppy that runs a program named "NTHQ" (which stands for NT Hardware Qualifier) upon bootup.

By itself, NTHQ is a useful program, because it can:

1. Produce a detailed report to document the configuration it finds.

2. Troubleshoot, if installation fails because of hardware problems (the program includes online help and trouble-shooting data).

3. Show all the hardware it detects when a computer will run DOS but won't load Windows NT (if something isn't detected, it's likely to be involved—if not the culprit).

But NTHQ's real "intelligence" comes from its incorporation of compatibility information that Microsoft also publishes separately in a document called the "Hardware Compatibility List," usually abbreviated HCL.

The HCL is updated monthly, whereas the version that's incorporated into the NTHQ represents the HCL at the time the latest version of the software was produced. Since this is August 1996 for Windows NT Server 4, the corresponding HCL in the NTHQ is aging rapidly. For machines newer than August 1996, it might be necessary to check a newer edition of the HCL to assess component compatibility.

The latest HCL is always available on Microsoft's Web site (www.microsoft.com) and on its anonymous FTP server (ftp.microsoft.com). It's also published monthly on the TechNet CD. Given a current HCL, you could still use the NTHQ to document what it finds on a system, and then use the HCL to make sure that elements that the program marks as unsupported have since joined the latest HCL.

When it comes to assessing the results from NTHQ, or similar results by inspection of a more current HCL, there's only one thing to say about unsupported hardware: "If the item is not on the HCL, and the vendor does not have a known good, working Windows NT driver for the item, remove the offending item and replace it with something equivalent that *does* appear on the HCL." In most cases, trying to use incompatible hardware with Windows NT results in a failed installation or an unusable device. Save yourself some grief; do the homework in advance, and use only compatible system components.

Preparing The System

Before installing Windows NT, most experts—including Microsoft—recommend that you install DOS on the target machine (or machines), where that makes sense. Then, make sure you get the system's hardware components working. This includes all hard disks, CD-ROM drives, floppy disks, video cards, network interfaces, tape drives, and anything else that might make up part of your server.

Here's why: Because DOS is a much more forgiving operating system than Windows NT, making components work with DOS is merely a positive indication of potential success, rather than any kind of guarantee that those same components will work with Windows NT. But because DOS is more compact and easier to install, and a great many high-quality, DOS-based troubleshooting and diagnostic tools are available, bringing a system up under DOS first is your best shot at a successful Windows NT installation—assuming, of course, that all system components are on the latest HCL (or you've obtained the necessary drivers for items that are missing).

For similar reasons, the same experts that recommend you get your server up and running under DOS first, also recommend leaving at least a small DOS partition on your Windows NT Server machine. If hardware or software problems ever prevent the machine from booting into Windows NT, there's still a good chance that you'll be able to boot it up under DOS and perform a variety of diagnostic tests and "idiot checks." In many cases, you'll be able to fix your problems and get the server back up much more quickly than otherwise. At a cost of a little extra preparation time and 20 to 100 MB of disk space, many system administrators find this approach quite worthwhile.

 Remember that Windows NT runs on several other CPU types besides the Intel x86 processor family (including MIPS, DEC Alpha AXP, and IBM PowerPC). But only Intel-compatible CPUs can run DOS. When reading test questions—or working with real machines—be sure that the hardware will run DOS before making any further assumptions about using DOS for diagnosis or troubleshooting. Just because over 95 percent of Windows NT installations run on Intel CPUs doesn't mean that Microsoft doesn't expect you to know about non-Intel installation and other issues, or that you'll never encounter such a machine in your work with the operating system. Consider this a friendly reminder to examine all installation circumstances and requirements carefully!

Installing Windows NT

Because some installation decisions must be worked out in advance, it's a good idea to know what happens during the Windows NT installation process. This helps prior planning, so here's a high-level, step-by-step version of the Windows NT 4 Server installation process (we provide some discussion and pointers to other chapters in this book, where applicable):

1. Boot the machine under any operating system that can access the network and communicate with a source of Windows NT installation files, or under any Microsoft operating system that can access a local CD-ROM drive.

2. Run the Windows NT installation program that's appropriate for the platform: WINNT.EXE for DOS, Windows 3.x, or Windows 95 machines; WINNT32.EXE for Windows NT machines running Workstation or Server 3.5 or better. This copies the files from the distribution media (or network drive) to local hard disk space.

3. Verify the software and hardware components recognized by the installation program, and make changes if necessary (and repeat Steps 1 through 3 to restart the process).

   This is also the point in the installation process when you can examine the results of NT's built-in hardware detection program (named "ntdetect"). If you've got new or exotic hardware (which is a polite way of saying "hardware that ntdetect can't recognize") you will have one of two options: either reading drivers from floppies and installing at that point, or waiting until the initial install is complete and adding the hardware later.

> If the hardware you need to add isn't essential to the installation (like a CD-ROM that works with DOS or Windows 95, but isn't recognized by NT, or a hard disk that you want to put the system files on), wait until the initial installation is complete, and add the hardware later. That way, unforeseen problems won't impede the installation.

4. Select the hard disk partition where Windows NT is to reside. That partition can be either FAT or NTFS, but most experts recommend it be NTFS if at all possible (see Chapter 3 for a discussion of these file systems).

5. Format the selected partition (this step is optional, but recommended, especially if creating one or more new NTFS partitions).

6. Select the Windows NT default directory (most installations use the default \winnt directory).

7. Enter name and organization when prompted.

8. Select the licensing mode for the server machine; the options are Per Server (good for small networks or Internet-attached machines), or Per Seat (good for larger, multiserver networks or private machines). Microsoft charges for licenses, and you may change from Per Server to Per Seat only once. Because of

potential expense issues, most organizations with more than one server elect Per Seat licensing (which allows users to connect to as many servers as they want without requiring a separate license for each connection). For single-server networks, it's okay to choose Per Server licensing, because it can be changed to Per Seat later.

9. Enter a name for the computer; it must be unique on your network (for large networks, this may take some planning or coordination).

10. Set the machine's security role. A Windows NT Server may be either a Primary Domain Controller (PDC), a Backup Domain Controller (BDC), or a Stand-Alone Server (called a member server in Microsoft documentation, but not in the installation utility). Only one machine can be a PDC for a given domain, so only the first domain controller for a domain is installed as a PDC; all other domain controllers for the domain will be installed as BDCs. Member servers usually play other roles on a network, such as database server, communications server, or some other service. For more information about domain controllers, see Chapter 5.

11. Enter a password for the Administrator account (write it down; you'll need it again).

12. Select the options to create an Emergency Repair Disk (unless you're doing an extremely vanilla installation, we recommend against this—it's smarter to wait until the system is fully configured and generate the ERD then).

13. Select from the Components To Install checkboxes; choices include Accessibility Options, Accessories, Communications, Games, MS Exchange, and Multimedia. It's best to install everything (it's easier to delete

extraneous stuff later than to rerun the install program to add more stuff).

14. Establish networking role; choices are Wired To The Network and Remote Access To The Network. The first choice is the overwhelming favorite for most server machines.

15. Install Microsoft Internet Information Server (IIS). This is optional, and should be chosen only for systems that plan to run a Web server.

16. Detect network adapters; choices are Auto-detect or Manual setup. Most network cards can be automatically detected, but some must be configured manually. Be sure to have drivers on hand for your network interfaces, should the latter condition prevail.

17. For each network interface, select the protocols to be used; choices are TCP/IP, NWLink IPX/SPX Compatible Transport, and NetBEUI. For most networks, TCP/IP is the predominant choice.

18. Select Network services; choices are Microsoft Internet Information Server (if installed in Step 15), RPC Configuration, NetBIOS Interface, Workstation, and Server. All are chosen by default; there is seldom any need to make changes here.

19. Supply network interface settings. These include IRQ number, memory base address, DMA settings, and more. A successful DOS installation documented by NTHQ can supply all this information, if you don't already have it recorded somewhere.

20. If either NWLink or TCP/IP protocols were selected in Step 17, you'll have to configure them now. This will take some preparation, especially for TCP/IP: Be sure to obtain the machine's IP address, one or more DNS server addresses, the IP gateway (router) address, and the WINS server address (if applicable).

21. If the machine was designated a PDC in Step 10, you must now supply its computer and domain names; otherwise, it just gets a computer name.

22. If you elected to install Internet Information Server in Step 15, you will select and configure its component options at this point.

23. You will be prompted for Date/Time properties; set the local date, time, and time zone information as requested.

24. You will be prompted for Display Properties; be sure to click the Test button (not just to make sure the display is working properly, but to be able to proceed with—and complete—the installation).

25. Create an Emergency Repair Disk (if selected in Step 12).

Based on the steps where user input or foreknowledge is required, some items deserve a bit more discussion. Here is additional information regarding the following steps in this preceding 25-step process:

4. Select FAT or NTFS for the Windows NT partition.

   Chapter 3 covers this subject in some detail, and provides other sources of further details and information. FAT is more accessible to different types of operating systems than NTFS, but NTFS is more robust and secure than FAT. Most production installations elect to store operating system files under NTFS for those reasons.

10. Select the security role for the server: PDC, BDC, or Stand-Alone Server.

    Three important observations apply here (more details are covered in Chapter 5):

    a. There can be only one PDC for any given domain. When installing domain controllers, only the first one can be a PDC (that's why including the domain name is an important part of the configuration information here—Windows NT won't permit a second PDC to be installed).

b. If there's any chance you might want to use the machine being installed as a domain controller, be aware that you must designate it as one now, or reinstall Windows NT later for it ever to attain such status.

c. A member server (Stand-Alone Server in the installation dialog) plays no role in domain management. The only way to convert a member server to a domain controller is to reinstall Windows NT Server and change the designation in Step 10.

17. Choose Protocols: TCP/IP, NetBEUI, NWLink.

Microsoft has been deemphasizing NetBEUI for a while, and is pushing TCP/IP strongly. NWLink is recommended primarily for networks where interaction with NetWare-based resources is required (NWLink supports NetWare's native IPX/SPX protocols).

Most network administrators choose protocols for compatibility with existing installations, but Microsoft has this to say about possible rationales for choosing the aforementioned protocols:

a. NetBEUI is now recommended only for small, single-server networks. It's nearly completely self-configuring and self-tuning, and requires little or no administrative effort for installation and up-keep. It's also limited in scope and capability, and not at all routable, which is why it's best used only on small networks.

b. NWLink makes it easy for Microsoft networking clients to access NetWare-based resources or applications, or NetWare networking clients to access NT-based resources or applications. NWLink thus provides the foundation for NetWare interactions of all kinds (from simple application access to making NetWare servers look like NT, or NT servers look like NetWare). NetWare does a good job of managing node addresses automatically, but requires management of network addresses as the number of physical networks increases. It's much simpler than TCP/IP to manage, but more work than NetBEUI.

c.   TCP/IP is the protocol of the Internet—and by extension, for intranets as well—and represents Microsoft's primary emphasis for large, complex, or geographically dispersed networks. TCP/IP supports global access and reach, and the richest set of address and network management services. It's also the most work to manage, and takes ongoing effort and involvement from network administrators. Microsoft has done an excellent job of providing good infrastructure elements for TCP/IP—including services like WINS, DNS, and DHCP—but most of these fall into the scope of the Server Enterprise test, rather than this one. What information we do supply about TCP/IP may be found in Chapter 6.

19.   Supply network interface settings.

To configure a network interface card (NIC) properly, you must determine which of the many settings that can be involved will work on your system. If you get the NIC working with DOS, you'll be forced to resolve those issues in advance. Just be sure to record all the relevant information, in case Windows NT's network detection software can't puzzle all the details out for itself.

For any PC adapter to work properly, it must be set to use a unique (and available) Interrupt Request Line (IRQ), memory base address (and associated block of memory), and, in some cases, I/O port addresses and Direct Memory Addresses (DMA) must also be supplied. It's imperative to understand how to resolve NIC configurations and how to install them successfully to make Windows NT work on a network (but you won't see many questions on this subject on the NT Server 4 test).

20. Configure NWLink and/or TCP/IP.

   Each of these two protocols has its own special configuration issues.

   For NWLink it's important to understand that the NWLink Auto Frame Type Detection setting picks the predominant IPX frame type as its default. This makes it necessary to configure mixed NetWare 3.x (for versions older that 3.12) and 4.x networking environments manually, so that network addresses for the segments that carry the older 802.3 frame types can be distinguished from those that carry newer 802.2 frame types. (We'll cover this in detail in Chapter 7.)

   For TCP/IP, it's essential to understand and obtain the following address information for a successful Windows NT installation:

   a. The IP addressing scheme in use on your network

   b. The subnetworking approach in use, and the subnet mask for each subnet to which the NT server will be attached

   c. The IP address for the server itself (and for each additional NIC that will handle IP), plus any IP address ranges that a DHCP server on the machine will handle

     d. The IP address for at least one Domain Name Service (DNS) server, if not a primary and a secondary server address

     e. The IP address for at least one Windows Internet Names Service (WINS) server, if not a primary and a secondary address

If you're working with an Internet Service Provider in a small-to-medium-sized network, you should be able to get most if not all of this information from them. On larger networks, you'll need to work with your WAN or organization-wide networking authorities to obtain this information. We will discuss TCP/IP concepts and information further in Chapter 6.

21. Select a computer name.

Part of Microsoft's NetBIOS networking heritage is its use of 15-character names for computers, user accounts, and shared network resources. Several questions appear on the NT Server 4 test related to evaluating naming schemes, so it's wise to consider carefully how to create names that are easy to read and understand, and also easy for users to deduce. Because asking for things by name is a very human way to behave (but computers require that names be unique and conform to certain rules), naming is the focus of one or two test questions.

23. Supply Date/Time properties.

During installation, you must set the Time and Date for the new NT server, and indicate the time zone where the server operates. Time helps Windows NT format dates and timestamps, and is particularly essential on domain controllers and replication servers. You also can set locale (and associated language) information for Windows NT at this point that formats date displays and currency information as well.

With all these steps completed, you will have installed Windows NT Server, along with whatever options for protocols and services you selected along the way. As the next step for most network administrators is to press on and define user accounts, groups, and install other applications to make a server ready for production use, we recommend against making an Emergency Repair Disk (ERD) at this point.

If you wait until the rest of the predeployment installation and configuration work is done before building an ERD, the ERD will contain all the work you've done on the system. On the other hand, if the post-NT install work is complex or significant, making an ERD at this point prevents you from having to reenter all the information you entered during the first install. This will help if any problems occur after the OS has been installed, but before other predeployment installation and configuration work is complete (and the final ERD is created).

A successful Windows NT installation in and of itself doesn't represent a complete NT Server installation by any means. There's usually quite a bit of additional work to do after NT is installed before a system is completely ready for use. We'll cover the topics and utilities involved in this post-installation, predeployment work in Chapter 5.

The WINNT/WINNT32 Commands Demystified

The programs that drive Windows NT installation come in two flavors:

➤ **WINNT.EXE** This version of the install program is a 16-bit program, built to run on machines with DOS, Windows 3.x, or Windows 95 installed.

➤ **WINNT32.EXE** This version of the install program is a 32-bit program, built to run on machines running some version of Windows NT already. Most often, it's used to upgrade an existing from a previous version, or to change the status of an NT machine from Workstation or member server to an NT Server of some kind (perhaps even a domain controller).

Other than the difference between 16- and 32-bit operating environments, the two programs are identical. That's why we can discuss the switches and options to both commands in the following Help message, which may be produced by entering WINNT /? or WINNT32 /? at the command prompt:

```
WINNT [/S[:]sourcepath] [/T[:]tempdrive] [/I[:]inffile]
     [/O[X]] [/X | [/F] [/C]] [/B]
/S[:]sourcepath
        Specifies the source location of Windows NT files.
        Must be a full path of the form x:\[path] or
        \\server\share[\path].
        The default is the current directory.
/T[:]tempdrive
        Specifies a drive to contain temporary setup files.
        If not specified, Setup attempts to locate a drive for
        you.
/I[:]inffile
        Specifies the file name (no path) of the Setup information
        file.
        The default is DOSNET.INF.
/O      Create boot floppies only.
/OX     Create boot floppies for CD-ROM or floppy-based
        installation.
/X      Do not create the Setup boot floppies.
/F      Do not verify files as they are copied to the Setup boot
        floppies.
/C      Skip free-space check on the Setup boot floppies you
        provide.
/B      Floppyless operation
/U      Unattended operation and optional script file
        (requires /S).
/R      Specifies optional directory to be installed.
/RX     Specifies optional directory to be copied.
/E      Specifies command to be executed at the end of GUI setup.
```

Following are some notes about the syntax used above:

1. Square brackets ([ ]) enclose optional terms. Among other things, this indicates that all the parameters and associated attributes are optional for both WINNT and WINNT32.

2. The string /S[:]sourcepath indicates that the value of sourcepath is optional, but if it appears, the colon must

appear also (that is, /S:X:\bin\source is legal, but /SX:\bin\source is not).

3. The vertical bar character (|)separates mutually exclusive options, so [/X | [/F] [/C]] means that if /X appears, neither /F nor /C can appear, and that if either /F or /C appears, then /X cannot appear, in any single invocation of WINNT or WINNT32.

4. The notation used in the sourcepath explanation \\server\share[\path] is a NetBIOS network name, called a UNC (Universal Naming Convention). Here, \\server is the NetBIOS computer name of the machine where the source files reside, \share is the NetBIOS name for the network share within which the files reside, and the optional \path designation can point to a subdirectory beneath the share itself. UNC names are quite common in Microsoft networks; they go back to MS-Net's origins.

Relevant Switches And Options

A significant number of the switches and options for these commands relate to unattended installations that can be ordered up across the network by an administrator to install Windows NT on servers elsewhere on a network. In the NT Server test, these switches do not appear, so you need to remember only the following ones for the test:

➤ /S   Appears seldom, but must be used when reading source files from any drive other than the current default drive.

➤ /T   Appears seldom, but must be used when the compressed files that WINNT or WINNT32 copies locally from the source directory is any drive other than the current default drive.

➤ /O   Appears regularly; use this switch with WINNT to create boot floppies after an installation that used the /X or /B switches. It will not install anything on the computer; it only builds a set of boot floppies.

➤ /OX Appears occasionally; used to create boot floppies for a CD-ROM installation, but does not start the install process.

➤ /X Appears occasionally; if you want to install NT on a computer, but not to create a set of boot floppies, this is the switch to use.

➤ /F Appears seldom, but can be used to skip the verify step after copying files to a set of boot floppies. Speeds the process, but not recommended. Only used with WINNT.

➤ /C Appears seldom; use only if using blank, preformatted floppies when creating a set of boot floppies. Only used with WINNT.

➤ /B Appears regularly; use when installing from a network drive or a CD-ROM drive, without using floppies.

The other switches safely can be ignored for this test, but they do appear on the Server Enterprise exam, in conjunction with a series of questions on unattended installs.

Common Uses And Combinations

In the most common test questions that include WINNT and WINNT32, you are required to remember that WINNT32 may be used only with machines running some version of Windows NT (3.5 and higher), and that WINNT must be used with DOS, Windows 3.x, and Windows 95. As for command and switch combinations, these occur most frequently in test questions:

➤ **WINNT /OX** Use this to create a set of boot floppies, sometimes called Setup disks, after an installation is complete.

➤ **WINNT /B** Use this to install Windows NT without using setup floppies, whether from a network drive or a (local) CD-ROM. Although you can map a CD-ROM drive as a network share, and read files directly across the network, this is painfully slow, and not recommended. For network installs, copy the files from the CD to directory on a hard drive, and create a share for that directory.

Of course, the same switches can be used with WINNT32, but only on machines running Windows NT 3.5 or higher.

NetBIOS Names And Network Naming Schemes

By design, NetBIOS names are limited to 15 characters in length. The first character in a NetBIOS name must be alphabetic, but all other characters can be letters, numbers, or certain punctuation marks. It's not a good idea to put spaces in NetBIOS names, either. Table 2.2 lists those characters that should not appear within NetBIOS names; they're not necessarily illegal, but they often cause problems on networks, especially those with DOS or Windows 3.x clients.

Some additional caveats and information about NetBIOS names are required. Neither DOS nor Windows 3.x users can handle NetBIOS names longer than eight characters. Therefore, when working in a hybrid environment, you should either define NetBIOS names eight characters or shorter, or define aliases eight characters or shorter for those resources that DOS or Windows 3.x users must access. It's a good idea to stay away from punctuation marks of all kinds in NetBIOS names, if only because some applications may otherwise have trouble with them.

Finally, it's time to reveal that dollar signs are legal in NetBIOS names, but should be used for one purpose only: When a dollar sign appears in the final position of a NetBIOS share name, that name will not appear in network browser lists or in response to NetBIOS network survey commands like **net view**. Such shares are called "hidden shares" and are used by Windows NT itself to create a class of administrative shares that only administrators can access (and no one can see on the network). You occasionally

Table 2.2	Problem characters for NetBIOS names.	
Character Name	**Character**	**Key Combination**
Bullet	•	Alt+0419
Dollar sign	$	Alt+0164
Vertical bar			Alt+0166
Section sign	§	Alt+0167
Paragraph marker	¶	Alt+0182

will see questions on the test that require knowledge of how to create and use hidden shares. Only those who know such shares exist, and know their exact names, can access them.

Networking Clients With Windows NT

When installing a network server, it's usually desirable to make that server's resources available to clients elsewhere on the network. Sometimes, the software that enables desktop machines to communicate with the network must be installed from scratch—especially when bringing up a network for the first time, or when adding new clients to an existing network. To that end, Microsoft has included a utility, called the "Network Client Administrator," that creates installation and startup disks. These disks enable a variety of operating systems to become clients on a Windows NT network, including:

➤ Network Client 3.0 for MS-DOS

➤ LAN Manager 2.2c for MS-DOS

➤ LAN Manager 2.2c for OS/2

➤ Windows for Workgroups 3.11 (the entire OS is included, in fact)

For more information on the Network Client Administrator, see Chapter 5.

The process of creating an installation or startup disk is quite simple: Once inside the Network Client Administrator utility, select the Make Network Installation Diskette option, and it will pilot you through the process. It's also necessary to point the utility at the proper subdirectory where the source files for the various operating systems reside.

The official use for the Network Client Administrator is to make it easy for network administrators to create disks that can enable networking for workstations running any of the aforementioned operating systems. The second DOS option is provided to provide backward compatibility with MS-DOS users who wish to maintain existing batch files built for LAN Manager networks. In practice, this utility makes it easy to set up multiple clients at the same time, and builds install disks that make the best use of DOS's limited memory management and networking capabilities.

Another excellent "guerrilla application" of this tool, however, makes it easy to install Windows NT Servers onto a bare machine. Here's how this is done:

1. Use a bootable DOS disk, with FDISK included, to create and format a DOS partition on the new server's boot disk. For best results (if space isn't too precious), 200 MB is plenty of room to handle all the NT files during installation; after that you'll have plenty of room for DOS, diagnostics, and even Windows 95, if you're so inclined.

2. Install DOS on the boot partition, and make it bootable. Install a network interface card, and make sure the computer continues to boot (if a test or diagnostics disk is included, make sure your work passes its tests).

3. Use the Network Client Administrator to create a DOS Network Client disk; install the software on the new server (you must have access to a working machine running Windows NT Server).

4. Create a share on the working server that points to a copy of the \i386 directory taken from the Windows NT distribution media (this directory includes subdirectories, so use the **xcopy** command, or some other utility that handles recursive copy).

5. Once the MS Network Client is running on your new server, simply map a drive to the \i386 share. For example, **net use x: \\server\i386** does the job quite nicely. Then, enter X: at the command prompt to point to the mapped drive where the install files reside.

6. At that point, you need only invoke winnt to start a network install of Windows NT, as follows:

```
winnt /b
```

Remember, this performs a floppyless install, right across the network. It may take a while to copy all the files (15 to 30 minutes is normal) but it's the easiest method of NT installation we've tried.

Common Install Dilemmas

There are two major parts of a Windows NT installation:

1. The initial portion of the install, until all the files are copied to the target machine, occurs inside a blue-screen, character mode interface that's familiar to anyone who's ever installed any version of Windows. This is called the character mode portion of the install.

2. The second portion of the install occurs about midway through the process. At this point, enough of Windows NT has been installed that the machine reboots itself and uses a graphical user interface to complete the rest of the process. This is called the GUI mode portion of the install.

When problems occur during the character mode portion of the install, it's frequently necessary to restart the process and begin afresh. If the install program has begun copying files when it fails, one or two temporary directories will be present on the computer:

1. **WIN_NT.~LS:** where the install program stores all the compressed Windows NT system files.

2. **WIN_NT.~BT:** where the install program stores compressed boot files for Windows NT (this directory appears only if the /B switch has been selected for the WINNT or WINNT32 command that launched the failed installation; otherwise these files are written to the three boot disks created during the installation process).

If you begin a reinstall of Windows NT without removing these directories and their contents, the install program will remove them for you. Experience has shown that it's faster to delete the files yourself—provided that you include the DOS program DELTREE.EXE on the DOS boot disk that you use to restart the machine (or in the DOS partition on the hard drive). Without DELTREE, it can take more than half an hour to delete these files; with DELTREE it seems to go somewhat faster (but be prepared to lose some time here).

Beyond the need to restart the process from time to time, there are a few other well-known dilemmas that may show up during a Windows NT installation. In the sections that follow, we'll cover two of the most common situations that you may encounter during installation.

To Upgrade Or Install Anew?

Windows NT can capture and use information from other, preceding Windows installations with degrees of success and fidelity that vary according to the difference between the information that's already on the machine, and the structure of Windows NT 4's native environment. According to the Microsoft literature, it's possible to instruct Windows NT Server 4 to capture configuration information from any of the following Microsoft operating systems (listed in decreasing order of difference):

➤ Windows 3.1, 3.11, or Windows for Workgroups (WfW)

➤ Windows 95

➤ Windows NT 3.5 and 3.51

As always, there are a few interesting terminological distinctions. Windows NT is not really considered an upgrade of Windows 3.x, WfW, or Windows 95, but if you install Windows NT in the same directory where the "earlier" version of Windows resides, the install program will grab as much configuration information as it can from either the .INI files (Windows 3.x) or from the Windows 95 Registry files. Most experts agree, however, that unless you have compelling reasons to leave parts of the previous installation alone (like no access to the application disks), you're better off backing up such a system, reformatting the drive, installing Windows NT, and then reinstalling the applications you want to keep on the machine. Because some 16-bit applications won't run under Windows NT anyway, this is by far the safest course of action.

The term "upgrade" really applies only to prior versions of Windows NT. The easiest upgrade is from a prior NT Server installation (3.5 or 3.51) to 4; in that case, the bulk of the configuration information, the security and accounts database, and most services will transfer intact into the new environment. If you're upgrading multiple servers, and one or more is a domain controller, always upgrade the PDC first, to keep the domain database correct and intact.

If you're upgrading an older version of NT Server to a newer version, the following information is left intact:

➤ Any edits made to the Registry using the Registry Editor

➤ Custom program groups, desktop layout, settings, and preferences set through the Control Panel

➤ Local security accounts (users and groups)

➤ Network adapter settings, protocols, and service configurations and addresses (including Macintosh and RAS services, if applicable)

➤ Preferences set for Accessories and Administrative Tools. But the upgrade process does copy new versions of system files and change settings and program groups to reflect new utilities, capabilities, and organization. During an upgrade, it's necessary to provide the following information:

The directory where system files will reside (the default for 3.5 and 3.51 is \winnt35, which differs from 4's \WINNT default)

Some new parameters (if you're already using TCP/IP, they will be requested). You'll want to create a new emergency repair disk as part of the upgrade process. Also, as with any major system changes, we recommend you begin the upgrade process by making a complete system backup of the current installation.

When it comes to upgrading from NT Workstations to NT Server, there's one well-known gotcha: If the resulting Server is to be used as a domain controller, it's necessary to reinstall Windows NT Server software from scratch. In other words, you can't use the upgrade option and obtain the desired result. If you do upgrade Windows NT to NT Server, it can only be a member server; in that case, to be able to use the new version of User Manager that comes with NT Server, you also must delete your old user profile. Even if you want to convert a Windows NT 4 Workstation machine to an NT 4 Server machine, all of these restrictions still apply. Likewise, if you are upgrading a Stand-Alone (member) server from an earlier version of Windows NT to 4, you must reinstall from scratch if it is to become a domain controller.

The Hardware Works Now, But Not With NT

You'll sometimes run into a situation where hardware that works fine with DOS, Windows 3.x, or Windows 95 is not on the HCL. This is especially common for older CD-ROM drives, many of which use proprietary interface cards and require custom drivers. Windows NT recognizes most SCSI CD-ROM drives, and many of the newer IDE CD-ROM drives, but it doesn't recognize all of them.

If this happens on a machine on which you're trying to install Windows NT, don't despair. You can always insert the Windows NT CD and simply copy the files from the \i386 directory to your hard drive, and use the copied files to perform the installation. If that doesn't work, as long as your machine can still access the network, you can always perform a network install by reading the necessary files from a mapped network drive.

Be sure to build the install floppies, though, just to make sure you can continue the process should the installation fail for some reason along the way. You'll want to be sure to back up the original system first, so you can always get back to where you started if you can't complete the installation for some reason.

You may sometimes encounter situations where Windows NT doesn't recognize hardware elements on your system during installation. If those elements aren't essential to the installation, you can always skip the problem-solving (or supplementary driver installation) that's usually required. But during the installation process, Windows NT will show you a list of the drives it recognizes on your system, and the overall system components; in both cases, it does give you options to install additional hardware, assuming that you've got the necessary driver software in hand.

Exam Prep Questions

Question 1

Which of the following elements of this PC's configurations do not meet Windows NT Server's minimum installation requirements for a network installation where source files will be copied to the machine's FAT partition? [Check all invalid entries]

❏ a. 95 MB free disk space on the FAT partition

❏ b. 12 MB RAM

❏ c. 486/100 DX4 CPU

❏ d. Paradise VGA card

❏ e. CD-ROM drive

Because Windows NT Server requires 124 MB of free disk space for all the files, plus room to decompress them, answer a is insufficient and should be checked. Windows NT Server requires a minimum of 16 MB of RAM; therefore, answer b should be checked. NT Server works on any Intel processor greater than or equal to a 486; answer c should not be checked. Indeed, Windows NT requires a VGA graphics card or better to work; answer d is correct, and should not be checked. Finally, Windows NT does not require a CD-ROM—but it's a good idea to have one, especially on machines for which a network install isn't possible—so having one is not a problem; answer e also should be unchecked.

Question 2

> Which of the following tools or techniques can you use to assess the suitability of a two-year-old Pentium PC for Windows NT installation? [Check all correct answers]
>
> ❑   a. Microsoft Windows NT Diagnostics
>
> ❑   b. System Sleuth
>
> ❑   c. NTHQ disk
>
> ❑   d. Obtain a current copy of the Hardware Compatibility List, and check every system component to be sure it appears therein.

Windows NT Diagnostics aren't available until Windows NT is installed successfully on a machine, nor does the program perform hardware checking on its own (rather, it reports the contents of the Registry written by the NTDETECT.EXE program that runs at bootup). This means answer a is incorrect. System Sleuth is an old PC diagnostics program that doesn't perform Windows NT hardware compatibility checks of any kind, making answer b incorrect as well. The Windows NT Hardware Qualifier disk may be constructed by running the MAKEDISK.BAT program in the \Support\Hqtool directory on the Windows NT CD ROM. Since NTHQ checks the machine against a built-in version of the HCL, it will do the job (except on machines with hardware newer than August 1996, which the software may not recognize). But because the machine is older than NTHQ, NTHQ should work correctly. This makes answer c correct. Finally, the HCL is indeed the source of the latest information on what works with Windows NT; even though checking by hand is more work than using NTHQ, it will produce a correct assessment of the machine, making answer d correct as well. We call this a trick question because it slyly mentions that the machine is two years old, which means that the HCL included on the distribution CD for Windows NT should be able to recognize all its components.

Question 3

Which of the following statements are true? When upgrading from Windows NT Workstation 3.51 to Windows NT Server 4 you can: [Check all correct answers]

❏   a. transfer Registry edits from the old version to the new.

❏   b. designate the machine as a domain controller.

❏   c. maintain custom program groups.

❏   d. maintain desktop layout, icon spacing and placement, and color scheme.

❏   e. maintain local groups and accounts.

Answer b is the only incorrect answer to Question 3. A Workstation upgraded to a Server only can be designated as a Stand-Alone Server (member server elsewhere in Microsoft's documentation) in the install program (a complete reinstall is necessary to change this status). Otherwise, the upgrade process maintains direct Registry edits, transfers any existing custom program groups, maintains the desktop as before, and preserves any existing local groups and accounts defined for that machine.

Question 4

> Even though Windows 95 can recognize the CD-ROM drive on a machine, it's not supported for Windows NT Server 4. How can you install Windows NT Server 4 on that machine anyway?
> [Check all correct answers]
>
> ❑ a. Create a set of installation disks from another Windows NT Server machine, and use the disks to perform the install.
>
> ❑ b. Use the xcopy command to copy the files from the \i386 directory onto the Windows 95 machine's hard disk, and run WINNT.EXE from there.
>
> ❑ c. While running Windows 95, change to the \i386 directory on the NT CD, and run WINNT32.EXE.
>
> ❑ d. Copy the installation files from \i386 to a server, map a drive from the Windows 95 machine to that directory, and run WINNT.EXE from there.

Since the machine can recognize and use the CD-ROM while it's still running Windows 95, the easiest approach is to copy the files from the \i386 directory to a directory on the machine's hard disk. But this will work only if the drive is formatted to permit creation of another partition for NTFS, or if the FAT partition where the files are deposited may later be converted to NTFS (see Chapter 3 for a discussion of FAT and NTFS). That's why b is a correct answer. Answer d also is correct, because if the drives on the machine need to be completely reformatted—as often will be the case when upgrading from Windows 95 to Windows NT—it might be smarter to copy the installation files to a server, and perform a network install. This leaves the drives on the machine free to be reformatted completely, but it will require a boot floppy (that you might build using the Network Client Administrator). Answer a is incorrect because the install disks alone don't convey all the Windows NT installation files; there's still a need to gain access to the CD-ROM or a copy of its contents. Answer c is incorrect because the 16-bit installation program, WINNT.EXE, works with Windows 95; WINNT32.EXE only works with versions of Windows NT 3.5 and higher.

Question 5

During Windows NT installation, Setup fails to recognize one of your SCSI drives, but this affects neither the boot nor the system drive. How can you solve this problem? [Choose all correct answers]

❏   a. Use the Search For Devices option during installation, right after the hardware detection phase is complete.

❏   b. Press S to specify additional devices during installation, at the phase when the list of "Mass Storage Devices"appears.

❏   c. Complete the installation, then add the missing SCSI drive, using the Control Panel afterwards.

❏   d. Stop the installation. Remove the problem drive and replace it with one that's listed on the HCL.

There is no Search For Devices option during installation, so this is patently false, as is answer a. On the other hand, during the phase when the list of Mass Storage Devices appears, it is possible to press S to specify additional devices, which makes answer b correct, but it requires that you have a copy of the driver software on hand. A better approach is described in answer c, where the option of installing the drive for the errant device in the SCSI Devices applet in Control Panel is mentioned. Because the drive is not essential to a successful installation, it's probably best to wait until installation is complete to add it to a working Windows NT Server. Thus, answer c is not only correct, it's recommended. Finally, answer d also is correct. If you remove an unsupported device, install a supported replacement, and restart the installation, it should complete successfully. In fact, answer c is recommended because it lets you complete the installation immediately, and helps you make sure a driver is available for the errant drive; if not, d becomes the only viable alternative.

Question 6

> Select the installation recipe that permits you to install Windows
> NT Server across the network onto a Windows 95 computer.
>
> ○ a. Connect to the network directory that contains the
> Windows NT installation files and run WINNT32.EXE.
>
> ○ b. Connect to the network directory that contains the
> Windows NT installation files and run WINNT.EXE.
>
> ○ c. Connect to the network directory that contains the
> Windows NT installation files and run SETUP.EXE.
>
> ○ d. Create a client installation disk using Network Client
> Administrator, boot the machine with that disk, and run
> NETWORK.EXE.

WINNT32.EXE works with Windows NT only, not with Windows 95;
this disqualifies answer a. Answer b accurately describes a network install
scenario, and cites the correct version of the install program, so it is correct.
SETUP.EXE is not the name of a program used to install Windows NT, so
answer c is incorrect. Likewise, d is incorrect because NETWORK.EXE
will not perform a networked Windows NT installation.

Question 7

> A RAID array and its SCSI controller must be installed on a new
> Windows NT Server machine. Which of these activities is required
> to make these devices available on your system? [Check all cor-
> rect answers]
>
> ❑ a. Install the driver for the SCSI controller.
>
> ❑ b. Install the driver for the RAID array.
>
> ❑ c. Use the Services applet in Control Panel to start the
> SCSI controller and RAID array.
>
> ❑ d. Restart the machine.

For any hardware components to work on a Windows NT machine, drivers
must be installed and operating. Thus, answers a and b are both correct,
and should be checked. Devices are started by the operating system itself
when the computer boots up, so there's no way to start a SCSI controller or

a RAID array in the Services applet in Control Panel. Therefore, answer c is incorrect and should be left unchecked. Because hardware changes are recorded in the Registry and such changes cannot take effect until the next time a system boots, it's necessary to restart Windows NT anytime you add new hardware components to the system. Of course, this means that answer d also must be checked.

Question 8

What is the correct way to upgrade a computer running Windows for Workgroups to Windows NT Server 4?

○   a. Install Windows NT in a separate directory and reinstall all applications.

○   b. Install Windows NT in a separate directory and import WIN.INI and SYSTEM.INI into the registry.

○   c. Run WINNT32.EXE and install Windows NT into WfW's home directory, c:\windows.

○   d. Run WINNT.EXE and install Windows NT into WfW's home directory, c:\windows.

Trick! question

Strictly speaking, upgrading from Windows for Workgroups (WfW) to Windows NT Server is not an installation option. But by installing Windows NT Server into the same directory where WfW resides, the install program is smart enough to grab what information it can carry into the Windows NT environment by detecting and reading the WIN.INI and SYSTEM.INI files, and converting program and group information into corresponding Windows NT Registry entries. This means, of course, that answer d is correct. It's also a trick question because this really isn't an upgrade, per se, but rather a new installation that's smart enough to preserve some old configuration information. Answer a does not give the install program the implicit directive to convert the WfW.INI files and fails the "upgrade" requirement. Answer b apparently assumes that some magic import function for .INI files is available; since there isn't one, this answer also is incorrect. Finally, answer c provides the correct directory placement, but calls the 32-bit version of the install program, which works only with Windows NT, not with WfW.

Question 9

> Windows NT permits creation of a network startup installation disk. Which of these activities is necessary to create such a disk? [Choose all correct answers]
>
> ❏   a. Create the disk using Client Manager.
>
> ❏   b. Create the disk using User Manager For Domains.
>
> ❏   c. Specify the shared directory where the installation files reside.
>
> ❏   d. Choose Make Network Installation Startup Disk within the Network Client Administrator utility.

There is no Client Manager utility in Windows NT Server; answer a is incorrect. User Manager For Domains has nothing to do with network installation, making answer b incorrect as well. To build a network installation startup disk using Windows NT Server, it's necessary to identify the proper directory where the installation files reside, and to choose the Make Network Installation Startup Disk option immediately after launching the Network Client Administrator utility. Therefore, both c and d are correct, and should be checked.

Question 10

> There are 25 Windows 95 machines on your network. You want to
> upgrade them to Windows NT Workstation with a minimum of
> effort. The installation files reside in a shared directory named
> \\Server5\Wks4. What is the best way to handle the installation
> across the network?
>
> ○ a. Attach to the shared directory and run WINNT.EXE
>   across the network.
>
> ○ b. Attach to the shared directory and run SETUP.EXE
>   across the network.
>
> ○ c. Install the Windows NT Workstation client using
>   Network Client Administrator.
>
> ○ d. Use Network Client Administrator to create a DOS
>   Installation Startup Disk, attach to the shared directory,
>   and run SETUP.EXE across the network.

To perform a network installation of Windows NT on a computer running
Windows 95, it is necessary to obtain access to and run the WINNT.EXE
program. Thus, a is the only possible correct answer. Both answers b and d
refer to SETUP.EXE, which is the install program for Windows 3.x and
Windows 95, not for Windows NT (you must choose WINNT.EXE because it is the only version of the NT installation program that works on
non-Windows NT systems). Answer c is incorrect because it assumes that
NCA includes support for installing Windows NT Workstation; because
this is not the case, this answer is wrong.

Question 11

> When you installed Windows NT Server 4, you opted not to make a set of startup disks. How can you make a set of startup disks on that machine, now that the operating system's already installed?
>
> ○   a. You can't; you have to reinstall Windows NT Server 4 again.
>
> ○   b. Run WINNT.EXE /O from the installation CD-ROM.
>
> ○   c. Run WINNT32.EXE /O from the installation CD-ROM.
>
> ○   d. Run the System applet in Control Panel.

To build a set of startup disks only, both WINNT.EXE and WINNT32.EXE support the /O switch, which instructs these programs to build only a set of startup disks, nothing more. Thus, answer a is patently false. Answer b comes very close, but invokes the 16-bit version of the install program, which won't work on a machine running Windows NT. Answer c therefore is the correct answer. Finally, answer d is incorrect because the System applet includes no options to create a set of startup disks for Windows NT.

Need To Know More?

 Heywood, Drew: *Inside Windows NT Server*. New Riders, Indianapolis, IN, 1995. ISBN 1-56205-472-4. Chapters 3 through 5 provide all kinds of planning and installation information and advice, along with some useful troubleshooting tips.

 Siyan, Karanjit S.: *Windows NT Server 4 Professional Reference*. New Riders, Indianapolis, IN, 1996. ISBN 1-56205-731-6. Chapters 3 and 4 cover basic and advanced installation topics; all of this information is valuable, but some of it—particularly the data about unattended installs—is more appropriate for the Server Enterprise exam rather than this test. The detailed description of a Windows NT installation on pp. 82 through 94 is the best we've ever seen in print.

 Strebe, Matthew, Charles Perkins, and James Chellis: *MSCE: NT Server 4 Study Guide*. Sybex Network Press, San Francisco, CA, 1996. ISBN 0-7821-1972-7. Chapters 2 through 4 cover planning, hardware, and installation respectively. Chapter 17, "Troubleshooting," includes an informative section entitled "New Windows NT Installations."

 The Windows NT Server 4 manuals cover planning, configuration, and installation issues quite well. Both the *Start Here Manual* and the *Concepts and Planning Manual* are worth perusing, at least once.

   The Windows NT Server Resource Kit contains lots of useful information about Windows NT system planning and installation. You can search the TechNet CD or the CD accompanying the *Resource Kit*, using keywords like "installation" and "hardware compatibility." In the *Resource Guide* volume, Chapter 1, "Deploying Windows NT Server," and Chapter 4, "Planning a Reliable Configuration," include information that is both germane and useful.

File Systems

Terms you'll need to understand:

√ File Allocation Table (FAT)

√ New Technology File System (NTFS)

√ High Performance File System (HPFS)

√ Compact Disk File System (CDFS)

√ Long File Names (LFNs)

√ Virtual FAT (VFAT)

√ FAT32

√ Share

√ No Access

√ Read

√ Change

√ Full Control

√ Add

√ Add & Read

√ List

√ CONVERT.EXE

Techniques you'll need to master:

√ Selecting a file system for NT

√ Securing system resources

√ Establishing access permissions

√ Creating shares and implementing share permissions

√ Understanding the difference between copying and moving files

√ Using CONVERT.EXE to convert FAT to NTFS

Windows NT supports two primary file systems to save and retrieve data from storage systems of all kinds (primarily hard disks):

1. File Allocation Table (FAT)
2. New Technology File System (NTFS)

In this chapter, we'll review these file systems and explore the key aspects of features, functions, and behavior that you're likely to encounter on an exam. We'll also examine a couple of other special-purpose file systems that work with Windows NT, so that you're familiar with all the Microsoft Windows NT file systems alphabet soup. Then we'll conclude with some example file-system-related test questions and some good places to go looking for more information on this fascinating subject.

FAT Comes In Many Flavors

FAT stands for File Allocation Table and refers to a linear table structure used to represent information about files. The information represented includes file names, file attributes, and other directory entries that locate where files (or segments of files) are stored in the FAT environment; this information points to the actual location on disk where the beginning of a physical file resides.

Original FAT

FAT is the file system originally used with DOS. FAT represents a nearly unbroken chain of capability back to the earliest days of the first DOS-based PCs. The file allocation table from which FAT draws its name stores directory information in a simple table structure that must be searched from beginning to end, one entry at a time, when users access directories or the files that reside within them.

 Although FAT is both primitive and simple, FAT implementations abound: A variety of versions for DOS, Windows 3.x, Windows NT, many flavors of Unix, and Macintosh are available. Numerous other, more exotic operating systems also support FAT file structures. For this reason, Microsoft recommends using FAT volumes with Windows NT Server or Workstation whenever many different types of clients must exchange data through a single file system. (Volumes are discussed in more detail in Chapter 4.)

One of the most important characteristics of original FAT is its use of so-called 8.3 (pronounced "eight-dot-three") file names, where the name of a file can be up to eight characters long, all extensions must be preceded by a period, and file extensions can be no more than three characters long. This latter specification has led to the proliferation of many common three-character file extensions, such as .TXT for text files, .DOC for word processing files, .XLS for Excel spreadsheet files, and more. For many users, this is a defining characteristic for DOS, but it's really a requirement of the FAT file system.

Because the size of files and partitions that FAT can manage has grown with each new version of DOS, FAT uses two kinds of pointers in its allocation tables. Partitions smaller than 50 MB use 12-bit pointers, while larger partitions require the use of 16-bit pointers. That's why sometimes you'll see FAT volumes labeled as either "FAT12" (the volume's FAT uses 12-bit pointers) or "FAT16" (the volume's FAT uses 16-bit pointers). As shown in Figure 3.1, a FAT12 or FAT16 label appears in disk partition management utilities like the FDISK command that ships with most versions of DOS. For versions of DOS from 3.0 to 6.22, all FAT drivers are 16-bit only (but this does not affect whether a volume is called FAT12 or FAT16—that's purely a function of the size of the FAT volume itself).

Today, in addition to ordinary FAT, there are two other flavors of FAT in use in the most modern Microsoft operating systems (Windows 95 and

Figure 3.1   The DOS FDISK utility indicates whether a FAT volume is FAT12 or FAT16.

Table 3.1 Vital statistics for the FAT file system.	
Feature	**Capability/Maximum**
Maximum volume size	2 GB
Maximum file size	2 GB
Maximum files in root directory	512
Maximum files in nonroot directory	65,535
File-level security	No
Long file name support	No
Self-repairing	No
Transaction logging capabilities	No
File-level compression	No
File-level security	No
Dual file fork support (Macintosh)	No
POSIX support	No

Windows NT, to be precise): Virtual FAT (VFAT) and the FAT32 File System. We'll cover those in the sections that follow.

Virtual FAT (VFAT)

The Virtual FAT file system was first introduced with Windows for Workgroups 3.11 to process file I/O in protected mode. With the introduction of Windows 95, VFAT added support for long file names (LFNs). Nevertheless, VFAT remains backward compatible with original FAT, which means that it supports access using 8.3 file names as well as LFNs, and in fact, maintains an equivalence mechanism that maps 8.3 names into LFNs, and vice versa.

 VFAT is the version of FAT that the original releases of Windows 95, Windows NT 3.51, and Windows NT 4 currently support. When using VFAT file systems, it's absolutely essential to use file management utilities that understand VFAT in general and LFNs in particular. That's because earlier DOS file management utilities will happily reorganize what appears to them as an original FAT structure, and will often lose or damage any LFN information that the FAT table maintained by VFAT (or FAT32 for that matter) contains. Therefore, with VFAT volumes, you must be certain to use file management utilities that can understand and preserve VFAT file structures.

In the initial release of Windows 95, the 32-bit VFAT file system is the primary file system. VFAT can use either 32-bit, protected-mode drivers or 16-bit real-mode drivers. Actual allocation on disk is still 12- or 16-bit (depending on the size of the volume), so FAT on the disk uses the same structure as earlier implementations of FAT. VFAT handles all hard drive requests, and uses 32-bit code for all file access to hard disk volumes.

 As Table 3.2 should illustrate, the primary differences between VFAT and original FAT are an increase in maximum volume and file sizes, an increase in nonroot directory container size, and addition of long file name support to 8.3 file names. VFAT also supports both 16- and 32-bit calls, whereas original FAT supports only 16-bit calls.

The FAT32 File System

FAT32 is a 32-bit successor to VFAT that was introduced with Microsoft Windows 95 OEM Service Release 2, in September 1996. You sometimes will see this release called Windows 95 OSR2 in Microsoft publications. FAT32 is a completely native 32-bit file system (much like NTFS) and supports numerous updates and enhancements compared to other FAT implementations.

Table 3.2 Vital statistics for the VFAT file system.	
Feature	**Capability/Maximum**
Maximum volume size	4 GB
Maximum file size	4 GB
Maximum files in root directory	512
Maximum files in nonroot directory	No limit
File-level security	No
Long file name support	Yes
Self-repairing	No
Transaction logging capabilities	No
File-level compression	No
File-level security	No
Dual file fork support (Macintosh)	No
POSIX support	No

Most important, FAT32 uses disk space more efficiently than other FAT implementations. FAT32 can use smaller disk clusters than earlier implementations, which were limited to a maximum of 65,635 clusters per volume (so as drives got bigger, cluster sizes had to increase as well). This means that even for drives up to 8 GB in size, FAT32 can use 4 K clusters. This results in a 10 to 15 percent savings in storage allocation and uses disk space more efficiently compared to FAT16 drives.

FAT32 also can relocate the root directory and use a backup copy of the FAT, rather than the default copy. FAT32 supports an expanded boot record to include copies of critical data structures, making FAT32 drives less susceptible to failures owing to FAT corruption than earlier implementations. FAT32 even represents the root directory as an ordinary cluster chain, which means that the directory can be located anywhere on a drive, and the prior limitation of 512 entries on a root directory no longer applies (as it does to earlier FAT implementations). Planned implementations of FAT32 may even support dynamic resizing of FAT32 partitions, but this is not supported in Windows 95 OSR2.

Windows 95 OSR2 is the only current Microsoft operating system that supports FAT32. This means that not even Windows NT 4, with the latest service pack applied, supports this file system. If you create a multiboot configuration on a machine with Windows 95 OSR2 and Windows NT installed, NT will not be able to access any files that reside in a FAT32 partition. Windows 95 OSR2 can, however, access the VFAT partitions that Windows NT creates.

The same proviso about using VFAT utilities on VFAT volumes applies to FAT32 volumes. Because earlier FAT utilities (including both FAT and VFAT, where FAT32 is concerned) can damage or lose critical disk information, *never* use anything but FAT32 file management utilities on FAT32 volumes.

In addition to increasing FAT's storage capacity (to a whopping 4 terabyte maximum for files and volumes), FAT32 makes some much-needed improvements to the root directory structure for FAT. Previous implementations required that all information in a FAT root directory fit into a single disk cluster. To all intents and purposes, this limited the number of files in the root to a maximum of 512 entries.

Table 3.3 Vital statistics for the FAT32 file system.	
Feature	**Capability/Maximum**
Maximum volume size	4 TB
Maximum file size	4 TB
Maximum files in root directory	No limit
Maximum files in nonroot directory	No limit
File-level security	No
Long file name support	Yes
Self-repairing	Yes*
Transaction logging capabilities	No
File-level compression	No
File-level security	No
Dual file fork support (Macintosh)	No
POSIX support	No

The introduction of LFNs further limited what the root directory could hold. Since the maximum length of an LFN is 256, a single full-length LFN can consume 25 entries in a FAT (1 for the 8.3 name, 24 more for the LFN itself). This reduces the number of entries possible in a VFAT root directory to 21. Microsoft recommends that LFNs be avoided in FAT root directories unless FAT32 is in use.

Then, too, full file specifications, which require both path names and file names (whether LFNs or 8.3 names), are limited to a total of 260 characters. FAT32 does away with the problems that LFNs in root directories can pose, but it does nothing to increase the 260-character limit on full file specifications. For that reason, Microsoft recommends that even LFNs not be allowed to exceed 75 to 80 characters in length, to leave plenty of room for path designations (up to 180 to 185 characters).

Finally, FAT32 delivers several improvements to FAT's fault tolerance. For one thing, FAT32 boot records now capture important file system data (such as partition table information). For another, FAT mirroring can be disabled in FAT32, so that another copy of the FAT can be used to drive file lookup and access. That's why the Vital Statistics table for FAT32 includes a "Yes" under the Self-repairing category. (It gets an asterisk, though, because these characteristics, while useful, fall short of NTFS's broader set of self-repair capabilities.)

The New Technology File System (NTFS)

In keeping with the New Technology part of its name, NTFS incorporates significant improvements and changes to the file system native to Windows NT. From a user's point of view, files remain organized into directories (often called "folders" in the Windows environment). But unlike FAT, there is no special treatment for root directories, nor limitations set by underlying hardware (such as the ability to access only a maximum number of disk sectors or clusters, as is the case with FAT). Likewise, there are no special locations on an NTFS volume, like the file allocation table that gives FAT its name.

NTFS was designed to provide the following characteristics:

➤ **Reliability** Desirable on high-end or shared systems, such as file servers, reliability is a key element of NTFS design and behavior.

➤ **Added functionality** NTFS is designed to be extensible and incorporates advanced fault tolerance, emulates other file systems easily, supports a powerful security model, handles multiple data streams, and permits addition of user-defined attributes to files.

➤ **POSIX support** Because the U.S. Government requires minimal POSIX compliance in all systems it buys, NTFS provides them. Basic POSIX file system capabilities include optional use of case-sensitive file names, an additional timestamp for time of last file access, and an aliasing mechanism called "hard links" that lets two or more file names (potentially in different directories) point to the same file.

➤ **Flexibility** NTFS supports a highly flexible clustering model, with cluster sizes from 512 bytes to 64 K, based on a multiple of the hardware's built-in disk allocation factor. NTFS also supports LFNs, the Unicode character set, and maintains 8.3 file names for all files for backward compatibility with FAT.

NTFS Advantages

NTFS is constructed to handle large collections of data particularly well (see Table 3.4 for the details), and also works well for volumes of 400 MB or greater. Because the directory structure for NTFS is based on a highly efficient data structure called a "B-tree," search time for files under NTFS does not degrade as the number of files to be searched increases (as it does for FAT-based systems).

NTFS also has been designed with sufficient recoverability so that users never should need to employ any kind of disk repair utility on an NTFS partition. Among other things, NTFS maintains a Recycle Bin so that users ordinarily can retrieve their own deleted files without having to run an Undelete utility of any kind. But NTFS also supports a variety of file system integrity mechanisms, including automatic transaction logging, which permits all file system writes to be replayed from a special system log.

Table 3.4 Vital statistics for the NTFS file system.	
Feature	**Capability/Maximum**
Maximum volume size	16 EB
Maximum file size	16 EB
Maximum files in root directory	No limit
Maximum files in nonroot directory	No limit
File-level security	Yes
Long file name support	Yes
Self-repairing	Yes
Transaction logging capabilities	Yes
File-level compression	Yes
File-level security	Yes
Dual file fork support (Macintosh)	Yes
POSIX support	Yes

NTFS also supports Windows NT's native object-level security, and treats all volumes, directories, and files as individual objects. Every time users request a file system object, they will be subjected to a security check that matches their right to access the requested object against a list of permissions for that object. Requests from users with sufficient rights will be granted; requests from users with insufficient rights will be denied. This security applies whether users are logged into an NT machine locally or they make their requests across a network.

The vital statistics for NTFS show it as the powerhouse it is. In addition to a staggering capacity of 16 exabytes for volumes or files (an exabyte is 2^{64}, or approximately 16 gigabytes' worth of gigabytes), NTFS offers built-in compression that can be applied to individual files, entire directories, or complete volumes (and selectively removed or applied thereafter).

NTFS offers file-level security, which means that access to volumes, directories, and files can be controlled by an individual's account and the groups to which that account belongs. LFNs are customary with NTFS, but NTFS can map to 8.3 names to maintain support for FAT-based users. In addition to maintaining multiple copies of file system information, Windows NT offers multiple mechanisms to repair and restore an NTFS volume, should problems arise. Likewise, NTFS's transaction logging helps minimize the potential for data loss.

Finally, NTFS supports a much richer file structure, which means it's easy to graft support for other file systems onto an NTFS foundation. Microsoft exploits this capability to provide native support for the Macintosh Hierarchical Filing System (HFS) in NTFS, when Windows NT's Services for Macintosh are installed. Likewise, third parties have built native implementations of Sun's Network Filing System (NFS) that run on top of NTFS (NFS is a popular distributed file system on Unix networks).

Differences Between FAT And NTFS

Where file system overhead is concerned, FAT is more compact and less complex than NTFS. Most FAT volumes impose an overhead of less than

1 MB for the file allocation table structures that represent the directory entries for all files stored in the volume. Because of this low overhead, it is possible to format small hard disks and floppy disks with FAT. NTFS, on the other hand, requires a higher-end system than FAT, partly because each directory entry requires 2 K (this has the advantage, however, of enabling NTFS to store files of 1,500 bytes or less entirely within their directory entries).

NTFS cannot be used to format floppy disks, and shouldn't be used to format partitions smaller than 50 MB. Its relatively high overhead means that for small partitions, directory structures would consume as much as 25 percent of the available storage space.

 Microsoft recommends always using FAT for partitions of 50 MB or smaller, and NTFS for partitions of 400 MB or larger. In the "gray area" between 50 and 400 MB, other factors come into play. Chief among these is file-level security: If this is important, NTFS is the way to go, although FAT will work as well (but gets slower as the size increases).

In relation to file size, FAT partitions can be up to 2 GB, VFAT 4 GB, and FAT32 4 TB; however, FAT partitions work best when they are 200 MB or less, because of the way the FAT itself is organized. NTFS partitions can be as much as 16 EB; however, they currently are restricted to 2 TB by hardware and other system constraints.

FAT partitions may be used by Windows 95, Windows NT, MS-DOS, and WfW, not to mention other operating systems with added FAT support (for example, both Unix and Macintosh can accommodate such add-ons). With a few notable exceptions, NTFS partitions may be accessed directly only using Windows NT. NTFS information is readable across the network by many operating systems (including DOS, Windows 3.X and 95, and other operating systems), partly because of its backward compatibility with FAT, and because of its ability to host other file systems. Also, a recently released utility called NTFSDOS makes it possible to read NTFS data on a PC booted into DOS.

Local security is not an option when you are using FAT partitions (see the next section for more details). NTFS partitions, on the other hand, allow both files and directories to be secured locally. Another difference is that

FAT partitions are required for Windows NT to dual boot with other operating systems; likewise, at least one FAT partition is required to install and operate Windows NT on RISC-based systems.

Securing FAT And NTFS Resources

FAT partitions cannot support local security. This helps explain why the default for Windows NT server is to disallow all local logins except for accounts with administrative or operator privileges. However, FAT partitions can use share permissions, which may be imposed when directories are shared on a network. This does not prevent someone who is logged on locally from accessing files located on a particular machine, but it can protect even FAT-based files from unauthorized network access.

For security purposes, NTFS is the wiser choice. NTFS partitions can lock out or limit access both for remote and local users. All files and directories on an NTFS partition can be locked using NTFS security. This means that the only people who can access protected files are the users that have been granted explicit access to them.

Directory shares and NTFS security are controlled by security properties associated with a directory to be shared, or with any NTFS file system object (which may be either a directory or an individual file). By selecting the Properties entry in the File menu, or right-clicking on a file name and selecting the Properties entry in the resulting pop-up menu, users can examine Sharing (for directories only) and Security (for files and directories) tabs, shown in Figures 3.2 and 3.3.

The default for the system group Everyone is Full Control for both shares and secured resources. Only a network administrator, the owner, or a user who has been granted the Change Permissions permission can reset the access levels on an NTFS or shared resource.

Access Permissions

It is possible for a single user to belong to more than one named group in Windows NT. Access to resources may be assigned to groups or individual

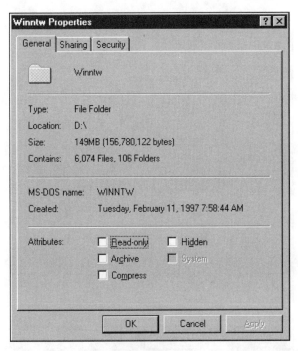

Figure 3.2   Only directories show both the Sharing and Security tabs.

users. This makes it possible for a single user or group to be assigned different levels of access for any particular resource. For example, User A may be a member of two different groups—one that assigns User A **Read** access, and the other that assigns User A **Change** access. We explain how to resolve this apparent conflict in the sections that follow.

Share Permissions

A share may be created for a directory that will be given a share name, so users can connect to this directory across the network. The following list names the share permissions that can be assigned in the Windows NT environment:

➤ **No Access** Users can see the directory name, but have no access to its contents.

➤ **Read** Users can see the directory name, and read and execute files within the directory, but can make no changes.

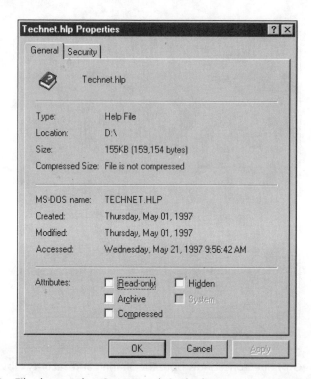

Figure 3.3 Files have only a Security tab (only directories can be shared).

> ➤ **Change** Users can read, write, execute, and delete files within the directory, but cannot change permissions for the directory or the files within it.

> ➤ **Full Control** Users can read, write, execute, and delete files within the directory, delete the directory, and change permissions for the directory and the files it contains, as long as the permissions in the contents haven't been restricted further.

For users that belong to more than one group, these permissions are cumulative, except the No Access permission. When the No Access permission is assigned, all other permissions become obsolete. In other words, the broadest permission always will apply, unless No Access appears anywhere; when that happens, No Access always "wins."

For example, assume that User A belongs to both GroupOne and GroupTwo. Assume further that a ForEveryone directory exists and has been shared under the same name. Finally, assume that members of

GroupOne have Read permission and members of GroupTwo have Change permission for the ForEveryone share.

In this scenario, User A has both Read (by virtue of membership in GroupOne) and Change (by virtue of membership in GroupTwo) access to the ForEveryone share. Since Change is a broader right than Read, this translates into Change permission for User A to ForEveryone.

If we assume that, instead, GroupOne was assigned No Access to ForEveryone, even though User A still has Change access by virtue of his membership in GroupTwo, User A will not be permitted to access the contents of the ForEveryone share because of the No Access assignment.

NTFS Permissions

NTFS treats directories (folders) and files as different types of objects and maintains a separate (but overlapping) set of permissions for each type. Here is a list of the NTFS permissions that can be assigned to folders (the corresponding permissions for files appear on the next page):

- ➤ **No Access** (None)
- ➤ **Full Control** (All) (All)
- ➤ **Add** (WX)
- ➤ **Add & Read** (RWX) (RX)
- ➤ **List** (RX)
- ➤ **Change** (RWXD) (RWXD)
- ➤ **Read** (RX) (RX)

Where two sets of values appear in parentheses after a permission name, the first value applies to the folder itself, and the second applies to any files that may be created within the folder. For instance, Full Control grants all rights to a folder, but it also means that for any file created within that folder, a user with Full Control to the folder will also have Full Control over files created within that folder (unless a file's permissions are reset explicitly by an administrator or the file's owner). In other words, NTFS works like this: Files and folders inherit the permissions set for their parent folders by default, but they can be overwritten by any user with the right to change permissions for the NTFS objects in question.

Here is the list of NTFS permissions for files:

➤ **Full Control** (All)

➤ **No Access** (None)

➤ **Change** (RWXD)

➤ **Read** (RX)

Like share permissions, NTFS permissions are cumulative, except the No Access permission which overrides all others. NTFS permissions and share permissions are used together when users connect over a network. When share and NTFS permissions combine, the most restrictive permission applies.

For example, through the NTFS Security tab, User A is assigned Full Control permission to the ForEveryone folder. Through the Sharing tab, however, User A is assigned Read permission for the same folder.

This means that if User A tries to access the ForEveryone folder across the network, he or she will have Read permission only, because it is the most restrictive of the combination of share and NTFS permissions. However, if User A were to access the folder from the computer where the file resides, he or she would have Full Control. That's because share permissions apply to network access only.

 For remote users, both share and NTFS permissions apply (pick the most restrictive). For local users, only NTFS permissions apply (pick the least restrictive). But remember, No Access always wins. Because Windows NT's default NTFS permission is Full Control, the default is to deny anyone except administrators or operators local access to a Windows NT Server machine.

Moving NTFS Secured Files

Higher-level folders usually share NTFS permissions with the files and folders that they contain. For example, if you create a folder within a folder where administrators have Full Control and backup operators have Read Only permission, the new folder will inherit those same permissions. The same goes for files that are copied from another folder or moved from a different NTFS partition.

However, if you move a folder or a file into another folder on the same NTFS partition, security attributes are not inherited from their new container object. For example, if you move a file from a folder with Read permissions for the Everyone group to a folder on the same partition with Full Control for the Everyone group, the moved file retains its original Read permission. That's because an NTFS move operation within the same partition changes only the object's location pointer, not any of the object's other attributes (including security information).

These three important rules will help you decide if permissions will be inherited or retained when performing move or copy operations on NTFS objects:

1. If you move files within the same NTFS partition, they will *retain* their original permissions.

2. Other operations such as file creation, file copy, and moves from one NTFS partition to another will *inherit* the parent folder's permissions.

3. All NTFS permissions are lost when files are moved or copied from NTFS to a FAT partition.

A Matter Of Conversion

Windows NT includes a utility named CONVERT.EXE that converts FAT volumes to NTFS equivalents, but there is no utility to perform a conversion from an NTFS volume to a FAT version. To do this, you'd have to create a FAT partition, copy the files from an NTFS partition to that FAT partition, and then delete the NTFS originals. Remember that when files are copied from NTFS to FAT, they lose all their NTFS security attributes (FAT lacks the ability to associate and store security attributes with the files under its care). When installing Windows NT across a network, files are copied to a FAT partition, and the install program automatically invokes the CONVERT.EXE utility just before the install switches from character mode to the GUI interface (which occurs about halfway through the Windows NT installation process).

What About HPFS?

HPFS stands for High Performance File System. Originally introduced with OS/2 1.2 and LAN Manager, HPFS was the first PC-compatible file system that supported LFNs. Like FAT, HPFS maintains a directory structure, but it adds automatic sorting of the directory and includes support for special attributes to better accommodate multiple naming conventions and file-level security.

With the introduction of Windows NT 4, NT no longer supports HPFS directly. Also, HPFS file security is not directly compatible with NTFS security. However, a special conversion utility, ACLCONV.EXE, is available from Microsoft; this utility converts HPFS volumes (from LAN Manager, LAN Server, or Windows NT 3.51 or earlier NT versions) to an NTFS equivalent. The utility's readme file also explains how HPFS security is mapped into an NTFS near-equivalent.

 Anytime you see HPFS mentioned in a question with regard to Windows NT Server 4, be prepared for a possibility of a trick question. Remember, HPFS is no longer supported in Windows NT 4.

CDFS

Both Windows 95 and Windows NT 3.51 and higher-number versions (including 4) support a special read-only file system called the Compact Disk File System (CDFS) to permit easy access to CDs in these operating systems. Since all of these operating systems primarily are distributed in that format, it should come as no surprise that CDFS is an important, if limited, file system in the Windows NT environment. One interesting enhancement that CDFS confers is the ability to boot a PC directly from the CD that contains the Windows NT distribution media.

Exam Prep Questions

Question 1

You have a 50 MB partition you wish to use as a share for users to store document files. What is the best file system type to format this partition with?

○ a. FAT

○ b. CDFS

○ c. NTFS

○ d. HPFS

FAT is the best choice because it requires much less overhead than NTFS, and Microsoft does not recommend NTFS on partitions smaller than 400 MB. Therefore, answer a is correct. CDFS is not a file system type that can be used to format a hard drive; it is the format of a CD-ROM. Therefore, answer b is incorrect. NTFS has too much overhead for a partition of this size. Therefore, answer c is incorrect. HPFS is not supported by NT 4.0. Therefore, answer d is incorrect.

Question 2

As you install Windows NT Server 4 on a brand-new machine, you decide to set up two 500 MB partitions, one where Windows NT and other server software will reside, the other where your users will keep their personal files, some of which are confidential. You would:

○ a. set up both partitions using VFAT.

○ b. set up both partitions using NTFS.

○ c. set up the system partition using NTFS and the user partition using FAT.

○ d. set up the system partition using FAT and the user partition using NTFS.

The correct answer is b—to set up both partitions using NTFS. That's because file-level security is just as important for NT's own files as it is for user files that must be kept confidential (that is, secure). The first answer provides no file-level security, while c and d omit file-level security for the user and system partitions, respectively.

Question 3

> While configuring a new 8 GB drive for Windows NT Server 4, your manager requests that you set up a large FAT partition for exchanging extremely large desktop publishing and graphics files with a print bureau. He asks you to configure the entire drive for such use, since your monthly newsletter and advertisements routinely require as much as 6 GB of uncompressed space. To meet his requirements, your best choice is to:
>
> O a. set up a single 8 GB VFAT partition.
>
> O b. set up two 4 GB VFAT partitions.
>
> O c. set up four 2 GB VFAT partitions.
>
> O d. set up sixteen 500 MB VFAT partitions.

The only wrong answer is the first one, since VFAT is limited to a maximum partition size of 4 GB. The second answer is the best choice, because you know the files in question are extremely large (and therefore there will not be a large number of them). If there were a lot of small files, the third answer would be the best choice. The final answer, while theoretically possible, would require searching too many partitions to locate individual files (and the partitions might be too small for "extremely large" files as well).

Question 4

You're upgrading a Windows NT Server from 3.51 to 4. The H: partition on the 3.51 server is formatted using HPFS. After upgrading Windows NT, you can use the CONVERT utility to convert H: from HPFS to NTFS.

○ a. True

○ b. False

The correct answer is b, False. Since Windows 4 no longer supports HPFS, you'll have to obtain the ACLCONV utility from Microsoft to convert the HPFS partition into NTFS. For Windows 4, you can only switch FAT partitions into NTFS partitions. Since NT 3.51 CONVERT will switch HPFS to NTFS, it might be even better to convert HPFS to NTFS before installing the upgrade to 4.

Question 5

User JimBob is a member of the Accounting, Managers, and PrintOperators groups. For a share named SalesFeb, these groups have the following permissions:

- Accounting: CHANGE

- Managers: READ

- PrintOperators: FULL CONTROL

In addition, JimBob's NTFS permissions for the SalesFeb directory are READ. JimBob can do the following with files in the SalesFeb share:

○ a. Nothing; he has no access.

○ b. Read and execute the files in the SalesFeb directory only.

○ c. Read, write, execute, and delete files in the SalesFeb directory, but not change permissions for the directory or its contents.

○ d. Read, write, execute, delete, and change permissions for SalesFeb and its contents.

To calculate share and NTFS permissions combined, take the most permissive of each kind and then the least permissive of the remaining share and NTFS permissions. If **No Access** appears anywhere, the resulting permission will always be **No Access**. Of the three share permissions that pertain to SalesFeb by virtue of JimBob's group memberships, **Full Control** is the most permissive, so that becomes his share permission. His NTFS permission is **Read**. The less permissive of **Read** and **Full Control** is **Read**, so Bob's effective permission to SalesFeb is **Read**. This makes b the only correct answer.

Question 6

User JimBob remains a member of the Accounting, Managers, and PrintOperators groups as before, but is added to the Dangerous group. For a share named SalesFeb, these groups have the following share permissions:

- Accounting: CHANGE

- Managers: READ

- PrintOperators: FULL CONTROL

- Dangerous: NO ACCESS

In addition, JimBob's NTFS permissions for the SalesFeb directory are READ. JimBob can do the following with files in the SalesFeb share:

○ a. Nothing; he has no access.

○ b. Read and execute the files in the SalesFeb directory only.

○ c. Read, write, execute, and delete files in the SalesFeb directory, but not change permissions for the directory or its contents.

○ d. Read, write, execute, delete, and change permissions for SalesFeb.

Because No Access always takes precedence over everything, poor JimBob has no access to SalesFeb and its contents. Thus, the first answer is correct. Remember, No Access always wins.

Question 7

> If you put confidential data onto a FAT partition on a Windows NT
> 4 Server machine, any user can access the data from that parti-
> tion, providing that: [Check all conditions that must apply]
>
> ❏   a. the user can log into the machine remotely.
>
> ❏   b. a share is defined for the folder that contains the
>   confidential materials.
>
> ❏   c. the user has READ permissions for that share (or
>   better).
>
> ❏   d. the user's file permissions are also READ (or better).

The correct answer is to check boxes a, b, and c. If users cannot log into the
machine across the network, they can't get to any partitions on that
machine, whether FAT or NTFS. If a share is not defined where the confidential data resides, no user can obtain access to the data across the network. Finally, the user's share permissions must permit them at least to
Read the data in that share, or they still won't be able to access it. The final
element, d, is irrelevant because FAT partitions do not support file-level
security—hence, they have no associated permissions.

Need To Know More?

 Heywood, Drew: *Inside Windows NT Server*. New Riders, Indianapolis, IN, 1995. ISBN 1-56205-472-4. Chapter 11, entitled "Sharing Drives, Directories, and Files," deals very nicely with issues relating to shares and NTFS permissions and access information.

 Siyan, Karanjit S.: *Windows NT Server 4 Professional Reference*. New Riders, Indianapolis, IN, 1996. ISBN 1-56205-731-6. Chapter 3 contains a section entitled "Comparing the FAT and NTFS"; Chapter 9 is entitled "Managing Network Files and File-System Security." Both of these sections contain materials germane to this discussion.

 Strebe, Matthew, Charles Perkins, and James Chellis: *MSCE: NT Server 4 Study Guide*. Sybex Network Press, San Francisco, CA, 1996. ISBN 0-7821-1972-7. Chapters 4 and 5 both contain useful information about FAT and NTFS, including descriptions of their characteristics and differences.

 Search the TechNet CD (or its online version through www.microsoft.com) using the keywords "FAT," "VFAT," "FAT32," and NTFS. KnowledgeBase articles Q154997 "Description of the FAT32 File System" and Q100108 "Overview of FAT, HPFS, and NTFS File Systems" are particularly informative.

 The Windows NT Server Resource Kit contains lots of useful information about NTFS and share permissions. Here again, you can search the TechNet CD or the CD accompanying the *Resource Kit*, using keywords like "NTFS permissions," and "share permissions." The section in Chapter 3, "Disk Management Basics," of the *Resource Guide* entitled "Windows NT File Systems" is a particularly good resource.

Windows NT
Fault Tolerance

4

Terms you'll need to understand:

√ Fault tolerance

√ Disk partition

√ RAID (Redundant Array of Inexpensive Disks)

√ Disk mirroring

√ Disk duplexing

√ Disk striping

√ Disk striping with parity

√ Disaster recovery

√ UPS (Uninterruptible Power Supply)

Techniques you'll need to master:

√ Using Disk Administrator to implement fault tolerance

√ Creating a volume set

√ Creating a disk mirror

√ Implementing disk striping (with and without parity information)

Fault tolerance embraces a wide variety of system capabilities and functionality. This topic is covered broadly in this chapter, across all subject areas, but the relevant details necessary to answer exam questions also are provided.

The specific topics that fall under the general heading of fault tolerance for Windows NT Server include: disk mirroring, disk duplexing, and disk striping (both with and without parity). Other relevant fault tolerance topics include disaster recovery (using NT's built-in Disk Administrator utility) and several general storage, controller, and bootup matters. Some of the information in this chapter repeats information from other chapters. This should help you correlate various aspects of fault tolerance as implemented in Windows NT's overall system design and architecture.

Disk Administrator

All the fault tolerant features of NT are focused on, or at least related to, the Disk Administrator utility. That makes it imperative to examine this tool thoroughly, so that you may understand Microsoft's implementation of fault tolerance for Windows NT Server 4. The better your knowledge of Disk Administrator's tools and menus, the more likely it is that you will understand the fault tolerance-related questions that appear on the exam (see Figure 4.1). Remember, Disk Administrator appears beneath the Start Menu, in the Programs|Administrative Tools (Common) fly-open menu.

Take time to familiarize yourself with the layout of Disk Administrator's menus, the locations of commands, and resulting dialog boxes. If you are visually inclined, you may be able to work with the tool for a short time and then be able to "see" it in your mind's eye. Those of you unable to visualize the utility must memorize its menus. Table 4.1 is a chart that will help you with that task. (*Note:* We omitted the Help menu.)

One important command is Commit Changes Now. This command instructs Windows NT to make your requested changes to the affected storage devices. In other words, partitions and drives will not be created or changed in Disk Administrator until this menu option is chosen.

Figure 4.1   The Disk Administrator utility.

Table 4.1	Disk Administrator's menus and options.			
Partition	**Fault Tolerance**	**Tools**	**View**	**Options**
Create	Establish Mirror	Format	Volumes	Toolbar
Create Extended	Break Mirror	Assign Drive Letter	Disk Configuration	Status Bar
Delete	Create Stripe Set with Parity	Eject	Refresh	Legend
Create Volume Set	Regenerate	Properties		Colors and Patterns
Extend Volume Set				Disk Display
Create Stripe Set				Region Display
Mark Active				Customize Toolbar
Configuration				
Commit Changes Now				
Exit				

Obviously there are many commands in the five menus found in Disk Administrator. Many of these commands are discussed in further detail when a specific fault tolerance exam issue warrants such a discussion. But if a menu selection is not discussed further in this text, it's safe to assume you need know little (if anything) about it.

Disk Structure 101

Hopefully, you are already familiar with storage devices and the terminology used to describe their configuration and operation. But just to be sure you're equipped with the bare minimum of such information, a short refresher follows.

Partitions

Hard drives are subdivided into partitions. A partition can contain one or more file systems, each of which enables an NOS or OS to store and retrieve files. Even though NT only supports FAT and NTFS natively, partitions that support other file systems can reside on a machine that runs Windows NT (even if NT cannot access them). For instance, it's possible that a drive on a dual-boot machine running Windows 95 OEM release 2 and Windows NT Server 4 could contain a FAT32 partition; in that case, only Windows 95 could access that partition (see Chapter 3 for a more detailed discussion of this topic).

In general, a hard drive can contain between 1 and 32 separate partitions. Thus, a single physical hard drive can appear as multiple logical drives. Hard drives should be partitioned to maximize their usage by the underlying NOS and its applications. If you attempt to change a partition, any information stored in that space on disk will be destroyed. If there is free unpartitioned space on a drive, you may create new partitions without damaging existing partitions. Likewise, deleting any one partition does not affect other partitions on a drive.

The NTFS file system supports a variety of partition schemes. A single drive may contain up to four primary partitions, or one to three primary partitions and a single extended partition. An extended partition can be subdivided further into multiple logical drives. The total number of primary partitions plus logical drives, however, cannot exceed 32 on any one physical hard drive under NT's control.

Volumes

An NTFS volume is an organizational structure imposed upon one or more partitions that supports file storage. If you select one or more partitions on a physical drive and format them with a specific file system, the resulting disk structure is a volume. Under Windows NT, volumes can span multiple partitions on one or more physical drives.

A volume set is a volume comprised of 2 to 32 partitions. A volume set may be extended at any time by adding another partition to the set without damaging existing stored data. However, a volume set and its data must be destroyed to reduce the size of a volume. All the partitions in a volume set must use the same file system, and the entire volume set is assigned a single drive letter. A volume provides no fault tolerance for its data. If any one of the partitions or drives within a volume set fails, all of the data is lost.

 The best way to remember the impact of losing a volume set element is the phrase "You lose one, you lose them all." This also means that the only way to recover the data in a damaged volume set is to restore the data from a backup.

Drive Letters

Nearly every volume on a Windows NT machine has an associated drive letter; in fact, Windows NT cannot access a volume unless it has an associated drive letter. Drive letters simplify the identification of an exact physical drive, partition, and volume for any referenced folder or file. NT can assign drive letters to storage devices using the letters C through Z (A and B are reserved for floppy drives). Since this only covers 24 potential drives, and Windows NT supports as many as 32, the assumption is that some volumes will span multiple physical drives (which all share a single drive letter).

NT automatically assigns the next available drive letter to each new volume that is created. You can reassign dynamically or shuffle drive letters using the Assign Drive Letter option on the Tools menu in Disk Administrator.

Another exception to association of volumes with drive letters applies to volumes formatted with file systems not supported by Windows NT. These volumes generally are not assigned drive letters because NT cannot access them.

Master Boot Record

The Master Boot Record (MBR) is a BIOS bootstrap routine used by low-level hardware-based system code stored in Read-Only Memory (ROM), to initiate the boot sequence on a PC. This in turn calls a bootstrap loader, which commences loading the machine's designated operating system. The MBR directs the hardware to a so-called "active partition" whence the designated operating system may be loaded (for more information on this topic, consult Chapter 13).

Only a primary partition can be made active, by using the Mark Active command on Disk Administrator's Partition menu. The system partition is where the MBR and boot loader reside; for Windows NT, the boot partition is where the Windows NT system files reside. It's backwards!

Fault Tolerance

The resilience of a system in the presence of errors, mistakes, or disasters without causing damage or loss to its data is its fault tolerance. Windows NT's fault tolerance features vary from disk partition organization to high-level file system operations to backup techniques. When all of these are combined, they make NT a reliable and solid network operating system.

The NTFS file system supports internal and automatic fault tolerance. Using a method called "hot fixing," every storage device write is monitored and written sectors checked for integrity. If any verification fails, the question-able sectors are flagged and the data is rewritten to another working location on disk. This is performed automatically by the file system and does not report error messages to any applications. NTFS also logs all changes to the file system so that changes may be undone or reapplied if a discrepancy is found, or if damage is caused by a system failure or power loss.

Windows NT Server 4 supports three types of fault-tolerant disk structures—disk mirroring, disk duplexing, and disk striping with parity. These
structures may be implemented using the Fault Tolerance menu in the Disk
Administrator utility. But, as you'll soon learn, only disk striping with parity qualifies as fault tolerant; disk striping without parity does not qualify,
even though it's another legal way to aggregate multiple partitions in Disk
Administrator.

Disk Mirroring

Disk mirroring creates an exact duplicate of one physical and logical storage device on a separate physical storage device. Both the original drive and
the backup (mirrored drive) are attached to the same hard drive controller.
If the original disk fails, there is no loss of data because everything written
to the original disk also is written to the mirror. Barring other physical
component problems, when the original drive fails, the system automatically switches to the mirrored drive to continue operation.

Disk mirroring's drawbacks include:

> **Slow performance** The act of writing the same data twice takes longer
> than writing it just once.

> **Increased cost** Every mirror must be a separate physical device; thus,
> you must purchase twice the storage capacity.

> **No protection from controller failure** If the disk controller fails, the
> mirrored drive is just as inaccessible as the original drive.

 The boot and system partitions can be the original disk in a disk
mirror set. But if the original fails, that makes it necessary to
hand-edit the BOOT.INI file on the boot drive to point to the ARC
(Advanced RISC Computing) name for the mirror instead. (ARC
names and BOOT.INI editing are both covered in Chapter 13.)

Disk Duplexing

Disk duplexing is similar to disk mirroring, but more robust. Like mirroring, disk duplexing uses a duplicate physical and logical drive on a separate
hard disk; unlike mirroring, the drive is connected to the system via a separate controller. If the original drive or controller fails, the system continues
to operate using the duplexed drive. There is no system performance

degradation, because writing the same data twice through two disk controllers requires no additional time, and both writes occur simultaneously.

One significant drawback to disk duplexing is the cost: It requires double the storage space and a second disk controller.

 As with mirroring, the boot and system partitions can be the original disk in a disk duplexing set. If the original fails, however, you must edit the BOOT.INI file by hand to point to the ARC name for the duplexed drive.

Disk Striping

Disk striping stores data across multiple physical storage devices. In a stripe set, multiple partitions of equal size on separate devices are combined into a single logical device. When data is stored to a stripe set, it is written in 64 K chunks—stripes—across the drives, starting at the drive on the left with data block 1, then on the middle drive with data block 2, and so on (see Figure 4.2 for an example of a stripe set).

Disk striping is fast, especially when the individual storage devices are attached to separate disk controllers. Disk striping does not have the same cost drawbacks as mirroring and duplexing, since all or most of the storage space you purchase is fully available to you. You only need two devices to create a stripe set without parity, and such a stripe set can include as many as 32 devices. Disk striping can be implemented using either FAT or NTFS.

Figure 4.2   A stripe set using three physical disks.

However, disk striping without parity provides no fault tolerance. Should any one of the drives in a stripe set without parity fail, all of the data on all disks is lost (once again, it's "Lose one, lose them all!"). If any of the drive controllers fails, none of the data is accessible until that drive controller is repaired.

The boot and system partitions cannot be part of a disk stripe set without parity (or with parity, either, as you'll see in the next section). *Warning!* If the test says anything about a stripe set but does not mention the parity (with or without), you must assume that this means a stripe set without parity, and answer accordingly.

Disk Striping With Parity

Disk striping with parity offers most of the benefits of parity-free disk striping without the same risk of data loss. Parity defines a storage method where the data that's written across the stripes is recorded so that data stored on any one drive is duplicated across all the other devices in the stripe set. The duplicate data is called parity information. Then, if any one of the drives in a parity stripe set fails, that data can be rebuilt from the parity information on the remaining devices without loss.

To record parity information within a stripe set, additional space is required. Unfortunately, this means that the total amount of storage capacity is smaller than the sum of the partitions on each member of the stripe set. To calculate the total capacity (T) of a stripe set with parity, use the following formula (where P is the size of any single partition and n is the number of partitions in the set):

```
T = P * (n - 1)
```

When you create a stripe set using the Create Stripe Set With Parity option on the Disk Administrator's Fault Tolerance menu, you will be presented with a dialog box that displays the total size of the set. This number is P * n, which equals the size of the smallest partition multiplied by the total number of partitions. This number does not reflect the amount of actual usable storage space of a stripe set with parity. That number is determined by the preceding formula, which takes the space requirements for parity information into account.

Here are a few important items to remember about disk striping with parity:

➤ All partitions within a stripe set must be of equal size (or nearly so).

➤ Each partition must be on a separate physical disk.

➤ NTFS or FAT can be used as the file system on a stripe set with parity.

➤ A minimum of three devices is required to build a stripe set with parity; as before, the maximum number of devices remains set at 32.

➤ Writing performance is slightly slower than disk striping without parity, but faster than disk mirroring.

➤ If one drive in a set fails, the data set can be rebuilt from the remaining devices.

Neither the boot nor system partitions can reside in a disk stripe set, even with parity.

RAID

The four partition organizations we've described for Windows NT represent software implementations of RAID (Redundant Array of Inexpensive—or Individual—Disks). In other words, RAID is a storage method that uses numerous devices in combination to store large amounts of data.

RAID also addresses various levels of fault tolerance and recoverability for specific configurations and storage techniques. There are six distinct levels recognized in RAID subsystems, starting with 0 (zero) and ending with 5 (five). Windows NT Server supports RAID Levels 0, 1, and 5. Here's an explanation of these levels:

➤ **RAID 0 is disk striping without parity.** This level provides no fault tolerance, but it is the fastest method. RAID 0 includes nonstriped volume sets as well as disk striping without parity.

➤ **RAID 1 is disk mirroring.** This level provides a reasonable level of data protection, but has some performance consequences. Disk duplexing also is sometimes categorized as

RAID 1 because it provides the same level of data protection with improved performance. Both mirroring and duplexing require twice as much physical storage as the data to be stored (because there are two identical copies of everything).

➤ **RAID 5 is disk striping with parity.** This level provides the highest level of data protection with only a minor dip in performance and modest overhead storage requirements for parity information.

Remember that NT's software implementation of RAID requires additional system overhead, especially when large numbers of devices are involved. Software RAID is convenient and inexpensive (it is included with NT), but hardware RAID is faster and offers more options and reliability (like "hot-swappable" drives and controllers).

Comparing RAID Levels

On the exam, you'll encounter questions that ask you to designate a level of fault tolerance for a particular system or configuration. Remember first and foremost that disk striping without parity (RAID 0) offers no fault tolerance whatsoever. In addition to the RAID levels and fault tolerance features of the various partition organizations, remain aware of expense and hardware requirements.

When comparing disk mirroring (or duplexing) to disk striping with parity, remember:

➤ Two physical disks per mirror set are required for disk mirroring.

➤ No less than 3 or more than 32 physical disks may be used with disk striping with parity.

➤ You can mirror (or duplex) the volumes where system and boot files for Windows NT are stored (these are the Windows NT boot and system partitions, respectively).

➤ You cannot use disk striping (with or without parity) for Windows NT system and boot partitions.

➤ Disk mirroring and disk duplexing require half the disk space for copies that might otherwise be used for data storage.

➤ Disk striping with parity uses 1/n of the total disk space available to store parity information (where n is the number of partitions in the stripe set).

➤ If a disk stripe set with parity or a mirror set loses more than one physical drive, data from the entire set will be lost; the set then must be repaired, rebuilt, and the data restored from backup.

Recovery

As long as the physical disk(s) that contain the system and boot partitions do not fail, recovery from disk failure is relatively simple. However, recovery without resort to a backup is possible only with a disk mirror, disk duplex, or stripe set with parity. All other partition structures offer no "live recovery" for the data they store.

Fixing Broken Mirrors And Duplexes

When the original member of a disk mirror (or duplex) set fails, NT automatically uses the other member of the set to continue operation. But whenever a member of a mirror or duplex set fails, you must replace the failed member and reestablish the mirror or duplex, or you no longer will benefit from the data protection. In fact, the NT Server will be unable to reboot at all if the original set member fails, because the BOOT.INI file points to that member (that's why it's necessary to hand-edit the ARC name in the boot file to point to the other member of the set to restart the system at all).

The first step in repairing a mirrored set is to break the mirror. This is accomplished in the Disk Administrator utility, using the Break Mirror option in the Fault Tolerance drop-down menu. Once the mirror is broken, you must reassign the drive letter to the remaining member of the (now broken) mirror set. For example, if Drives 1 and 2 are mirrored and assigned drive letter D, and Drive 1 fails, you must break the mirrored set, and then assign drive letter D to Drive 2.

The second step is to replace the failed drive and create a partition on the new drive equal in size to the drive to be mirrored. Then, you must re-create the mirror by using the Establish Mirror option from the Fault

Tolerance drop-down menu. (*Note*: This effectively switches the roles of the previous original and mirrored drives. Once NT reboots, the mirror set will be rebuilt using the new member, but the original drive now will be Drive 2, based on the example in the preceding paragraph.)

 If the mirror set includes a boot partition, and the drive that failed was the original member of the set, you must boot with a floppy to regain access to the system to run the Disk Administrator utility to repair the set. You must create an up-to-date boot floppy for the system so this process can work. That boot floppy should contain the following files:

➤ BOOT.INI

➤ NTLDR

➤ NTDETECT.COM

➤ NTBOOTTDD.SYS—only if you are using a SCSI controller with BIOS translation disabled (or missing)

➤ BOOTSECT.DOS—only if you need to boot into MS-DOS or another operating system present on your system

You may need to edit the BOOT.INI file to match new parameters and the new location of boot and system partitions. For further information, read "Special Boot Considerations" later in this chapter.

Restoring With Parity Information

Recovering from a device failure with disk striping with parity is easy. Once the device fails, the system is able to rebuild data on the fly from parity information stored on the still-operational devices. Because regeneration is CPU-intensive, performance slows dramatically. However, the system continues to operate, even with a failed set member.

 Once a set member fails, it's important to replace it quickly to restore fault tolerance and system performance levels to normalcy. First, fix the hardware by replacing or repairing the failed drive. Next, using Disk Administrator, create a new partition equal in size to the one that failed (if the original disk is brought back online without losing its partition structure, skip this step). Select the stripe set and the partition that replaces the failed member (which could be the original partition if it wasn't destroyed), then

> select the Regenerate command from the Fault Tolerance drop-down menu. Once NT reboots, the stripe set will be rebuilt by copying parity information to re-create the new member.

Special Boot Considerations

If the partition that contains Windows NT's system files fails, you will find where those mirrored system files are mapped in BOOT.INI, which uses ARC name syntax to map a path to the system files. This path designation starts by identifying the hard disk controller, and finishes with the name of the folder that contains the Windows NT system files.

Here are some examples of BOOT.INI entries:

```
multi(1)disk(0)rdisk(1)partition(2)\WINNT=
  "Windows NT Server Version 4.00"
scsi(0)disk(0)rdisk(0)partition(1)\WINNT=
  "Windows NT Server Version 4.00"
```

Should a boot or system partition fail, these entries may need to be changed, especially if the order, number, or configuration of your drives and partitions change, or if the Windows NT system files must be accessed from an alternate location (like the other member of a mirror or duplex set).

If the original drive in a mirror set fails and that drive was the boot partition, BOOT.INI on the mirror drive (which must now function as the boot partition) must be edited to reflect the new, correct location of these files. You might also edit the BOOT.INI file on a boot floppy to perform the same function, especially if you plan to restore the original drive quickly and return the system to its previous state.

BOOT.INI lives in the system partition, usually on drive C, on your Windows NT machine. BOOT.INI is a text file, which means you can edit it with any text editor. BOOT.INI attributes are set as a system and read-only file; therefore, you must turn off these attribute settings before you can edit the file, and then reset them once your changes are complete. Here's an example of a BOOT.INI file:

```
[boot loader]
timeout=10
default=scsi(0)disk(0)rdisk(0)partition(1)\WINNT
```

```
[operating systems]
scsi(0)disk(0)rdisk(0)partition(1)\
   WINNT="Windows NT Server Version 4.00"
scsi(0)disk(0)rdisk(0)partition(1)\WINNT="Windows NT
   Server Version 4.00 [VGA mode]" /basevideo /sos
C:\="MS-DOS 6.22"
```

To edit the BOOT.INI file properly—and there are specific test questions on this topic—you must know the following about ARC names:

➤ To change the BOOT.INI file to point to the proper location, you must edit both the default= line and the main NOS line (which is scsi(0)disk(0)rdisk(0)partition(1)\WINNT= "Windows NT Server Version 4.00" in the preceding example). Both ARC names must match exactly.

➤ The first four elements of an ARC name are always lowercase in the BOOT.INI file. We use uppercase in this discussion to set them off from normal body text

➤ The first element in an ARC name, either SCSI or MULTI, is the controller type. SCSI indicates that a SCSI disk controller is being used that does not support BIOS translation. If SCSI appears, it also means that a driver file named NTBOOTDD.SYS must appear in the system partition to handle BIOS translation for the controller. MULTI indicates any other controller type that supports BIOS translation, including IDE and SCSI (among others).

➤ The number immediately following SCSI or MULTI identifies the position of the controller within the system, numbered ordinally. Thus, the first controller is numbered zero (0), the second is one (1), and the third is two (2).

➤ The second element in an ARC name, DISK, designates the device number for a SCSI controller with no BIOS translation abilities. DISK will appear in an ARC name. But if SCSI is the first element in the name, the number that follows DISK identifies the storage device, numbered ordinally. Thus, the first device also is numbered zero (0), the second is one (1), and so on. If MULTI appears first in an ARC name, DISK is ignored and will always be set to a zero (0).

➤ The third element, RDISK, designates the device number for a BIOS translating SCSI controller, or for any other controller. RDISK always appears in any ARC name. But only if MULTI is its first element does the number following RDISK identify the storage device, numbered ordinally. Again, the first device is numbered zero (0), the second one (1), and so on. If SCSI appears first in an ARC name, RDISK is ignored and is always set to zero (0).

➤ The fourth element in an ARC name identifies a disk partition. PARTITION indicates the partition where system files reside, numbered cardinally. Unlike the other terms, the first partition is one (1), the second is two (2), the third is three (3), and so on.

➤ The fifth element in an ARC name is the name of the folder where the system files reside. "\WINNT" indicates that the folder (or directory) on the specified partition named "WINNT" is where system information may be found. Whatever the directory is named, this element must reflect that exact name.

➤ The data following the folder name provides the information that appears in the Windows NT boot menu. The equals sign and the quotes that enclose the text string must follow the folder name without any additional spaces outside the quotes.

➤ After the Boot Menu name, additional command line parameter switches may be added to control how Windows NT boots. These switches include /SOS and /BASEVIDEO. /SOS causes Windows NT to display the names of drivers on screen as they are loaded during system boot. /BASEVIDEO puts Windows NT into VGA mode, which is useful when troubleshooting video configuration problems.

One important item to remember for the exam is that Microsoft reversed what you might expect the terms "boot partition" and "system partition" to mean. As it happens, boot files are stored on the system partition, that is, the active partition where BOOT.INI and NTLDR reside. System files are stored on the boot partition, where the default WINNT directory resides. When a question requests the ARC name of a partition that contains boot files, remember that these files reside on the system partition, and vice versa. We can only guess at Microsoft's thinking—that system files are for low-level hardware initiation of the boot process, and thus reside on the boot partition, and boot files supply bootup intelligence for Windows NT itself, and therefore reside on the system partition. Just remember that it's the opposite of common sense, and you'll do just fine.

Exam Prep Questions

Question 1

Using free unpartitioned space on a SCSI drive, you create a new partition. You highlight the free space, select Create from the Partition menu, specify the size of the partition, and click OK. Now the new drive appears in the Disk Administrator display. What should you do next in your endeavor to create a new place to store data?

○ a. Assign drive letter

○ b. Select Configuration, Save

○ c. Format

○ d. Commit Changes Now

It is not possible to assign a drive letter to a partition unless it is formatted; therefore, answer a is incorrect. The Configuration, Save command stores the current configuration status as stored in the registry to an Emergency Repair Disk; this is not a step toward creating a usable volume, so answer b also is incorrect. Formatting a partition to create a volume is required, but this cannot occur until partition creation changes are committed, making answer c incorrect as well. You must use the Commit Changes Now command to save the partition creation changes as your next step; then you can proceed to format the partition and assign it a drive letter. Therefore, answer d is correct.

Question 2

> You have two IDE hard drives on a single drive controller in your Windows NT Server computer. There is only one partition on each of the two drives. The first drive's partition is formatted with FAT, and the second drive's partition is formatted with NTFS. The boot files are located on the second drive. What is the ARC name for the system partition?
>
> ○ a. multi(0)disk(1)rdisk(0)partition(1)
>
> ○ b. multi(0)disk(0)rdisk(1)partition(1)
>
> ○ c. multi(1)disk(0)rdisk(1)partition(1)
>
> ○ d. multi(0)disk(0)rdisk(1)partition(0)
>
> ○ e. multi(1)disk(0)rdisk(0)partition(1)

Answer a displays an improperly composed ARC name: When MULTI is used, the disk(n) number must be set to zero. Therefore answer a is incorrect. Answer b indicates the first partition of the second hard drive on the first multitype drive controller. Because this is indeed the location of the system partition for this configuration, answer b is correct. Answer c points to a second drive controller that doesn't exist in this example, and consequently must be incorrect. Answer d supplies an incorrect number for the partition element—because partitions are numbered cardinally, a partition number never can be zero. Because the first partition is numbered one, answer d is wrong. Answer e names a second, nonexistent drive controller, and points to the first drive on that controller. Because the system partition for this question is attached to the first—and only—disk controller, on the second hard drive, answer e is incorrect. Remember that the system partition must be active, but it does not have to be on the first drive or the first partition on a drive.

Question 3

> What is the best method for implementing fault tolerance on a Windows NT Server computer with two high-speed SCSI drives, each on a separate controller card?
>
> O   a. Disk duplexing
>
> O   b. Disk striping without parity
>
> O   c. Disk mirroring
>
> O   d. Create a volume set across both drives.

Disk duplexing is the fault tolerance method that utilizes two drives, each on separate controllers. Therefore answer a is correct. Disk striping without parity offers no fault tolerance, making answer b incorrect. Disk mirroring utilizes two drives on the same controller, making answer c incorrect as well. Finally, a volume set offers no fault tolerance either, making answer d incorrect.

Question 4

> Which items below describe disk striping with parity?
> [Check all correct answers]
>
> ❏   a. Requires three physical drives.
>
> ❏   b. Can be implemented with FAT.
>
> ❏   c. Provides fault tolerance.
>
> ❏   d. Has faster read-write performance than disk mirroring.
>
> ❏   e. Data cannot be recovered if a single drive within the set fails.

Disk striping with parity requires a minimum of three physical drives, so answer a is correct. Disk striping with parity can be implemented with either NTFS or FAT. Therefore, answer b is correct. Because disk striping with parity is indeed a fault tolerant storage method, answer c also is correct. Because it spreads the load across more drives, disk striping with parity offers better performance than disk mirroring. Thus, answer d is correct as well. And because disk striping with parity can recover from a single drive failure, answer e is incorrect. Therefore, answers a, b, c, and d are correct.

Question 5

Which of the following ARC names indicates the third partition of
the fourth SCSI drive on the second controller that has its BIOS
disabled?

○   a. multi(1)disk(3)rdisk(0)partition(3)

○   b. multi(1)disk(0)rdisk(3)partition(3)

○   c. scsi(1)disk(3)rdisk(0)partition(3)

○   d. scsi(1)disk(3)rdisk(0)partition(4)

Answer a indicates a BIOS-enabled controller, which makes this answer
incorrect. Answer b indicates the same condition and is equally wrong.
Answer c indicates the third partition on the fourth drive on a non-BIOS
SCSI controller, so this answer is correct. Answer d is close, but indicates
the fourth partition, and therefore is incorrect.

Question 6

You want to implement fault tolerance on your Windows NT Server
computer so your data will be protected in the event of a power
failure or hardware malfunction. Which of the following techniques
will provide you some type of fault tolerance? [Check all correct
answers]

❏   a. RAID 1

❏   b. Disk duplexing

❏   c. Volume set

❏   d. Disk striping without parity

❏   e. RAID 5

RAID 1 indicates disk mirroring, which provides some fault tolerance; therefore, answer a is correct. Disk duplexing is another fault tolerant storage
method, so answer b also is correct. A volume set is not fault tolerant, making
answer c incorrect. Disk striping without parity is not fault tolerant, either;
therefore, answer d is incorrect. RAID 5 is the same thing as disk striping
with parity; because this scheme provides fault tolerance, answer e is also
correct. The complete set of correct answers to this question is a, b, and e.

Question 7

> Your Windows NT Server computer has two physical disks. What
> forms of storage can be implemented with only two drives?
> [Check all correct answers]
>
> ❑   a. Disk striping with parity
>
> ❑   b. Disk mirroring
>
> ❑   c. Disk duplexing
>
> ❑   d. Volume set
>
> ❑   e. Disk striping without parity

Disk striping with parity requires a minimum of three drives, which makes
answer a wrong. Disk mirroring uses only two drives, but they must be on
the same controller, so answer b is correct. Disk duplexing uses only two
drives, but as both must be on different controllers, answer c also is correct.
A volume set can consist of from 2 to 32 partitions on any number of
drives, so answer d also is correct. Disk striping without parity requires a
minimum of two drives, therefore answer e also is correct.

Question 8

> Which of the following drive sets supported by Windows NT Server
> can contain the system and/or boot partitions? [Check all correct
> answers]
>
> ❑   a. Disk mirroring
>
> ❑   b. Disk striping without parity
>
> ❑   c. Volume set
>
> ❑   d. Disk duplexing

Disk mirroring can contain either system or boot partitions, or both, on the
original disk. Therefore answer a is correct. No kind of stripe set can contain either system or boot paritions, so disk striping without parity cannot
contain the system or boot partitions. Of course, this means that answer b
is incorrect. A volume set cannot contain either system or boot partitions,

making answer c incorrect. Finally, disk duplexing can accommodate either the system or boot partitions, or both, on the original disk, so answer d also is correct.

Question 9

What files should be placed on a boot disk to boot to the duplicate drive of a disk duplex from a floppy in the event of a failure of the original drive? Assume the drive controller is SCSI that does not support BIOS translation. [Check all correct answers]

❑   a. NTDETECT.COM

❑   b. BOOT.INI

❑   c. NTLDR

❑   d. WINA20.386

❑   e. NTBOOTDD.SYS

NTDETECT.com is required on the boot floppy, so answer a is correct. BOOT.INI is required on the boot floppy, so answer b also is correct. NTLDR is required on the boot floppy; therefore, answer c also is correct. WINA20.386 is a Windows device driver that is not needed on the boot floppy, so answer d is incorrect. NTBOOTDD.SYS is the driver for SCSI translation required for non-BIOS controllers, making answer e correct as well. The full set of correct answers to this question is a, b, c, and e.

Question 10

> The original disk of a disk mirror fails. The mirror did not contain the system or boot partitions. What steps are required to restore the mirror set?
>
> ○ a. Replace the failed disk, reformat both drives, re-create a mirror set, and restore the data from a backup tape.
>
> ○ b. Replace the failed disk; Windows NT Server will automatically restore the mirror set.
>
> ○ c. Replace the failed disk, break the mirror set, and re-create the mirror set.
>
> ○ d. Replace the failed disk, select the mirror set and the replaced drive, and select Regenerate from the Fault Tolerance menu.

Answer a causes you to perform many long and unnecessary steps: Neither formatting the two drives nor restoring from tape backup is required; therefore, answer a is incorrect. Windows NT will not automatically restore a mirror set, so answer b also is wrong. The steps in answer c will restore a mirror set properly, with the roles of the drives reversed, making answer c correct. The steps in answer d are used to repair a stripe set with parity, so answer d is incorrect.

Question 11

> You have a Windows NT server where the system partition is the original drive of a disk duplex set. If your system partition fails, what modification should you make to a boot floppy to boot to the mirrored partition?
>
> ○ a. Add the /MIRROR switch to the default line of the BOOT.INI file.
>
> ○ b. Edit the ARC name in the BOOT.INI file to reflect the location of the mirrored partition.
>
> ○ c. A boot floppy is not needed.
>
> ○ d. Change the PATH statement in AUTOEXEC.BAT.

The /MIRROR switch is not a valid command parameter, so answer a is incorrect. Editing the ARC name enables you to boot the mirrored partition; this means that answer b is correct. A boot floppy is required, so answer c is incorrect. There is no AUTOEXEC.BAT file on an NT boot floppy, making answer d incorrect.

Question 12

You add four new drives to your Windows NT Server computer of sizes 800, 600, 500, and 300 MB. You want to establish a disk stripe set with parity. What is the total size of the largest set you can create using any or all of these drives?

○　a. 1200 MB

○　b. 1000 MB

○　c.　800 MB

○　d. 1500 MB

1200 MB would be the size of the set if you used all four drives with 300 MB on each one. Because this is not the largest possible sum using this set of drives, answer a is incorrect. 1000 MB is indeed the amount of data that could be stored on the largest set created from these drives, but the question requested the total size of the set, making answer b incorrect. Although 800 MB represents the size of the largest individual drive, you must use three drives to create a disk stripe set with parity. This means answer c is incorrect as well. As it happens, 1500 MB is the total size of the largest set that may be created from these drives, using only the 800, 600, and 500 MB drives, making answer d the only correct reply.

Question 13

> Your Windows NT Server computer has four hard drives: a 1200 MB drive that supports the system partition, an 1800 MB drive with two unformatted partitions, and two empty 800 MB drives. How much data can you store on a disk stripe set with parity created on this system? Choose the largest and best performing.
>
> ○   a. 2400 MB
> ○   b. 3400 MB
> ○   c. 1600 MB
> ○   d. 3200 MB

Always assume the simplest configuration; even though this question did not state the 1800 MB drive was partitioned into two equal segments, this is the easiest and most commonsense arrangement. Plus, you are not given the option to repartition. 2400 MB is the total size of a set created using both of hte 800 MB drives and 800 MB from one of the 900 MB partitions on the 1800 MB drive. Because a stripe set with parity requires one third of the space for parity data in this case, answer a is incorrect—it neglects to account for this reduction in actual storage capacity. 3400 MB is the size of a volume set created using both 800 MB drives and both 900 MB partitions on the 1800 MB drive. But the question requested creation of the fastest possible stripe set with parity; selecting two partitions on the same drive slows performance and is not legal with disk striping with parity configurations, so answer b is incorrect. 1600 MB represents the amount of data that can be stored on a stripe set with parity created using all of the two 800 MB drives plus 800 MB from one of the 900 MB partitions from the 1800 MB drive. This makes answer c correct. 3200 MB is a set size that's not possible with these drives (because it would require five 800 MB partitions on five drives); therefore, answer d is wrong.

Question 14

If you do not care about fault tolerance, what is the best method
to maximize your data storage space on your Windows NT Server
computer?

○   a. Disk mirroring

○   b. Disk striping with parity

○   c. Volume set

○   d. Disk stacking

Disk mirroring cuts storage capacity in half to implement fault tolerance,
making answer a incorrect. Disk striping with parity reduces storage capacity by one full partition to implement fault tolerance, making answer b
incorrect also. A volume set maximizes storage capacity and allows you to
add additional space as needed, so answer c is correct. Disk stacking is not
a valid Windows NT storage technology, so answer d is incorrect.

Need To Know More?

 Heywood, Drew: *Inside Windows NT Server*. New Riders, Indianapolis, IN, 1995. ISBN 1-56205-472-4. Chapter 10 discusses fault tolerance issues, implementation tips, and troubleshooting techniques for storage under Windows NT Server.

 Siyan, Karanjit S.: *Windows NT Server 4 Professional Reference*. New Riders, Indianapolis, IN, 1996. ISBN 1-56205-731-6. Chapter 9 has extensive coverage of NT's storage capabilities and fault tolerant features.

 Strebe, Matthew, Charles Perkins, and James Chellis: *MSCE: NT Server 4 Study Guide*. Sybex Network Press, San Francisco, CA, 1996. ISBN 0-7821-1972-7. Chapter 5 takes a detailed look into the file systems and storage features of NT; it's well worth reading.

 The Windows NT Server 4 manuals cover planning, configuration, and installation issues quite well. The *Concepts and Planning Manual* contains useful fault tolerance issue discussions.

 The Windows NT Server Resource Kit contains lots of useful information about Windows NT's fault tolerance. The TechNet CD or the CD accompanying the *Resource Kit* can be searched using keywords like "fault tolerance," "disk mirror," and "stripe set." In the *Resource Guide* volume, Chapter 3, "Disk Management Basics," Chapter 4, "Planning a Reliable Configuration," and Chapter 5, "Preparing for and Performing Recovery," contain useful background, implementation, and reference information on NT's fault tolerance features.

Managing Windows NT Resources

5

. . . .

Terms you'll need to understand:

√ User accounts

√ User rights and permissions

√ Primary Domain Controller (PDC)

√ Backup Domain Controller (BDC)

√ Policies

√ Profiles

√ Logon scripts

√ Replication

Techniques you'll need to master:

√ Setting up and maintaining user accounts

√ Setting up user rights and permissions

√ Establishing System policies and user profiles

√ Implementing directory replication

The main impetus behind setting up a network is to share resources among users. Windows NT makes managing such resources fairly intuitive. In this chapter, we examine what you need to know for the resource management section of the Microsoft Certification exam. We begin with a discussion of how to manage user accounts, which is where you assign rights to individual users. From there, we move on to examine domains, domain controllers, and local and global groups. For further user management, we explore how to set up user policies, profiles, and logon scripts to accommodate special needs for users. Finally, we turn to server-oriented topics such as replication, managing shared resources, and setting up client-based management.

Managing Users And Accounts

For most networks, user management on a per-user basis is frustrating. To relieve this administrative burden, Windows NT 4 comes equipped with an administrative tool for managing users., This tool is the User Manager for Domains (accessed from the Start menu—Start|Programs| Adminstrative Tools (Common)|User Manager For Domains).

The User Manager For Domains (for simplicity's sake, referred to hereafter as the User Manager) is where administrators create and manage user and group accounts. After you have familiarized yourself with this tool, the User Manager will be your primary access control tool for users and groups.

To simplify management—and to save your wits—the trick for managing users is the group administration philosophy. Rather than managing users one-by-one, it's easier to place individual users into groups and assign rights to the groups, not the users. Once a user is a member of a group, he or she inherits the access rights and restrictions assigned to that group.

To simplify matters further, Microsoft had the foresight to provide built-in groups (both local and global) for user management. Please note that you cannot delete or rename the built-in groups. It is a good idea to make use of these groups for administering users rights and restrictions. In addition, these built-in groups have certain users assigned to them by default. You may add or remove users from these groups as needed. Group concepts, as well as NT's built-in local and global groups, are discussed later in this chapter.

Working With The User Manager For Domains

The User Manager is the primary tool for controlling users' rights. Here are the various functions and tasks of User Manager:

➤ Produce, change, duplicate, and remove group accounts

➤ Produce, change, duplicate, and remove user accounts

➤ Enable account policies (this establishes defaults for password requirements, account lockouts, and disconnect status, etc.)

➤ Create user rights and audit policies

➤ Establish trust relationships

Creating New Users And Groups

To create a new user or group account in User Manager, perform the following steps:

1. Open User Manager, then click the User menu.

2. Select New User (or New Group, as desired).

3. Complete the New User dialog box by performing the following steps: Type in the User Name, Full Name (optional), Description (optional), Password, and Confirm Password.

4. Select the relevant buttons from the four checkboxes at the bottom of the New User dialog box if:

   ➤ The user must change password at first logon.

   ➤ The user cannot change password.

   ➤ The password never expires.

   ➤ The account is disabled.

In addition to these checkboxes, there are six option buttons at the bottom of the dialog box. These buttons govern many of the user's capabilities, as described in the following list:

➤ **Groups** This button enables you to add and remove users that are to be members of a certain group or groups.

➤ **Profiles** This button enables you to define the path to the user profiles for individual users, to logon scripts, and to a user's home directory.

➤ **Hours** This button allows you to set the hours during which a user can log on to the network. By default, if a user is already logged on when the restricted time is reached, the user may remain on the network, but may not log back on until the allowed time. You can change this to log the user off forcibly at a specific time. This is done through the user's account policy (discussed later in this chapter).

➤ **Logon To** This button restricts the user to log on to the network only from certain machines. However, because users tend to move around, it's a good idea to leave it set at the default (to log on to all workstations).

➤ **Account** Here you can set expiration dates for accounts (useful for temporary or contract workers). The default is Never, but you can type in a specific date. You also can assign the account as local (for users from untrusted domains) or global (for regular user accounts in the domain).

➤ **Dialin** This is where you establish the right for a user to dial in to the network, as well as establish callback security if desired.

Modifying Existing User Accounts

A common action for network administrators is setting up accounts for users. Often, new users take the place of existing users—it is easier to rename an account for an employee who is taking the place of another than to create a new account. To do this, simply select User, Rename from the User Manager. Just be sure to instruct the new employee to change the account's password at first logon because the old employee's password will be retained along with all other settings.

It is (unfortunately) common to accidentally delete a user's account. The only way to remedy this is to start anew and create a user account with the same name, rights, and restrictions. This is not as bad as it sounds because you can create user right templates for departments or groups. Then, from the User menu you can copy the template, rename it for the new user, and go from there if additional rights or restrictions are needed.

If you change the access rights for a user, that user must log off and then log back on for the new rights to take effect.

A Simple Look At Domains And Controllers

Put simply, a domain is a collection of networked workstations and servers that are managed as a group. In Windows NT, each domain must have a domain controller to administer user rights for that domain. The first NT Server installed in a domain is the Primary Domain Controller (PDC); this means that the server is responsible for authenticating that domain's users at logon, because the PDC houses the security policy and database for the domain.

The next server to be installed should take on the role of Backup Domain Controller (BDC). The BDC maintains a copy of the security policy and domain database (it synchronizes with the PDC at specified intervals to maintain up-to-date copies of these security features). If the PDC goes down for any reason, the BDC is not automatically promoted to a PDC. However, users can continue to log on to the network. Although it is not required that you have a BDC, it is highly recommended.

You can promote a BDC to a PDC manually if you need to take the PDC down for maintenance purposes. It is important, however, to promote the BDC *before* downing the PDC, or else some account information which may not have yet been replicated between the controllers may be lost. BDC promotion is performed with the Server Manager tool (Start|Programs| Administrative Tools (Common)|Server Manager).

To promote a BDC, follow these steps:

1. Launch Server Manager.

2. Select the Computer menu.

3. Select Promote To Primary Domain Controller.

4. Confirm the promotion.

 You should be certain that you want a server to be a domain controller, because if you want to demote it to be a member server later, you must reinstall Windows NT Server.

To allow workstations to log on to a domain, you must perform three steps:

1. Add the computer names of all domain Windows NT Workstations using Server Manager.

2. Add user accounts to the domain using User Manager.

In addition to PDCs and BDCs, Windows NT Servers can be member servers. This means that the server just provides resources upon request to clients and does not participate in the authentication of users.

PDCs and BDCs control access to resources on a particular domain, but what if a user needs access to a resource on another domain? Then you must establish a trust relationship between domains.

By establishing a trust relationship, secure access between domains is allowed. But users in one domain are not required to be defined in another domain. Trusted domains make Windows NT a more scaleable network scheme, especially in enterprise-wide networks. If it weren't for the use of trusted domains, large NT-based networks would not be workable due to the huge amount of administration involved. With the trusted domain concept, for example, the Sales department can have its own little part of the network, separate from the rest of the network. If it's necessary for the Sales domain to share information and resources with the Marketing department domain, NT can easily provide the cross-access needed via domain trusts.

To establish trusts between domains, perform the following steps:

1. Launch the User Manager For Domains.
2. Select the Policies menu.
3. Select Trust Relationships.
4. In the Trust Relationships dialog box, select the domains that you want to be trusted or trusting domains.

It is important to note that trusts are one-way by default. This means that although the Production domain (the trusting domain) grants a trust to the Engineering domain (the trusted domain) to access the Design share, Production does not have any additional rights to the Engineering domain unless this is defined in the Trust Relationships dialog box. Two-way trusts are simply two one-way trusts between domains.

Managing Local And Global Groups

Managing users would be difficult if it weren't for group administration. The group concept is to assign access rights only to groups, and then control access by adding and deleting users from the various groups as needed. By taking this approach, you rarely should have to adjust access rights for individual users to a resource. The user accounts by themselves have almost no rights assigned; all of these rights are inherited from the groups in which they are placed.

A good method for approaching user security in the NT is to create groups for each resource on the network so that each resource has a group that manages access for that particular resource. After establishing this setup of resource groups, you will spend most of your time managing the groups and their members, not the resources.

Windows NT has two types of groups: local and global. Local groups only are available on the local domain; global groups are available across domain lines. This distinction is very important to understand. Another important difference is that local groups can contain both users and groups, whereas global groups only can contain users. No local or global groups can be members of another global group.

So, if you want the Engineering domain to access the color printer in the Marketing domain, a global group (for example, EngnrPrint) should be created, with access rights to the color printer in Marketing. Note again that just because the Marketing domain trusts the EngnrPrint global group to access the color printer, it does not mean that either domain has any additional rights to other domain resources, unless explicitly defined.

As mentioned earlier, NT comes with some built-in local and global groups, which have default users and access privileges assigned. Table 5.1 describes these groups, whether they are local or global, the default members assigned, and their description.

Table 5.1   NT's built-in groups.

Group Name	Default Members	Local/ Global	Description
Account Operators	None	Local	Members can administer domain user and group accounts
Administrators	Domain Admins, Administrator	Local	Members can administer fully the computer/domain
Backup Operators	None	Local	Members can bypass file security to back up files
Domain Admins	Administrator	Global	Designated administrators of the domain
Domain Guests	Guest	Global	All domain guests
Domain Users	Administrator	Global	All domain users
Everyone	All	Global/Local	All users
Guests	Guest	Local	Users granted access to the computer/domain
Print Operators	None	Local	Members can administer domain printers
Replicators	None	Local	Supports file replication in a domain
Server Operators	None Administrator	Local	Members can administer domain servers
Users	Domain Users	Local	Ordinary users

In addition, each group can have a certain type of access at the directory level:

➤ **Full Control** Users can add files, read and change files, change directory permissions, and take ownership of directories and files.

➤ **List** Users can list the files and subdirectories within that directory.

➤ **Read** Users are able to read files and run applications within the directory.

➤ **Add** Users can add files to the directory, but cannot read or change them.

➤ **Add & Read** Users can add and read files in the directory, but cannot change them.

➤ **Change** Users can add, read, and change the contents of files in the directory.

➤ **No Access** Users cannot access the directory (even if the user is a member of a group that has been granted access).

 When a user belongs to multiple groups in a domain, the least restrictive rights take precedence. For example, if a user has Full Control of one resource, and Read to another, that user has Full Control privileges. By the way, no access means NO ACCESS!

Of Policies, Profiles, And Logon Scripts

There are a number of methods you can use to specify settings for network users. This type of customization is handled through Windows NT policies, profiles, and logon scripts, described in the following subsections.

System Policies

System policies control user environments and actions. System policies are created and administered via the System Policy Editor (Start|Programs| Administrative Tools (Common)|System Policy Editor).

The System Policy Editor allows you to specify what programs are available in users' Control Panels, customize users' desktops, specify network settings, control network logon and access, and customize users' Start menu options.

You can define a default system policy for all domain users, or you can apply different policies for users, computers, or groups. By setting up system policies, you modify Registry settings for computers or users—specifically, the current user and local machine Registry values.

To define a system policy as the default policy, perform the following: Save the policy in the path \WinNT\System32\Reply\Export\Scripts, with a file name of NTCONFIG.POL. Files stored in this directory are duplicated to other NT Servers and Workstations that are participating in Replication. The copied files are stored in \WinNT\System32\Reply\Import\Scripts, which is shared as the NETLOGON share.

If you define a system policy in the System Policy Editor, you must choose between two modes: Registry mode and Policy File mode. To do this:

1. Select the File menu in the System Policy Editor.

2. Select either Open Policy or Open Registry.
   Open Policy lets you edit an existing policy. Open
   Registry leads you to the Registry areas for Local
   Computer and Local User. Make changes to the policy
   directly in the Registry, then save the changes.

Whenever you change the Registry, you run the risk of reducing the Registry to ruins. Depending on what portion of the Registry is damaged, NT may not boot anymore. *Always back up the Registry before making changes, and take care when modifying the Registry.*

Profiles

You can set and manage individual users' desktop configuration information with user profiles. Settings such as screen savers, network connections, customized desktops, mouse settings, and program groups can be specified with a user profile. Profiles can be created for both users and groups. User profiles are located in the Winnt\Profiles\<USERNAME> directory.

User profiles protect your network resources from your users and your users from themselves. Establishing user profiles can help you when network users remove or relocate program items and groups. By forcing users to maintain settings with user profiles, you produce a nonmodifiable, consistent user interface, reducing your support costs as well as the users' frustration levels.

You can force a user to use a certain profile by creating a Mandatory User Profile that cannot be changed or saved by the user. These are produced by establishing a roaming profile for a user, copying that profile to a shared directory, assigning the appropriate users to the profile, changing the name of the NTUSER.DAT file to NTUSER.MAN, and entering the profile UNC path into the User Profile Path dialog box, located in the User Environment Profile screen for each user.

Incidentally, in the event of a PDC failure, the user will not receive the mandatory profile at logon. When this happens, Windows NT accesses the user's last locally cached profile or the default profile assigned to the user's workstation. The locally cached profile is used if the user has logged on to the domain successfully in the past. The default profile is used if the user never has logged on to the domain successfully.

Use the following steps to create a roaming profile:

1. Copy the user's profile from the workstation to a shared network path.

2. Open Control Panel, and double-click System.

3. Select the user's profile entry, select Copy To, and type in the full UNC path name to the server where the profile will reside.

4. In the User Profile dialog box, enter the full UNC path name for the profile in the User Profile path field.

You also can set the user's home directory settings in the user's profile. To do this for an existing account that currently has a local home directory, you must perform the following steps:

1. Select the Connect option in the User Environment Profile dialog box in User Manager.

2. Select a shared drive letter, and then enter the full UNC path name of the user's new home directory. The full UNC path name contains the server name on which the home directory resides (the domain name is not required). The variable %HOMEPATH% contains the user's home directory UNC path name only after the new home directory has been established.

If you have users who change settings constantly and/or inappropriately, it's a good idea to establish profiles and force users to stick to these settings. Although this can upset users, it's the best way to protect everyone.

Logon Scripts

When you consider all of the user configuration utilities and capabilities that come with NT Server, it seems strange to include logon scripts. However, to maintain backward compatibility, you must provide for the use of logon scripts—for several reasons. First, because user profiles only work with NT-based computers, DOS-based clients require logon scripts to provide consistent network connections. Also, if you still have an old LAN Manager server on your network, logon scripts preserve backward compatibility to those servers for all clients.

In addition, you can specify a user's network connections or network printer connections without developing a sophisticated user profile plan. In the event that you only have defined personal profiles but you want to define persistent network connections, logon scripts can do that too. Finally, if you don't want to spend an extensive amount of time developing a complex and coherent user profile strategy, logon scripts are a quick and easy alternative.

Utilizing logon scripts is beneficial in custom-building a user's environment without managing all aspects of it. For backup purposes, you should export logon scripts from the PDC to all BDCs on the network. That way, should the PDC go down, the BDCs maintain a copy of the logon scripts and make them available to users at logon. Logon scripts do not need to be exported to every workstation. Always place files that are to be exported into subdirectories of the Winnt\System32\Repl\Export directory. The default export directory for logon scripts on the PDC is Winnt\System32 \Repl\Export\Scripts.

Replication

Windows NT has provided a quick and efficient way to set up mirrored directory structures among servers through a process called "directory replication." A major boon of system file replication is logon and authentication load balancing between PDCs and BDCs. Replication of such files maintains current versions of logon scripts, system policy files, and user profiles.

The Directory Replicator Service is composed of an export server that serves as the master directory. The servers selected for importing receive the replicated master directory in their import directories.

By replicating logon scripts, system policy files, and user profiles to all domain controllers, true load balancing can be achieved. Therefore, when users log on to the domain, authentication of that user is handled by the first domain controller to respond to the authentication request. By having the replicated system files on that domain controller, the controller is able to authenticate the user and log him or her on to the network without having to contact another server. If the system files are located only on the PDC, the BDC must send for and receive copies of all applicable system files from the PDC. This increases the load on the network.

Note that only Windows NT Server computers are able to be configured to export files for replication. Machines that run Windows NT Server and Workstation can be configured to import files during replication. MS-DOS clients and Windows 95 clients do not support replication. Also, it's important to understand that a special account for the Directory Replicator Service must be created on the export server. You should configure this account with a password that never expires, and the account must be able to log on during all hours. Replication export servers have replication-specific entries in the Registry that control the timing of directory export notices. Windows NT workstations, Windows 95 clients, and MS-DOS clients cannot be configured as export servers.

Finally, only domain controllers should receive logon scripts. Because these are the only servers that can authenticate users, unnecessary network traffic is created when you replicate logon scripts to machines that don't authenticate users.

Managing Shared Resources

The customary method for sharing files, directories, and resources on Windows NT Server is by creating a share. The process is simple; use the following steps to share a resource or directory:

1. Select the directory or resource you wish to share in NT Explorer or via the My Computer icon.

2. Right-click the directory or resource, and select Sharing from the drop-down menu (the default is Not Shared).

3. Click the Share As button. When you do this, a dialog box pops up, and NT displays a default share name (this is usually the first eight characters of the selected directory name). You can change the share name if desired. It is important to note, however, that share names that are greater than eight characters long cannot be accessed from DOS-based clients.

You also can limit access to the share to a maximum number of users on the Sharing tab. It's a good idea to limit the number of users, to prevent users from overloading a slow computer or to ensure that other server processes can run unimpeded. Select the Maximum Allowed option if you do not want to impose this limitation. To set the number of allowed users, select the Allow button and a number appears in the Users box. You may use the up and down arrows to set this number, or type a number directly in the Users box.

 Subdirectories inherit the permissions of the parent directories as their default share permissions.

After creating the share, you can assign permission to the share. To do this, select the Permissions button or click the Security tab. Note that the default setting for newly created shares is Full Control for everyone. You have four levels of security available for the purpose of restricting access to server shares: No Access, Read, Change, and Full Control.

 You must always set explicit directory permissions on new shares. The default permissions grant Full Control to group Everyone!

You also can manage access to shares via the Server Manager utility by performing the following steps:

1. Launch Server Manager (Start|Programs|Administrative Tools (Common)|Server Manager).

2. Highlight the desired machine and choose Properties from the Computer menu.

3. Select one of the following radio buttons:

    ➤ **Users** This button shows you the number of users connected to the resource.

    ➤ **Shares** This button shows you all of the shares on the domain, the number of users accessing shared resources, and the local name of the resource being shared.

    ➤ **In Use** This button shows all the open resources on the domain, the users who have the resources open, the type of operation taking place on the resources, the number of locks on the resource, and the path for the open resource.

    ➤ **Alerts** This button allows you to build a list of all NT-based computers that are to receive administrative alerts.

To create a share in Server Manager, perform the following steps:

1. Launch Server Manager.

2. Highlight the computer name on which you want to create a new share.

3. Select Shared Directories from the Computer menu.

4. Click the New Share button, enter the share name and path of the share, and click OK.

 If you want to manage shares from a remote location, they must be managed from Server Manager, not Windows NT Explorer.

There are a number of administrative shares that are hidden from users but are accessible to the Administrator. These shares all have a dollar sign ($) appended to them to keep them hidden. Table 5.2 lists these shares and their purposes.

 NT's built-in administrative shares cannot be deleted or renamed.

Table 5.2   Windows NT's hidden administrative shares.

Share Name	Description
Admin$	The directory where NT Server (or Workstation) is installed, and the directory used for remote administration of NT.
Driveletter$	The letter of the drive on which a storage device is installed. This can be accessed remotely by members of the following groups: Administrators, Backup Operators, and Server Operators.
IPC$	IPC stands for Interprocess Communications, the resource used to share the named pipes interface, which is required by communications programs.
NETLOGON$	The share used by the logon server, set by default to %SystemRoot%\System32\Repl\Import. This share is utilized by the NETLOGON service for processing domain requests on NT Server.
Print$	Used for management and support of shared printers.
Repl$	The shared export directory, which is used for replication. It is set by default to the %SystemRoot%\System32\Repl\Export directory.

Setting Priorities

NT's multiprocessing environment requires that some processes have a higher execution priority than others. The kernel handles the setting of priorities for each process and has the ability to increase or decrease the priority of a process to improve or alter how it executes. There are 32 priority levels (0 through 31); the higher-numbered priorities are executed before the lower-numbered priorities. Although the system has the ability to use all 32 levels directly, you have only a limited ability to set priorities. By default, all user- and administrator-launched applications are assigned a base priority of 8 (/normal). However, users can launch applications with 4 (/low) or 13 (/high) priority, and an administrator can launch applications with 24 (/realtime) priority. To launch an application with an alternate priority level, use the following syntax at a command prompt:

```
start [/low|/normal|/high|/realtime] application
```

NT offers two other priority controls to alter the levels of running processes. The first is a slide bar that controls the performance boost for foreground applications. (A "foreground application" is the process operating in the active window on your screen—usually indicated by a colored title bar.) This slide bar control is located on the Performance tab in the System applet in the Control Panel. By default, foreground applications have a priority of 10 (maximum). Move the slider to the right to increase the priority for foreground applications, to the left to decrease priority (left =8, middle=9, right=10).

The second control is accessed via the Task Manager. By selecting any of the listed processes on the Process tab, you can change the priority to low, normal, high, or realtime via the Set Priority menu accessed through the right-click pop-up menu. However, only administrators have the ability to set a process's priority to realtime.

Client-Based Windows NT Management

Windows NT Server comes with a tool called the "Network Client Administrator," which helps you install the programs and tools that come with NT Server. It is located in the %systemroot%\system32 directory, and is accessible from the Start menu (Start|Programs|Administrative Tools (Common)|Network Client Administrator).

The Network Client Administrator comes with installation files for clients running Windows 95, the Microsoft Network Client for MS-DOS 3.0, LAN Manager for MS-DOS 2.2c, LAN Manager for OS/2 2.2c, Remote Access Client for MS-DOS 1.1a, and TCP/IP-32 for Windows for Workgroups.

You can use the Network Client Administrator to share installation files contained on the NT Server CD and copy the directories and files on the NT Server CD to a network server. The Client Administrator lets you efficiently install network client software by creating an installation disk set or a network installation startup disk. Depending on the kind of software you want to install, you can determine the type of installation disk you need to create with the Client Administrator (see also Table 5.3).

Use the Network Client Administrator to copy the files and directories in the \CLIENTS directory of the NT Server CD. To avoid using up too much hard disk space, you can delete the directories you don't need. However, do not delete \CLIENTS\MSCLIENT\NETSETUP. Those files are required for the creation of network installation startup disks for Windows 95, Windows for Workgroups, and the Microsoft Client for MS-DOS.

To use a network installation startup disk to install NT Server, NT Workstation, or Windows for Workgroups, you have to create the necessary subdirectories in the Clients directory and then copy the needed files. For specific instructions on copying the files, see the README.TXT file in the Clients\Support directory on the NT Server installation CD.

 Network installation startup disks are usable only on x86 or Pentium computers; they can't be used for Alpha, MIPS, or Power PC computers.

Table 5.3 **Determining the type of installation disk set or network installation disk you need.***

Client Type	Installation Disk Set	Installation Startup Disk
NT Server	—	X
NT Workstation	—	X
Windows 95	—	X
Windows for Workgroups	—	X
TCP/IP-32 for Windows for Workgroups	X	—
Network Client for MS-DOS	X	X
LAN Manager for MS-DOS	X	—
LAN Manager for MS OS/2	X	—
RAS for MS-DOS	X	—

*** Note**: × = is available or is supported
—= is not available or is not supported

Exam Prep Questions

Question 1

> What is the difference between local and global groups?
>
> ○   a. It is possible for local groups to contain global groups, but global groups cannot contain local groups.
>
> ○   b. Only user accounts from the local domain can be contained within a local group, whereas user accounts from both the local and trusted domains can be contained in global groups.
>
> ○   c. It is not possible to create a local group on the domain controllers, whereas global groups are created only on the domain controllers.
>
> ○   d. Local groups can only contain global groups, and global groups can only contain user accounts.

The correct answer is a. Global groups help organize domain users into logical units, whereas local groups provide users with permissions or rights to domain resources. The domain controllers of the domain are the only ones that can create global groups, while local groups can be created on any workstation or server within the domain. Global groups are limited to containing only user accounts for the domain.

Question 2

> Mary is leaving the company and David is her replacement. What is the best way to give David the same access to all of the resources previously used by Mary?
>
> ○   a. Create an account for David in Server Manager using Mary's account as a template. Then delete Mary's account.
>
> ○   b. Rename Mary's account in User Manager For Domains. Tell David to change the account password when he logs on for the first time.
>
> ○   c. Rename Mary's account in Server Manager. Tell David to change the account password when he logs on for the first time.
>
> ○   d. Create an account for David in the User Manager for Domains using Mary's account as a template, then delete Mary's account.

Renaming Mary's account through User Manager for Domains and instructing David to change the password is the best way to give David the same access as Mary; therefore, answer b is correct. Server Manager is not used to manage user accounts; therefore answers, a and c are incorrect. Although creating a new account by copying the existing account is a possible method, it is not Microsoft's current position that this is the best course of action. The text for answer d states the account is deleted once the copy is completed. If this action is followed, then there is no need to copy the account in the first place; it would be much simpler to rename it. An alternative not listed here is to retain the old account for the possible return of that user or for security audit purposes. Because answer d is more work than necessary and does not recommend changing the account's password, answer d is incorrect.

Question 3

> Which of the following built-in groups, other than Administrators, have the default right to log on locally to a Windows NT server?
>
> ○ a. Server Operators and Account Operators only.
>
> ○ b. Server Operators only.
>
> ○ c. Server Operators, Account Operators, Backup Operators, and Print Operators.
>
> ○ d. Server Operators, Account Operators, and Backup Operators only.

All of the following built-in groups have the right by default to log on locally to a Windows NT Server: Server Operators, Account Operators, Backup Operators, and Print Operators; therefore, choice c is correct.

Question 4

> How do you demote a BDC to a file server?
>
> ○ a. Choose the Network option in Control Panel, select the BDC, and click Demote.
>
> ○ b. Highlight the BDC in the Server Manager, and select Demote on the Computer menu.
>
> ○ c. Reinstall Windows NT Server.
>
> ○ d. Restart the BDC, and choose Member Server at the startup screen.

Although you promote a BDC to a PDC by using Server Manager, you need to reinstall Windows NT Server to change the role of the server from a domain controller to a member server. The converse also is true; therefore, choice c is correct. For this particular scenario, you must reinstall Windows NT Server and select Stand-Alone or Member Server when the system asks for a role for the server.

Question 5

Bill used to belong to the Production group. Now he has been reassigned to Engineering. Because of this change, he must be able to access program source files in the \Source directory on the file server. The Engineering and Administrators groups have Full Control permissions to the \Source directory. The Production group has No Access permission. After logging on as a member of the Engineering group, Bill notices that he still cannot access the files in the \Source directory on the file server. What is the best way for Bill's domain administrator to grant him the required access to the \Source directory?

○   a. Remove Bill's user account from the Administrators group.

○   b. Remove Bill's user account from the Production group.

○   c. Grant all permissions for the \Source directory to Bill's user account.

○   d. Add Bill's user account to the Administrators group.

If a user belongs to a group that has No Access permissions for a directory, then he or she will be denied access to that NTFS directory, because No Access always wins. Even if Bill was added to the Administrators group, he still would not be able to access files in the \Source directory. The only way to grant Bill full access to the \Source directory is to remove his user account from the Production group; therefore, choice b is correct.

Question 6

You want to modify user logon scripts to ensure that users have access to the latest shared resources. What is the best way to do this?

○ a. Save the logon scripts in a subdirectory of \Winnt\ System32\Repl\Export on the PDC and configure Windows NT to replicate these scripts to other domain controllers.

○ b. Put the scripts in the \Winnt\System32\Repl\Export directory on the PDC and have NT replicate these scripts to each domain workstation.

○ c. Place the logon scripts in a subdirectory of \Winnt\ System32\Repl\Export on the PDC and replicate these scripts to each domain workstation.

○ d. Store the logon scripts in the \Winnt\System32\ Repl\Export directory on the PDC and configure Windows NT to replicate these scripts to each domain controller.

Logon scripts should be exported from the PDC to all BDCs responsible for authenticating logons on the network. The default export directory for logon scripts on the PDC is the C:\Winnt\System32\Repl\Export\Scripts directory; therefore, choice a is correct. The Replicator Service only grabs files that appear in subdirectories beneath the ...\Export\Scripts directory. It's the presence of the subdirectory in answer a that makes it absolutely correct.

Question 7

What is the most efficient method for installing client administration tools on your network clients?

○ a. Copy the desired utilities onto a floppy disk and install them on each network client.

○ b. Install the utilities on each client using the NT Server installation CD.

○ c. Use the Network Client Administrator to copy the needed files from the CD, and place the files on a shared network server so they can be accessed from the clients that need them.

○ d. Upon request during installation, tell Windows NT which network clients need such files.

The Network Client Administrator is the best method for sharing installation files contained on the NT Server CD; therefore, choice c is the correct answer. The Client Administrator lets you efficiently install network client software by creating an installation disk set or a network installation startup disk for network clients.

Question 8

Which of the following is the best application to use to create a new shared directory on a domain server from your Windows NT workstation computer?

a. User Manager

b. Server Manager

c. Windows Explorer

d. Network Client Administrator

Server Manager allows users to create new shares on remote computers; therefore, choice b is correct. None of the other utilities will do the job, so answers a, c, and d are all incorrect. Server Manager is not a Windows NT Workstation utility; it is a Windows NT Server utility. However, it can be added to NTW by installing it from the administrative tools from the NTS distribution CD.

Question 9

Which of the following types of computers can be configured to export files during replication? [Check all correct answers]

❑   a. Windows NT servers that are configured as domain controllers

❑   b. Windows NT member servers

❑   c. Windows NT Workstations

❑   d. Windows 95 clients

Only those computers running Windows NT Server (member servers and Primary and Backup Domain Controllers) can be configured to export files during replication; therefore, choices a and b are correct.

Question 10

You want to force John to use the same user profile on any work-station; how do you do this?

○ a. Create a network profile on the PDC in the \Winnt\ Profiles directory named for John's account, followed by the .dat suffix. Remove any local profiles from John's workstation.

○ b. Rename John's current profile from NTUSER.DAT to NTUSER.MAN.

○ c. Using the Copy Profile To box from the System option in Control Panel, copy John's current profile from his workstation to a shared network path. Delete the current profile from his workstation.

○ d. Copy John's workstation profile to a shared network path using the Copy Profile To box. Then, type in the network path in the User Profile Path box on John's machine.

A user's profile first must be copied from his or her workstation to a shared network path to create a roaming user profile. This is accomplished by choosing the profile entry on a user's machine from the User Profiles tab in the System option in Control Panel, selecting Copy To, and providing the UNC name to the server where the profile will be located. The User Profile Path field on the User Environment Profile dialog box should then be set to the full UNC path name of the copied user profile. Choice d, therefore, is correct.

Need To Know More?

 Heywood, Drew: *Inside Windows NT Server*. New Riders, Indianapolis, IN, 1995. ISBN 1-56205-472-4. Chapter 11, entitled "Sharing Drives, Directories, and Files," deals very nicely with issues relating to shares and NTFS permissions and access information.

 Siyan, Karanjit S.: *Windows NT Server 4 Professional Reference*. New Riders, Indianapolis, IN, 1996. ISBN 1-56205-731-6. A nice discussion of using Server Manager to manage shared resources is located in Chapter 6: "Implementing Windows NT Server Domains."

 Strebe, Matthew, Charles Perkins, and James Chellis: *MSCE: NT Server 4 Study Guide*. Sybex Network Press, San Francisco, CA, 1996. ISBN 0-7821-1972-7. Chapter 9 contains useful information about creating and maintaining your user environment.

 Search the TechNet CD (or its online version through www.microsoft.com) using the keywords "user management," "replication," "domain controllers," and "groups."

 The Windows NT Server Resource Kit contains lots of useful information about shares and share permissions. You can search the TechNet CD or the CD accompanying the *Resource Kit*, using keywords like "shares," "resource management," and "user management."

Windows NT Networking

6

. . . .

Terms you'll need to understand:

√ Protocol

√ NetBIOS

√ NetBEUI

√ TCP/IP

√ IPX/SPX

√ DLC

√ AppleTalk

√ SNMP

√ DHCP

√ WINS

√ DNS

√ CSNW

√ GSNW

√ Frame type

√ SLIP

√ PPP

√ PPTP

√ FTP

√ Gopher

√ HTTP

√ Protocol binding

Techniques you'll need to master:

√ Installing and configuring network protocols

√ Implementing services that complement certain protocols

√ Understanding and configuring protocol bindings

√ Adjusting frame type settings

To enable communications on a computer network, you must tell NT how it's supposed to "talk" to other computers and peripheral devices. In the networking world, this is established through the use of protocols. Basically, a protocol is an agreed-upon set of standards which define how computers communicate. In this chapter, we explain what protocols are available with Windows NT Server and when to use what protocol, as well as the properties of each protocol. In keeping with the tone of this series, we cover only those details you need to pass the networking portion of the Microsoft Certification examination. Pointers are provided to additional resources for this topic.

Built-In Windows NT Protocols

Windows NT Server comes with a number of protocols that can be enabled for communications purposes:

➤ Network Basic Input/Output System (NetBIOS)

➤ NetBIOS Extended User Interface (NetBEUI)

➤ Transmission Control Protocol/Internet Protocol (TCP/IP)

➤ NWLink Internetwork Packet Exchange/Sequenced Packet Exchange (IPX/SPX)

➤ Data Link Control (DLC)

➤ AppleTalk

We define and explain all of these protocols and their uses in the following sections.

NetBIOS

NetBIOS is installed automatically when NT is installed. NetBIOS originally was developed in the 1980s by IBM. NetBIOS is an extremely fast protocol that requires very little communications overhead, which is why it's used by NT for basic operations (for example, browsing and interprocess communications between network servers). Unfortunately, however, it is not a routable protocol; therefore, it is unusable in networks that have routing capabilities.

NetBEUI

NetBEUI is a simple network layer transport protocol that was developed to support NetBIOS networks. NetBEUI, like NetBIOS, is not routable, so it really has no place on an enterprise network. NetBEUI is the fastest transport protocol available to NT. Benefits of NetBEUI include its speed as well as good error protection, and it is easy to implement, with small memory overhead. The disadvantages of NetBEUI include the fact that it's not routable, there is very little support for cross-platform applications, and there are very few troubleshooting tools.

TCP/IP

TCP/IP is the most widely used protocol in networking today, due in part to the vast growth of the global Internet, which is a TCP/IP-based network. TCP/IP is the most flexible of the transport protocols, and is able to span wide areas. In addition, it has excellent cross-platform support, excellent routing capabilities, and support for the Simple Network Management Protocol (SNMP), the Dynamic Host Configuration Protocol (DHCP), the Windows Internet Name Service (WINS), the Domain Name Service (DNS), as well as a host of other useful protocols discussed in "TCP/IP Connectivity Issues," later in this chapter.

NWLink (IPX/SPX)

NWLink is Microsoft's "clean room" implementation of Novell's IPX/SPX protocol suite for NetWare networks. This protocol was included with NT to enable communication with NetWare servers. With NWLink, NT clients can access resources located on a NetWare server, and vice versa.

Put simply, Windows NT server requires that NWLink be installed to enable communications with NetWare clients and servers. In addition, the File and Print Services for NetWare is also required for NetWare clients and servers to access NT files and printers. The Client Service for NetWare (CSNW) is designed for Windows NT workstations that require a direct link to NetWare servers. The Gateway Service for NetWare (GSNW) lets Windows NT servers map a drive to a NetWare server, which provides access to NetWare server resources for Windows NT workstations (via a gateway). Additional information about NWLink can be found in "NWLink Connectivity Issues," later in this chapter.

DLC

Windows NT uses the Data Link Control (DLC) protocol primarily for connectivity to SNA (Systems Network Architecture) gateways, and more importantly, for connecting to network-attached printers, such as the Hewlett-Packard JetDirect. The use of DLC for network printing is detailed further in Chapter 8.

AppleTalk

It should come as no surprise that the AppleTalk protocol is used for communication with Macintosh computers. By enabling AppleTalk, you allow Mac clients to store and access files located on an NT Server, print to NT printers, and vice versa. (*Note:* you must first install the NT Services for Macintosh before you can install AppleTalk; and remember, Mac support is available only from an NTFS partition.)

NWLink Connectivity Issues

Put simply, NWLink is IPX for Windows NT: IPX is the protocol, and NWLink is the networking component that provides the protocol. NWLink is provided for connectivity to NetWare networks—both to allow NetWare clients to access NT servers and to allow NT clients to access NetWare servers. It is important to note, however, that NWLink by itself does not enable this type of communication; you must first install Gateway Service for NetWare and Client Service for NetWare. Basically, CSNW is a redirector, whereas GSNW is what makes file and print sharing on NetWare servers available to Microsoft clients.

IPX has a number of benefits: It supports routing between networks, it's faster than TCP/IP, and it's easy to install and maintain. Unfortunately, IPX doesn't have a sufficient central addressing scheme to prohibit multiple networks from making use of identical addresses, and it doesn't support the Simple Network Management Protocol (SNMP).

Installing NWLink

Installing the NWLink protocol is much like installing other protocols in Windows NT. There are, however, some special issues. To install NWLink, perform the following steps:

1. Open the Control Panel (Start|Settings|Control Panel).

2. Double-click the Network icon.

3. Click the Protocols tab in the Network dialog box.

4. Click the Add button.

5. Select NWLink IPX/SPX Compatible Transport from the list of available protocols.

6. Enter the path to the Windows NT Server installation CD in the path field of the setup dialog box, then click Continue.
    If you have installed NT's Remote Access Service (RAS), NT then asks if you want to bind NWLink to RAS. Either click OK to enable binding, or click Cancel.

7. Click the Close button, then click Yes when NT asks whether to restart the computer.

 Although in most cases it's fine to leave the default frame type (auto) as is, some Ethernet adapters don't work well with this setting. For new installations, the Ethernet 802.2 setting is recommended.

To change the Ethernet frame type and IPX network number, perform the following steps:

1. Open the Control Panel.

2. Double-click the Network icon.

3. Click the Protocols tab in the Network dialog box.

4. Double-click NWLink IPX/SPX Compatible Transport from the list of available protocols.

5. Click the Manual Frame Type Detection button.

6. Click the Add button.

7. Select your preferred frame type.

8. Type in the IPX network number for the adapter in the Network Number field.

9. Click the Add button.

10. Repeat the previous three steps for each frame type.

11. Click OK, then click the Close button.

12. Click Yes when asked to restart the computer.

There are more issues to consider when establishing communications between NT and NetWare networks. We cover these details in Chapter 7.

TCP/IP Connectivity Issues

TCP/IP currently is the most used networking protocol, as well as the standard protocol of the Internet. The beauty of the TCP/IP protocol suite lies in its ability to link many disparate kinds of computers and peripheral devices. Using this protocol stack, you enable most TCP/IP clients to access NT-based resources and vice versa.

Windows NT provides for a number of useful TCP/IP services. Included are the following:

➤ **Dynamic Host Configuration Protocol (DHCP)** This service enables the assignment of dynamic TCP/IP network addresses, based on a specified pool of available addresses. When a network client configured for DHCP logs on to the network, the DHCP service assigns the next available TCP/IP address for that network session. This really simplifies address administration.

➤ **Windows Internet Naming Service (WINS)** This service enables the resolution of network names to IP addresses (similar to the Unix DNS). This way, you don't have to remember the IP address of the client with whom you are trying to communicate—you can enter the network name and NT does the rest. Also, if a TCP/IP-based network does not have a WINS server, each time one computer tries to

access another, it must send a b-node broadcast, which creates unnecessary network traffic and can slow a busy network to a crawl. WINS
servers provide computer-name-to-IP address resolution, reducing
these broadcast messages and improving network performance.

➤ **Serial Line Internet Protocol (SLIP)** SLIP originally was developed
for the Unix environment and is still widely used among Internet
providers. Although SLIP provides good performance with little system overhead requirements, it does not support error checking, flow
control, or security features. SLIP is good for connecting to Unix hosts
or Internet providers. This protocol is quickly being replaced by PPP.

➤ **Point-to-Point Protocol (PPP)** PPP addresses many of the insuffi-
ciencies of SLIP, such as providing the ability to encrypt logons, as
well as support for additional transport protocols, error checking, and
recovery. In addition, PPP is optimized for low-bandwidth connections and, in general, is a more efficient protocol than SLIP.

➤ **Point-to-Point Tunneling Protocol (PPTP)** Simply stated, PPTP is
a protocol that creates secure connections between private networks
over the Internet. Benefits of PPTP include lower administrative,
transmission, and hardware costs than other solutions for this type of
connectivity.

➤ **World Wide Web (WWW)** This service comes as a part of NT
Server 4. WWW makes it possible to publish Web pages, whether for
an Internet-based Web site or for an internal intranet.

➤ **File Transfer Protocol (FTP)** This protocol is great for the fast transfers of files to and from a local hard drive to an FTP server located
elsewhere on another TCP/IP-based network (such as the Internet).

➤ **Gopher** This service serves text and links to other Gopher sites.
This service predates HTTP (the Web protocol). Although Gopher
sites are still out there, Gopher's use has been lessened because HTTP
handles information transfer better than this out-dated method.

➤ **HyperText Transfer Protocol (HTTP)** This World Wide Web protocol allows for the transfer of HTML documents over the Internet or an
intranet, and responds to actions like a user clicking on a hypertext link.

Installing And Configuring TCP/IP

There are a few items that you need to have on hand when you install TCP/IP. The following list describes these items:

► **Your server's IP address** This is the unique address that identifies a particular computer on a TCP/IP network. This number consists of four numbers, separated by periods (i.e., 125.115.125.48). The first one to three numbers identify the network on which the computer is located, and the remaining numbers identify the computer on that network.

► **Your network's subnet masks for each network adapter on the network** The subnet mask is a number mathematically applied to the IP address. This number determines which IP addresses are a part of the same subnetwork as the computer applying the subnet mask.

► **Your server's default gateway** The gateway is the computer that serves as a router, a format translator, or a security filter for a network.

► **The domain name server for the network** This is a computer that serves as an Internet host and performs translation of fully qualified domain names into IP addresses.

► **Any DHCP and WINS information about your network** If you already have these services configured, the process of configuring TCP/IP is greatly eased.

If you did not install TCP/IP when you first installed Windows NT Server, you must perform the following steps to install and configure this protocol suite:

1. Open the Control Panel.
2. Double-click the Network icon.
3. In the Networks window, click the Protocols tab.
4. Click the Add button.
5. Select TCP/IP from the list of available protocols. NT may request the installation CD or the location of the installation files.

6. In the Network window, click the Close button.

7. Either enter the TCP/IP address of the computer or select Obtain An IP Address From A DHCP Server, whichever is appropriate for this installation. Then, specify the subnet mask and default gateway.

8. If your network has a DNS server or a constant Internet connection, click the DNS tab and enter the DNS address.

9. If your network has a WINS server, click the WINS tab and enter the WINS address.

10. Click OK to close the TCP/IP Properties dialog box. If you did not specify a primary WINS address, NT gives a warning.

11. Click the Close button.

12. Click Yes when NT asks to restart the computer.

NetBEUI Connectivity Issues

NetBEUI is by far the easiest protocol to install and configure on an NT network. To install this protocol, perform the following steps:

1. Open the Control Panel.

2. Double-click the Network icon.

3. In the Networks window, click the Protocols tab.

4. Click the Add button.

5. Select NetBEUI from the list of available protocols and click OK.

6. Enter the path to the installation CD, or the location of the installation files.

7. If you have RAS installed, NT asks if you want to support it with this protocol. Click Cancel to leave it unsupported.

8. In the Network window, click the Close button.

9. Select Yes when NT asks to restart the computer.

Protocol Bindings

Protocol binding is the process NT uses to link network components from various levels of the network architecture to enable communication between those components. To set the binding order for network protocols, double-click the network icon in Control Panel and click the binding tab. This is where the bindings of installed network components are listed in order of upper-layer services and protocols to lower-layer network adapter drivers.

Binding should be ordered to enhance the system's use of the network. For example, if your network has both TCP/IP and NetBEUI installed—and most network devices use TCP/IP—workstation bindings should be set to bind TCP/IP first and NetBEUI second. In other words, the most frequently used protocol should be bound first. This speeds network connections. Because servers use whatever protocol is sent to them by each workstation, the binding order needs to be changed on the workstations only. Network speed is affected by the binding order on the workstations but not on the servers.

Exam Prep Questions

Question 1

> Your TCP/IP-based network is experiencing drastic increases in broadcast traffic. What is the best way to decrease the amount of broadcast traffic on your network?
>
> ○   a. Divide your network into two physical subnets, and install a bridge.
>
> ○   b. Divide your network into two logical subnets, and install a gateway.
>
> ○   c. Install a DHCP server.
>
> ○   d. Install a WINS server.

If a TCP/IP network does not have a WINS server, each computer on the network has to send a broadcast message to other computers on the network, which increases network traffic. By making use of a WINS server, you provide computer-name-to-IP address resolution that reduces the number of broadcast messages. Therefore, answer d is correct.

Question 2

> Of the following, which are required for access to a NetWare server from a Windows NT workstation running Client Service for NetWare? [Select all that apply]
>
> ❑   a. A group on the NetWare server called NTGATEWAY containing the Windows NT workstation's user account
>
> ❑   b. Gateway Service for NetWare
>
> ❑   c. A user account on the NetWare server
>
> ❑   d. The NWLink protocol

It is necessary to place user accounts in the NTGATEWAY group on the NetWare server only if workstations are accessing the NetWare server via a gateway. That is not the case in this example; therefore, answer a is incorrect. If an NT server is to act as a gateway to a NetWare server, the Gateway Services for NetWare must be loaded onto a Windows NT server.

Because this scenario discusses an NT client accessing a NetWare server, answer b also is incorrect. Any user accessing a NetWare server directly will need a user account on that NetWare server; therefore, answer c is correct. An NT workstation running the Client Service for NetWare can access a NetWare server directly by using the NWLink protocol; therefore, answer d also is correct.

Question 3

Your network uses multiple protocols. Where in NT is the binding order of the protocols changed to increase network speed?

○   a. On the domain controllers only

○   b. On the workstations only

○   c. On the servers only

○   d. On both the workstations and servers (including the domain controllers)

Because NT servers use the protocol sent to them by workstations, the binding order needs only to be changed on the workstations; therefore, answer b is the correct choice. Network speed is affected by the binding order on the workstations but not on the servers; therefore, answers a, c, and d all are incorrect.

Question 4

What is an advantage of SLIP over PPP?

○   a. SLIP supports security, whereas PPP does not support security.

○   b. SLIP supports error checking, whereas PPP does not support error checking.

○   c. SLIP supports flow control, whereas PPP does not support flow control.

○   d. SLIP requires less system overhead than PPP.

SLIP does not support error checking, flow control, or security—these are features of PPP. So answers a, b, and c are incorrect. SLIP does, however, require less system overhead than PPP; therefore, d is the correct choice.

Question 5

> You want to install TCP/IP on a member server in a nonrouted network. You have already assigned an IP address manually to the server. What other parameter must you specify to install TCP/IP on the server?
>
> ○   a. The subnet mask
>
> ○   b. The default gateway
>
> ○   c. The DHCP server IP address
>
> ○   d. The WINS server IP address

When installing TCP/IP on a nonrouted network, the IP address and subnet mask parameters must be specified; therefore, answer a is correct.

Question 6

> Your Ethernet network consists of a Windows NT 4 server, several NT Workstation clients, a NetWare 3.12 client, and one NetWare 4.1 client. NWLink is running on the network. Each of the NetWare clients is using different frame types. How would you configure the NWLink IPX/SPX Properties dialog box on the Windows NT 4 server to enable the server to recognize both NetWare clients?
>
>
>
> ○   a. By enabling Auto Frame Type Detection
>
> ○   b. By selecting the Manual Frame Type Detection option and adding a NetWare client's network number and frame type to the frame type configuration list
>
> ○   c. By selecting the Auto Frame Type Detection option and adding both NetWare clients' network numbers and frame types to the frame type configuration list
>
> ○   d. By selecting the Manual Frame Type Detection option and adding each of the NetWare clients' network numbers and frame types to the frame type configuration list

If frame types other than 802.2 are being used on a network, Manual Frame Type Detection must be enabled. Frame types belonging to each client must be added to the frame type configuration list on the NWLink IPX/ SPX Properties dialog box. Therefore, answer d is correct.

Question 7

> Your network users need to access your network resources across the Internet. How can you allow Internet-based user access while still providing security?
>
> ○ a. Implement the SLIP protocol
>
> ○ b. Implement the FTP protocol
>
> ○ c. Implement the Point-to-Point Protocol
>
> ○ d. Implement the Point-to-Point Tunneling Protocol

The Point-to-Point Tunneling Protocol (PPTP) uses the Internet as a connection medium while still maintaining network security; therefore, answer d is correct.

Question 8

> To end the process of maintaining user accounts on two different types of servers, you have decided to migrate users from the NetWare server to a Windows NT 4 server. What must be installed on the Windows NT server to provide those clients with access to NetWare? [Check all correct answers]
>
> ❑ a. Gateway Service for NetWare
>
> ❑ b. The NWLink protocol
>
> ❑ c. Client Service for NetWare
>
> ❑ d. SAP Agent

GSNW must be installed on the Windows server; therefore, answer a is correct. For the Windows NT Server to communicate with the NetWare server, the NWLink protocol must be installed on the Windows NT server; therefore, answer b also is correct. When GSNW is installed, NWLINK will be automatically installed if it is not already present.

Need To Know More?

 Heywood, Drew: *Inside Windows NT Server*. New Riders, Indianapolis, IN, 1995. ISBN 1-56205-472-4. Chapter 9, "Using TCP/IP," discusses detailed issues relating to installing and configuring the TCP/IP protocol suite.

 Siyan, Karanjit S.: *Windows NT Server 4 Professional Reference*. New Riders, Indianapolis, IN, 1996. ISBN 1-56205-731-6. Chapters 13 through 16 all discuss various aspects of protocol management.

 Strebe, Matthew, Charles Perkins, and James Chellis: *MSCE: NT Server 4 Study Guide*. Sybex Network Press, San Francisco, CA, 1996. ISBN 0-7821-1972-7. Chapter 6, "Networking and Network Protocols," and Chapter 8, "Windows NT Networking Services," both cover a lot of useful information about managing network protocols.

 Search the TechNet CD (or its online version through www.microsoft.com) using the keywords "protocol management," "TCP/IP," "NWLink," and "internetworking."

  The Windows NT Server Resource Kit contains lots of useful information about shares and share permissions. You can search the TechNet CD or the CD accompanying the *Resource Kit*, using keywords like "protocols," "binding," and "networking services."

The Windows NT/NetWare Relationship

7

. . . .

Terms you'll need to understand:

√ NetWare

√ NWLink Internetwork Packet Exchange/Sequenced Packet Exchange (IPX/SPX)

√ Client Services for NetWare (CSNW)

√ Gateway Services for NetWare (GSNW)

√ File And Print Services For NetWare (FPNW)

√ Frame type

Techniques you'll need to master:

√ Adjusting frame type settings

√ Installing, configuring, and enabling GSNW

√ Installing, configuring, and enabling CSNW

√ Implementing File And Print Services For NetWare (FPNW)

√ Using Microsoft's NetWare Migration Tool

By making NetWare connectivity part and parcel of Windows NT Server, Microsoft has made it possible to integrate its products directly and easily with existing networks all over the world. Considering its built-in NetWare access capabilities, and the add-ins available at low cost from Microsoft for Windows NT Server to enhance these capabilities, it's clear that NetWare interoperability is an important concern in Redmond.

Even if you don't have any NetWare servers on your Windows NT network, you must still understand what Microsoft offers by way of NetWare compatibility and access to pass this test (and the NT Server 4 in the Enterprise test as well). While much of this material will be old hat to those who work in hybrid NetWare–Windows NT environments, those who don't have the benefit of direct exposure should study this chapter carefully. It will help you with the three to six NetWare-related test questions.

Protocols And Compatibility Issues

To avoid paying royalties to Novell, Microsoft built its own implementation of the Internetwork Packet eXchange/Sequenced Packet eXchange (IPX/SPX) protocols, called "NWLink" (to avoid infringing on Novell trade names). Surprisingly, some comparisons between Novell's IPX/SPX client implementations and Microsoft's NWLink have shown the latter implementation to be slightly faster than the former. In other words, these guys are serious about their NetWare compatibility, and have done a pretty good job.

Although NetWare does support multiple protocols—primarily IPX/SPX and TCP/IP—it's most common to find IPX/SPX used to communicate between NetWare's clients and its servers. In fact, Novell itself does not support any protocols other than IPX/SPX for versions of NetWare older than 3.x (which usually means version 2.2). Thus, if you see a test question that mentions NetWare 2.2, it's safe to assume that IPX/SPX is the protocol used to communicate between the NetWare server and its clients.

When it implemented IPX/SPX, Novell also elected to use a special frame format for the protocol, on Ethernet and other network types. Even though the emerging standard at the time (which has since become the official standard) was to use 802.2 frame formats for networked communications, Novell elected to use what's often called a "raw 802.3" frame format for its implementation of IPX/SPX on Ethernet.

To make a long and complex story as short as possible, the upshot of Novell's initial decision, and its subsequent divergence from industry standard frame types, introduced the possibility of a frame type mismatch when using IPX/SPX (or NWLink). You'll see one, or possibly two, questions on the test referring to problems communicating on a network, or requiring an understanding of NWLink's ability to detect automatically 802.2 IPX frame types on a Windows NT Server machine.

Here's what you need to know to deal with such questions:

1. Although NWLink is provided primarily for NetWare access and interoperability, Windows NT-based networks can use only NWLink, where no NetWare is present. Don't be surprised if this shows up on a test question!

2. Until NetWare 3.12 shipped, NetWare's default frame type was raw 802.3, which Microsoft calls simply "802.3 frame type."

3. For NetWare 3.12 and all 4.x versions (including IntranetWare), the default frame type uses 802.2 headers, atop the native frame type for the network technology in use. Microsoft calls this the "802.2 frame type," without regard to technology.

4. The total battery of frame types you're most likely to encounter is:

   a. 802.2 frame type (industry standard, default for NetWare 3.12 and higher-numbered versions)

   b. 802.3 frame type (so-called "raw 802.3 header" format, developed by Novell, default for older, pre-3.12 versions of NetWare)

c. 802.3 with SNAP header (sometimes called "Ethernet_SNAP frame type" in Microsoft terminology)

d. 802.5 frame type (the native format for Token Ring networks)

e. 802.5 frame type with SNAP header (sometimes called "Token_Ring_SNAP" in Microsoft terminology)

(*Note:* SNAP stands for SubNetwork Access Protocol, and provides a mechanism that permits nonstandard higher-level protocols to appear within a standard IEEE logical link control frame like the frame types previously mentioned. It's often used to transport AppleTalk or SNA in IP network environments. It's not necessary to understand the subtleties of this technology for this MCSE test, however.)

5. If any workstation (or server) is configured for an incorrect IPX frame type (that doesn't match the rest of the population), an improperly configured machine will not be able to interact with the network. This can occur even though the network may otherwise work properly, and all other machines may communicate successfully.

6. NWLink's default auto detect type setting is 802.2. If the initiation broadcast does not receive a 802.2 response, but does get some other frame type, then NT will attempt to use 802.3, Ethernet II, then SNAP in an attempt to detect the correct frame type in use. If a match is found, the default auto detect setting is set to the determined type. However, auto detect only functions in an environment with a single frame type.

7. For client/server applications like SQL Server database access, or NetBIOS-based applications, native NetWare clients using IPX/SPX can communicate directly with a Windows NT server running such an application without requiring anything other than NWLink and the server side of the application to be installed on that machine. In essence, the client side of the client/server application supplies everything the clients and server need to communicate, as long as they have a protocol in common. Because the assumption is that native NetWare clients use IPX/SPX, a Windows NT server must install NWLink to communicate with such clients across the network.

Gateway Service For NetWare

Microsoft often refers to this software component by its acronym, GSNW. But there's more to GSNW than meets the eye, and this can lead to some confusion. If you examine the listing in Figure 7.1 carefully, notice that the complete name of the software component as it appears in the Add dialog box, generated from the Services tab, Network applet, Control Panel is "Gateway (and Client) Services for NetWare."

Unless you've actually looked at this on screen at some point, or been warned of this subtlety, you may be surprised to learn that GSNW includes Client Service For NetWare (CSNW; discussed in the next section) in its capabilities and functionality. In English, this means that any Windows NT server with GSNW installed also can function as a client to a NetWare server. This explains why you must remove existing NetWare client software—especially Novell's NetWare Client for Windows NT—from any Windows NT server before installing GSNW on that machine.

Understanding GSNW

Test questions that touch on GSNW require that you understand what it does, and what's involved in installing it. Generically speaking, the term "gateway" refers to a software component permitting computers that do

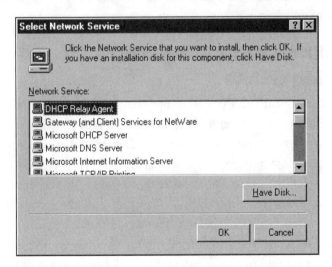

Figure 7.1   The unabridged expansion for GSNW is actually Gateway (and Client) Services for NetWare.

not share a common set of protocols and services to communicate with one another. In other words, the gateway translates from one protocol and service world to another, and vice versa.

GSNW is no exception: What GSNW does is make it possible for ordinary Microsoft Network clients (PCs running Windows 3.x, Windows 95, or even Windows NT Workstation or Server) to access resources on a NetWare server by translating requests from those clients stated in MS Network terms into NetWare terms and then translating the concomitant responses from the NetWare server from NetWare terms back into MS Network terms. The gateway is in the middle of these communications.

 This is the "trick" that makes this work: The Windows NT server where GSNW runs exports a logical volume from the NetWare server through the gateway that MS Network clients can access as if it were any other NT-based network share. The gateway also can create a similar fiction for NetWare-based printers, and make NetWare-based print services available to MS Network clients. The chief selling point for GSNW is that it provides access to NetWare resources for MS Network clients without requiring any additional software, or software changes, to be made to those clients themselves.

If you can understand and appreciate the material in the two preceding paragraphs, you'll know enough about GSNW to be able to answer any test questions in which it may appear.

Installing, Configuring, And Enabling GSNW

Gateway Service for NetWare is an optional network service included as part of Windows NT Server 4: This means it's included with the distribution media for the product, but not installed by default whenever you install the core operating system. To install GSNW you must open the Network applet in Control Panel, select the Services tab, and then click the Add button in the resulting display. This produces the screen shown in Figure 7.1, where GSNW appears as the second choice in the list. To begin the process of installing GSNW, highlight its entry, then click the OK button at the bottom of the Window. This will bring up a prompt for the NT Server CD.

Occasionally, a test question may reference NWLink separately from GSNW. It's important to note that if you elect to install GSNW on an NT server that does not already have NWLink running, NWLink will be installed automatically as a part of the GSNW installation process. Thus, while NWLink is required for GSNW to run, it's not necessary to install it in advance, nor is it a problem if NWLink has already been installed.

Here's a high-level overview of the GSNW installation process, emphasizing those elements and information that must be supplied during installation that are most likely to appear in GSNW-related test questions:

1. Before installing and configuring GSNW you must create the following accounts on the NetWare server where the gateway will connect:

    a. A user account on the NetWare server with rights to the NetWare file system directories that gateway users from the NT side will need.

    b. A group account named NTGATEWAY on the NetWare server with rights to all file and print resources that gateway users will need.

    [*Note:* All users who go through a single GSNW gateway have the same access and the same rights to the NetWare resources; the only way to create different collections of access and rights is to set up multiple gateways (only one instance of GSNW per individual Windows NT server is permitted).]

2. To install GSNW, you must log in to the Windows NT server as an Administrator. In the Network applet in Control Panel, select the Services tab, click the Add button, and select Gateway (and Client) Services For NetWare. Supply the NT Server CD or point to a copy of the \i386 directory where the necessary source code files reside. The software will more or less install itself.

3. To configure GSNW, double-click on the GSNW icon in Control Panel. The Gateway Service For NetWare dialog box appears.

   a. Click on the Gateway button, to elicit the Configure Gateway dialog box.

   b. Check the Enable Gateway box to enable the Gateway Service.

   c. In the Gateway Account field, enter the NetWare user name you created in Step 1a. Enter the Password into the Password field, then confirm that password in the Confirm Password field.

   d. Click the Add button to create a NetWare share for use by Microsoft networking clients. A New Share dialog box appears.

   e. In the Share Name field, enter a name through which the NetWare directory will be shared.

   f. In the Network Path field, enter a UNC name for the NetWare directory that's being shared. For the SYS:Public directory on a server named NETONE, the syntax is \\NETONE\SYS\ PUBLIC.

   g. In the Comment field, you can add an optional descriptive phrase that will appear in the Browse window for MS Clients on the network.

   h. In the Use Drive field, select a drive letter on the Windows NT server to be assigned to the NetWare directory. This drive letter remains taken as long as GSNW runs on the Windows NT server; by default, Z is the letter assigned to the first such share name.

    i.   The User Limit box permits administrators to limit the number of users who can access the NetWare share simultaneously. Because the gateway bogs down under increasing load, it's a good idea to limit the number of users to 10 or so (unless the server is extremely fast or only lightly loaded).

    j.   Click OK to save all changes. You'll return to the Configure Gateway dialog box. Click OK again to exit the Gateway Service for NetWare dialog box. All changes will take effect upon the next system logon.

4. The only way to create NetWare shares is through the interface described in Steps 3d through 3j (not through Explorer or My Computer, as is the case for normal Windows NT Server shares). Likewise, you must use the GSNW applet in Control Panel to set permissions for NetWare shares. Here's how:

    a.   From an administrative logon, launch the GSNW applet from Control Panel.

    b.   When the Gateway Service For NetWare dialog box appears, choose the Gateway button.

    c.   In the Configure Gateway dialog box that appears, highlight the NetWare share name and choose the Permissions button. Use this interface to set permissions for the NetWare share.

5. Using NetWare Print Resources through the Gateway requires none of the shenanigans needed to establish and set permissions for the NetWare shares. Instead, configure NetWare print queues through the Printers icon in Control Panel (as with any other Windows NT server-attached printer). Here's what's involved:

a. From an administrative logon, launch the Printers applet. Select the Add Printer icon. This will display the Add Printer Wizard window.

b. Select the Network Printer radio button, then click the Next button. This brings up the Connect to Printer dialog box.

c. In this dialog box, you will see two icons—one labeled "NetWare Or Compatible Network" and the other labeled "Microsoft Windows Network." You can expand and navigate this directory tree the same way you would the Microsoft Windows Network tree: Double-click Network, select a server, then double-click and select the printer you wish to manage.

Otherwise, the procedure is exactly the same as installing an ordinary Windows NT network printer (covered in Chapter 8 of this book).

Remember that it is necessary to map a drive on the Windows NT server for the NetWare share, and that NetWare shares and their permissions only can be managed through the GSNW applet, not through ordinary file management tools. NetWare printers, on the other hand, can be handled like any other network printers through the Printers applet, once GSNW has been installed on a Windows NT server.

Client Service For NetWare

GSNW makes NetWare resources available to ordinary MS Network clients, but CSNW works only with Windows NT machines in order to make them act as native clients to NetWare servers elsewhere on the network. This system component is called CSNW only on Windows NT Workstation 4, which ships without GSNW; however, CSNW is part and parcel of GSNW on Windows NT Server 4 machines. In either case, its job is to let Windows NT machines link up to and browse NetWare resources alongside Microsoft Windows Network resources.

File And Print Services For NetWare

FPNW, as it's usually called, is not included with Windows NT Server 4; it must be purchased separately (at the time of writing, it costs $100 in the U.S. market). What GSNW is to MS Network clients, FPNW is to native NetWare clients: It makes resources from a Windows NT server available to NetWare clients, without requiring any additional software or configuration changes to those clients. In other words, FPNW makes a Windows NT server look like a NetWare 3.11 server to any native NetWare clients on a network.

Microsoft's (NetWare) Migration Tool

The program, which ships as an optional element in the Windows NT Server 4 distribution media, is called NWCONV.EXE. It can take user and group definitions from a NetWare server, along with most of the associated rights and permissions that pertain to them, and re-create that information on a Windows NT Server 4 machine.

Likewise, NWCONV.EXE also can grab volumes, directories, and files from a NetWare server and copy them to a Windows NT server, translating and preserving most of the file system permissions involved at the same time. This program is fairly sophisticated and offers lots of bells and whistles for dealing with duplicate accounts and for converting information from its NetWare server incarnation to a reasonable Windows NT server facsimile, but for the purposes of this test, this is all you need to know. For more details about this utility, consult Karanjit Siyan's book (see "Need To Know More?" at the end of this chapter).

Exam Prep Questions

Unless you work in a mixed NetWare/NT environment, you'll want to review the basics about GSNW, CSNW, FPNW, and NWLink, before you take any NT Server test. If these sound like gibberish, check the Glossary first, then reread this chapter (and at least one of the references in the "Need To Know More?" section) before you even *think* about taking an NT Server test! For those who feel like they're better prepared, here are some questions for you to study.

Question 1

> At XYZ Corp., a handful of NetWare 3.11 clients remain in use. These machines need access to files on a newly installed Windows NT server. To support such access without changes to the existing clients, which of the following services and/or protocols must be available on the Windows NT server? [Choose all correct answers]
>
> ❑ a. Gateway Service for NetWare (GSNW)
>
> ❑ b. Client Service for NetWare (CSNW)
>
> ❑ c. File and Print Services for NetWare (FPNW)
>
> ❑ d. The NWLink Protocol
>
> ❑ e. The Migration Tool for NetWare

The correct answers are c and d. Here's why: GSNW provides mediated access to NetWare services for Microsoft Network clients, so it's not required, meaning answer a should be left unchecked. Likewise, CSNW makes it possible for NT workstations and servers to obtain direct access to a NetWare server; thus, answer b should remain unchecked as well.

File and Print Services for NetWare make an NT server look like a NetWare server to NetWare network clients, so it's what provides file access; this means that answer c must be checked. But native NetWare 3.x clients need IPX/SPX to access real NetWare servers, or Windows NT servers running FPNW; since NWLink is Microsoft's implementation of IPX/SPX, answer d must be checked as well.

Finally, the Migration Tool may be used to copy account and group information, security settings, and files from a NetWare server to a Windows NT server. It does NetWare 3.x clients no good whatsoever, meaning that answer e must be unchecked.

Question 2

The Palmer Food Cooperative struggles by with donated equipment for its network. The keystone of its network is Windows NT Server 4. Because of a recent gift of a NetWare server, the coop's Windows for Workgroups machines now need access to resources on that machine. How can these client machines access the new server without adding any additional software?

○ a. Install Gateway Service for NetWare on the Windows NT server, and make those users members of an NTGATEWAY group on that server.

○ b. Install NWLink and File and Print Services for NetWare on the Windows NT server.

○ c. Install Gateway Service for NetWare on the Windows NT server, and create a group that has permission to access the NTGATEWAY group on the NetWare server.

○ d. Install Gateway Service for NetWare on the NetWare server, and NWLink on the Windows NT server.

The key to answering this question is to understand GSNW and what must happen on the NetWare side of a connection that uses GSNW. In essence, GSNW provides a way to "translate" ordinary Microsoft Network client traffic bound for a Windows NT server into a usable kind of NetWare equivalent. This prevents administrators from having to add software to network clients that need access to NetWare resources, which is especially useful on older machines (like those running Windows for Workgroups at the coop) where memory and system resources are already at a premium. The correct answer to this question requires you to recognize that GSNW does the job, but also requires you to know that it's necessary to set up a group account on the NetWare server to handle GSNW requests from the Windows NT server. This means that c is the only correct answer.

Answer a is incorrect because it places the NetWare group on the Windows NT server. Answer b is incorrect because it provides a way to make Windows NT services available to NetWare clients, not vice versa. Finally, answer d is incorrect because it puts the gateway on the NetWare server (a highly unlikely place to run a Windows NT service, in fact).

Question 3

QXR Co. has a NetWare 4.11 network, but it's adding a Windows NT server, to provide access to a SQL Server client/server application for its NetWare clients. What elements and/or protocols must be available on the Windows NT server so that NetWare clients can use the SQL Server application?

- ❍ a. NWLink IPX/SPX Compatible Transport
- ❍ b. Gateway Service for NetWare
- ❍ c. Client Service for NetWare
- ❍ d. Migration Tool for NetWare
- ❍ e. File and Print Services for NetWare

The presence of a client/server application means that the application's clients already have whatever software is necessary to communicate with the server, assuming clients and the server share a common protocol. Given that QXR has a predominantly NetWare network, the protocol that's necessary is IPX/SPX, known on the Windows NT server as NWLink. This makes a the only correct answer to this question.

Answer b is incorrect because it makes NetWare resources available to Microsoft Network clients (and QXR wants to go in the other direction). Answer c is incorrect because it makes NetWare resources available to NT Server and Workstation clients (and QXR still wants to go in the other direction). Answer d is incorrect because nobody said anything about migrating from NetWare to Windows NT. And finally, answer e is incorrect because the client/server application supplies its own client-side intelligence, and no need for additional file and print services was requested from the Windows NT server.

Question 4

One of the PCs on a network is unable to establish a working connection, but all other computers are working correctly. The only protocol in use on the network is NWLink. Of the following possibilities, which is the most likely cause of this problem?

○   a. Faulty network interface devices

○   b. A protocol mismatch

○   c. A PC memory conflict

○   d. An incorrect IPX frame type

Trick! question

The key to answering this question correctly is careful reading. Anyone who knows anything about networks knows that "loose connections" is the most common cause of problems, but that appears nowhere in this list of choices. Because the problem statement includes an indication that only *one* PC is having problems, and gives "faulty network interface *devices*" as a possibility, this knocks out what typically might be the next most obvious cause, namely a faulty network interface card, thereby eliminating answer a from further consideration.

Answer b patently is false because the only protocol in use is NWLink (or IPX/SPX, if you prefer). Answer c is possible, but unlikely, because most memory conflicts will cause a machine to crash rather than simply rendering network access inoperative.

The clue to answering the question correctly lies in the statement that "the only protocol in use on the network is NWLink." Because IPX does not require a fixed frame type, but works with multiple frame types, a frame type mismatch easily can render a machine unable to communicate successfully with the network, even though the hardware is working correctly. Thus, answer d is correct.

Question 5

On a network that contains multiple versions of NetWare, some clients are configured for NetWare 2.2, while others are configured for NetWare 4.11. Among other protocols, NWLink is in use on this network. The NetWare 2.2 clients use an 802.3 raw frame type, whereas the NetWare 4.11 clients use the 802.2 frame type. What kinds of information must be supplied in the NWLink IPX/SPX Properties dialog box to allow the same Windows NT server to recognize both flavors of NetWare clients on this network?

O a. Select Auto Frame Type Detection, and add the clients' IPX network numbers and frame types to the frame type configuration list.

O b. Select Manual Frame Type Detection, and add the network numbers and frame types for both 2.2 and 4.11 clients to the frame type configuration list.

O c. Select only Auto Frame Type Detection; the rest is automatic.

O d. Select Manual Frame Type Detection, and add the 2.2 clients' network numbers and frame types to the frame type configuration list.

The secret to answering this question is to understand how automatic frame type detection works in Windows NT Server. As long as the only frame type in use is 802.2, automatic detection works fine. But since older NetWare clients—especially NetWare 2.2 clients—use only 802.3 frames, Manual Frame Type Detection must be selected during the configuration process. This eliminates answers a and c from consideration. Answer d is incorrect, because Manual Frame Type Detection requires entry of all frame types and network numbers in use. Only answer b covers all these requirements; that's why it's correct.

Question 6

> XYZ Corp. seeks to make its NT Workstation and Windows 95 clients able to access a NetWare server without installing NetWare client software on those machines. How can this objective be met most effectively?
>
> ○   a. Install Gateway Service for NetWare on a Windows NT server on the same network.
>
> ○   b. Install NWLink on the NT Workstation and Windows 95 computers.
>
> ○   c. Install Gateway Service for NetWare on the NetWare server.
>
> ○   d. Install File and Print Services for NetWare on a Windows NT server on the same network.

The whole point of a gateway is to permit clients to access services that their current configurations would otherwise make inaccessible. For that reason, answer a is the only correct answer, because it opens a gateway for the Windows NT and Windows 95 workstations to access NetWare resources with no change to their current configurations.

Answer b is incorrect, because by adding NWLink to the workstations, it not only violates the requirement that no NetWare client software be added to those machines, it does not do the complete job (additional software would be necessary to make it possible for these machines to communicate with a NetWare server). Answer c mentions the right software product, but puts it on a NetWare server rather than on a Windows NT server, where it was designed to be run. And finally, File and Print Services for NetWare let native NetWare clients access Windows NT, not native Microsoft Networking clients access NetWare (thus completely missing the point of the question).

Question 7

QXR Corp. operates a NetWare 4.11 network, but wants to add a Windows NT server to provide access to a NetBIOS application for NetWare clients to use. What protocols and/or software elements must be available on the Windows NT server to enable successful access to this application? [Choose all correct answers]

❑   a. IPX routing (RIP for NWLink)

❑   b. Client Service for NetWare

❑   c. File and Print Service for NetWare

❑   d. NWLink

❑   e. Gateway Service for NetWare

Answer d is the only correct choice. Like client/server applications, NetBIOS applications include their own client-side capabilities. This eliminates higher-level services from consideration, disqualifying answers b, c, and e. Answer a is incorrect because the question doesn't mention the need to manage IPX traffic flow across multiple network segments (the only reason to use RIP for NWLink). This leaves only the transport protocol on top of which NetBIOS will run between the Windows NT server and the NetWare clients—namely, IPX/SPX, known to Windows NT Server as NWLink, as specified in answer d.

Question 8

On a mixed network that includes both Windows NT Server and NetWare server machines, the Windows NT servers are configured to autodetect the IPX frame types in use. What kinds of frame types will the Windows NT server be able to identify successfully? [Choose all correct answers]

❑   a. 802.2 frame type

❑   b. 802.3 frame type

❑   c. 802.3 frame type with SNAP header

❑   d. 802.5 frame type

❑   e. 802.5 frame type with SNAP header

The secret to this question is understanding that Auto Detect is aimed at newer versions of NetWare (3.12 and higher), which support only 802.2 headers by default, in keeping with common practice for most networks. Auto Detect will not be able to detect anything but 802.2, which means that the only correct answer to this question is a.

Question 9

> Once you've successfully enabled a Windows NT Gateway Service for NetWare, what additional steps are necessary to actually use the gateway? [Choose all correct answers]
>
> ❑　a. Choose Bindery Emulation on the Windows NT server.
>
> ❑　b. Map a shared drive letter on the Windows NT server for the NetWare volume available through the gateway.
>
> ❑　c. Create user accounts that can access the gateway through the NTGATEWAY group on the NetWare server.
>
> ❑　d. Create an NTGATEWAY group on the NetWare server.

As it happens, enabling the Gateway Service for NetWare handles many of the elements in the preceding list of items. Part of the installation process requires creating the necessary user accounts in the NTGATEWAY group on the NetWare server, thereby eliminating answer c from consideration. In the same vein, the NTGATEWAY group itself also must be defined for the gateway to be enabled, so answer d also is incorrect.

Answer a refers to the method of directory information access chosen for the Windows NT server, and also is selected during installation of the Gateway itself. The necessary follow-up step to gateway installation that lets users with access to the NetWare server obtain files through a drive mapped through the Windows NT Server side of the gateway is contained in answer b; therefore, it is the only correct answer.

Question 10

> Which of the following software elements and/or protocols are required for a Windows NT workstation running Client Service for NetWare to successfully access NetWare-based resources? [Choose all correct answers]
>
> ❑ a. Gateway Service for NetWare
>
> ❑ b. File and Print Service for NetWare
>
> ❑ c. NWLink
>
> ❑ d. A valid account on a NetWare server
>
> ❑ e. Membership in the NTGATEWAY group on the NetWare server to which Gateway Service for NetWare is connected

This may seem like an irrelevant question on a Windows NT Server test. But the complete name for the gateway appears as Gateway (and Client) Services for NetWare in the Services applet in Control Panel under Windows NT Server. This means that CSNW is a subset of GSNW, strictly for use by the server where GSNW is installed. Whether explicitly supplied on a Windows NT workstation or implied in the contents of GSNW on a Windows NT server, the answers to this question are the same: None of the gateway or access services is required to use CSNW capabilities. This automatically eliminates answers a, b, and e.

As it happens, both of the remaining elements—that is, answers c (NWLink) and d (a valid account on a NetWare server)—are necessary to make successful use of CSNW. Answer c supplies the necessary protocol to communicate from client to server; answer d provides the necessary permission to access the NetWare server once communication commences.

Need To Know More?

 Gaskin, James E.: *The Complete Guide to NetWare 4.11/ IntraNetWare*, 2nd Edition. Sybex Network Press, Alameda, CA, 1997. ISBN 0-7821-1931-X. For a comprehensive look at NetWare networking, there's no better reference than this one. Use it to deal with NetWare specifics and the NetWare side of any NetWare-to-NT connection.

 Heywood, Drew: *Inside Windows NT Server*. New Riders, Indianapolis, IN, 1995. ISBN 1-56205-472-4. Chapter 16, "Windows NT Server and NetWare," explains the salient software, communications issues, and connectivity concerns likely to appear on the test.

 Minasi, Mark, Christa Anderson, and Elizabeth Creegan: *Mastering Windows NT Server 4*, 4th Edition. Sybex Network Press, Alameda, CA, 1997. ISBN 0-7821-2067-9. Minasi's been an NT guru ever since the product appeared; his experience and practical orientation show in Chapter 13, "Novell NetWare in an NT Server Environment." Worthwhile because of the tips and tricks it provides, and a good overview as well.

 Siyan, Karanjit S.: *Windows NT Server 4 Professional Reference*. New Riders, Indianapolis, IN, 1996. ISBN 1-56205-731-6. Chapter 12, "Integrating NetWare with Windows NT Server," brings Siyan's usual depth of coverage and details to this topic; this is the best available preparation material for NetWare questions for this test and the Server Enterprise test.

 Strebe, Matthew, Charles Perkins, and James Chellis: *MSCE: NT Server 4 Study Guide*. Sybex Network Press, San Francisco, CA, 1996. ISBN 0-7821-1972-7. Chapter 13, "Interoperating with NetWare," covers this ground well (only Siyan offers more depth and details).

Search the TechNet CD (or its online version through www.microsoft.com) using the keywords "NetWare," "NWLink," "Gateway Services," and related product names. The Windows NT *Concepts and Planning Manual* also includes useful information on making NT to NetWare connections, and vice versa.

The Windows NT Server Resource Kit contains lots of useful information about NetWare and related topics. You can search the TechNet CD or the CD accompanying the *Resource Kit*, using the keywords "NetWare," "NWLink," "Gateway Services." Useful NetWare-related materials occur throughout the *Networking Guide* volume of the Resource Kit.

Windows NT Printing

8

Terms you'll need to understand:

- ✓ Client application
- ✓ Connecting to a printer
- ✓ Creating a printer
- ✓ Network interface printer
- ✓ Print client
- ✓ Print device
- ✓ Print job
- ✓ Print resolution
- ✓ Print server
- ✓ Print server services
- ✓ Print spooler
- ✓ Printer driver
- ✓ Printer/Logical printer
- ✓ Queue/Print queue
- ✓ Rendering

Techniques you'll need to master:

- ✓ Installing and configuring a printer
- ✓ Managing printing clients
- ✓ Managing the print spooler
- ✓ Setting up print priorities
- ✓ Establishing logical printers and printing pools

It is the job of the network administrator to make sure that users have access to needed resources—and the printer is one of the most often-used resources. One of the biggest complaints about other network operating systems has been the inability to handle printers effectively and efficiently. Microsoft has developed an intuitive and simple way to manage these much-used resources. This chapter focuses on the Microsoft approach to printing and defines a few Microsoft-specific printing terms—both with an eye toward preparing you for the printing section of the Microsoft Certification exam.

The Windows NT Print Lexicon

The following list contains Microsoft-specific printing terminology that must be mastered. It is very important for successful exam taking that you know and fully understand all of these terms and concepts. Exam questions about printing can be tricky, especially when they deal with this specialized terminology.

➤ **Client application** A network program that originates print jobs (this can be located on a print server or client computer on the network).

➤ **Connecting to a printer** The process of attaching to a network share that resides on the computer on which the logical printer was created (performed through the Add Printer Wizard, accessed from the Start menu, Printers option).

➤ **Creating a printer** The process of naming, defining settings for, installing drivers for, and linking a printing device to the network. In Windows NT, this process is performed through the Add Printer Wizard.

➤ **Network interface printer** Built-in network interface cards for print devices that are directly attached to the network (for example, the Hewlett-Packard JetDirect). (*Note:* Unless a question specifically mentions the TCP/IP lpd service, it's wise to assume that the DLC protocol must be installed to communicate with directly attached print devices.)

➤ **Print client** A computer on a network (called a "client computer") that transmits the print jobs to be produced by the physical printing device.

➤ **Print device** The print device is commonly referred to as the printer—in other words, the print device is the physical hardware device that produces printed material. This is very confusing to most people. Just remember that the print device is the piece of hardware that actually spits out paper with your material printed on it.

➤ **Print job** The code that defines the print processing commands as well as the actual file to be printed. Windows NT defines print jobs by data type, depending upon what adjustments must be made to the file for it to print accurately (i.e., one data type can be printable as-is, whereas another may need a form feed to conclude the data stream for the print job to be executed properly).

➤ **Print resolution** The measurement of pixel density that is responsible for the smoothness of any image or text being printed. This is measured in dots per inch (DPI)—the higher the DPI, the better the quality of the printed material.

➤ **Print server** The server computer that links physical print devices to the network, and manages sharing those devices with computers on the network.

➤ **Print server services** Software components located on the print server that accepts print jobs and sends them to the print spooler for execution. These components, such as Services For Macintosh, enable a variety of client computers to communicate with the print server to process print jobs.

➤ **Print spooler** The collection of Dynamic Link Libraries (DLLs) that acquires, processes, catalogues, and disburses print jobs. A print job will be saved to disk in a spool file. Print despooling is the process of reading what is contained in the spool file and transmitting it to the physical printing device.

➤ **Printer driver** Programs that enable communications between applications and a specific print device. Most hardware peripherals, such as printers, require the use of a driver to process commands.

➤ **Printer/logical printer** The logical printer (Microsoft calls this "the printer") is the software interface that communicates between the operating system and the physical printing device. The logical printer handles the printing process from the time the print command is issued. Its settings determine the physical printing device that renders the file to be printed, as well as how the file to be printed is sent to the printing device (e.g., via a remote print share or local port).

➤ **Queue/print queue** In printing terms, a queue is a series of files waiting to be produced by the printing device.

➤ **Rendering** The rendering process in Windows NT is as follows: A client application sends file information to the Graphics Device Interface (GDI), which receives the data, communicates that data to the physical printing device driver, and produces the print job in the language of the physical printing device. The printing device then interprets this information and creates a file (bitmap) for each page to be printed.

Printing With Windows NT Server

Windows NT print settings are managed through the Printers folder, which is accessible from the Control Panel or the Start menu. (*Note:* The Printers folder replaces the old Windows NT 3.51 Print Manager.) This approach is extremely straightforward when compared to earlier versions of NT and other network operating systems.

Windows NT takes a modular approach to printing, as shown in Figure 8.1; each component has a specific use and interfaces with the other components in the print architecture.

The following list defines each component of the NT printing architecture:

➤ **Graphics Device Interface (GDI)** The component that provides network applications with a system for presenting graphical information. The GDI works as a translator between the application's print requests and the device driver interface (DDI) to make sure a job is rendered accurately.

➤ **Print device** The physical hardware device that produces printed output.

Figure 8.1   The Windows NT print architecture components work together to render print jobs for the user.

> ➤ **Print driver** The software component that enables communication between the operating system and the physical printing device.

> ➤ **Print monitor** The component that passes the print job, which has been translated to the print device's language, to the physical printing device.

> ➤ **Print processor** The component that makes any necessary modifications to the print job before passing the job to the print monitor. NT actually has two print processors, one for the Windows platform and one for the Macintosh.

> ➤ **Print router** The component that directs the print job to the appropriate printing device.

> ➤ **Print spooler** (also called the **print provider**) The component that accepts print jobs from the router, calls the processor to make any needed changes to the print job, and transfers the jobs one at a time to the print monitor.

Printing From Windows NT Clients

This is where NT's approach to printing really shines. Client computers need access to print devices, so they must add the printer via the Add Printer Wizard. Previously, all client computers required that the print driver be installed on each client machine that needed access to a printing device. No more! All that is needed for printing from an NT client is that the driver be installed on the print server. This simplifies the printing process, because if an updated print driver is released, it just needs to be installed on the server, not on every client machine.

Printing From Windows 95 Clients

This process is the same as for NT clients. All that is needed is a connection between the client computer and the print device, and that the print driver is installed on the server.

Printing From MS-DOS And Windows 3.x Clients

Unfortunately, the simplicity of printing from Windows NT and 95 clients does not extend to other client machines, such as DOS, Windows 3.x, and Macintosh clients. It is best to create a central repository for print drivers for these computers. You may then use this central repository for these types of clients.

Spooling

When a user sends out a print job, it goes to the print spooler, which is responsible for tracking the print job through the printing process, routing jobs to the correct ports, and assigning priorities to print jobs.

Print Priorities

By default, the spooler prints jobs in the order in which they are received. It is possible, however, to ensure that print jobs from certain users are printed before any other job. To adjust priority levels for individual users or groups, you must create a different logical printer to a particular printing device (this is discussed in detail in the "Logical Printers And Printing Pools" section, later in the chapter). To assign higher priority to print jobs from certain users, these steps must be performed on a logical printer:

1. Go to the Printers Folder (Start|Settings|Printers).

2. Select Server Properties from the File menu for the logical printer to be adjusted.

3. Select the Scheduling tab.

4. Adjust the slide bar to assign a higher priority (this can be set anywhere from 1 to 99, with 1 being the lowest—as well as the default setting).

Separate Spool Files

If the printers on your network are hit pretty hard with many print jobs at a time, the print spooler can get fairly large. It is important to make sure that the spooler file is big enough to handle all of the jobs that are sent to it. It may become necessary, therefore, to create individual spool files for each printer on the network. This is performed through the Registry by creating files under the following Registry key:

```
HKEY_LOCAL_MACHINE\SYSTEM\CurrentControlSet\Control\Printers
```

Stopping And Restarting The Spooler Service

It is possible for print jobs to get stuck in the spooler. To remedy this, stop and restart the spooler service by performing the following steps:

1. Go to the Control Panel.

2. Double-click the Services icon.

3. Highlight the entry labeled "Spooler" in the list of services.

4. Click the Stop button, and confirm that you want to stop the service.

5. Click the Start button.

6. Click Close on the Services dialog box.

Changing The Spool Location

The default directory for the print spooler is *SystemRoot*\\System32\\Spool. Here are the steps for changing the location of the spooler directory:

1. Go to the Printers Folder.

2. Select Server Properties from the File menu.

3. Select the Advanced tab.

4. Enter the path to the new spool directory in the Spool Folder text box.

The reason why you may want to change this setting is that the drive for the default path has limited space for storing print jobs. (*Note:* You must restart the print server before these changes take effect.)

Logical Printers And Printing Pools

A logical printer is the software interface that enables communication between Windows NT and the physical printing device. You can create multiple logical printers that send print jobs to a single print device (and, conversely, a single logical printer that sends jobs to multiple print devices).

It is necessary to create different logical printers (with different share names) to assign priorities to print jobs from various groups and users to a single print device. All of this is defined through the Add Printer Wizard in the Printers folder. You simply provide different settings (such as access rights, access times, and priorities) for different shares that attach to the same physical print device.

When a printer services multiple printing devices, it creates what is called a "printer pool." Put simply, a single logical printer spools out jobs to the next available printing device in the printer pool. It is necessary for all of the print devices in a printer pool to be of the same type. With this setup, the printer assigns files to be printed to whichever print device is free in the printer pool.

Exam Prep Questions

Question 1

> Several users are trying to print to a print server. You receive many complaints from the users that they have sent several jobs to the print server, but the jobs have not printed and cannot be deleted. How do you resolve this problem?
>
> ○   a. Verify that the Pause printing option is not checked on the print server.
>
> ○   b. Delete the stalled printer from the print server, create a new printer, and tell your users to resend their jobs to the new printer.
>
> ○   c. Delete all files from the spool folder on the print server, and tell your users to resend them.
>
> ○   d. Stop the spooler service, and then restart it.

The Pause printing command will prevent print jobs from printing, but it will not prevent jobs from being deleted, so this is not the problem. Therefore, answer a is incorrect. There's no need to re-create the printer from scratch, so answer b is also incorrect. You should never have to involve users in the problem-solving process (other than to gather information from them); therefore, answer c is also incorrect. Choice d is the correct answer. This scenario is a quintessential example of a stalled print spooler. To fix the problem, select Services in Control Panel, stop the spooler service, and then restart it.

Question 2

You have a Windows NT Server that provides print services to 20 Windows NT computers on your network. You have an HP LaserJet attached to the Windows NT print server. Hewlett-Packard has just released an updated printer driver. What must be done to distribute the updated driver to all the computers that print to this print server?

○   a. Install the updated driver on all client computers; there is no need to update the server.

○   b. Install the updated driver on the print server, and do nothing more.

○   c. Install the updated driver on the print server and on all client computers.

○   d. Create a separate logical printer with the updated driver on the print server, and tell all your users to print to the new printer.

○   e. Install the updated driver on the print server, and instruct all client computers to download the updated driver from the server.

The best way to update a printer driver is to update the driver on the print server; therefore, b is the only correct answer. There is no need to update the driver manually on each client computer that is running NT; therefore, answer a is incorrect. When a client computer sends a print job to the print server, the updated driver is automatically copied to the client; therefore, answers c and d are also incorrect.

Question 3

You run a network for a small consulting firm. You have only a single printer on the network. The company executives have asked that you configure printing so that all documents from the executives print before other documents. How is this performed?

○ a. Create a separate logical printer, assign rights to the executive group, and set the printer priority to 1.

○ b. Create a separate logical printer, assign rights to the executive group, and set the printer priority to 99.

○ c. Create a separate logical printer for the executive group, and configure the printer to start printing immediately.

○ d. Create a separate logical printer for the executive group, and configure the printer to print directly to the physical print device.

Trick! question

It is possible to set priorities between groups of documents by creating different logical printers for the same physical print device and setting different priority levels on the printers. To set printer priority, select the Scheduling tab in Printer Properties. The lowest priority is 1; therefore, answer a is incorrect. The highest priority is 99; therefore, b is the correct answer. The "start printing immediately" setting will not give the executives print priority over others. It simply instructs the print server to print without waiting for the entire print job to be saved to the spooler; therefore, answer c is incorrect. Printing directly to the printer will not offer print priority. It just instructs the print server to print without storing the print job to the spooler at all; therefore, answer d is incorrect.

Question 4

You have just installed a new printer on your print server. You send a print job to the printer, but it comes out as pages of nonsense. What is the most likely cause of the problem?

○ a. The DLC protocol is not installed.

○ b. The print spooler is corrupt.

○ c. An incorrect printer driver has been installed.

○ d. There is not enough hard disk space for spooling.

A print job won't print at all if the wrong protocol is in use, so answer a is incorrect. Likewise, nothing will print without the spooler; therefore, answer b is incorrect. If an incorrect printer driver has been installed, documents may print illegibly. Therefore, choice c is correct. As in answer b, a print job won't print without proper spooling; therefore, answer d is incorrect.

Question 5

You want to create a printer pool with five print devices. Which condition must be present for you to create this printer pool?

- ○ a. All print devices must use the same protocol.
- ○ b. All physical print devices must be connected to the same logical printer.
- ○ c. All print devices must use the same printer port.
- ○ d. All print devices must be located in the same room.

It is not necessary that all print devices use the same protocol; therefore, answer a is incorrect. To create a printer pool, all print devices must be connected to the same print server; therefore, answer b is the correct choice. All print devices also should be identical. Answers c and d are both incorrect because you don't have to use the same port for multiple printer devices, and printers don't have to be in the same room.

Question 6

You have a printer pool that consists of Printer 1 and Printer 2. Printer 1 is printing a job and Printer 2 is idle. A paper jam occurs on Printer 1's print device. What will happen to the rest of the job that was being printed?

- ○ a. The print job will be completed on Printer 2.
- ○ b. The print job will be canceled.
- ○ c. The print job will be completed on Printer 2 because Printer 2 has a higher priority level.
- ○ d. The print job is held for completion by Printer 1 until the device is fixed.

The print job will not be sent to Printer 2; therefore, answer a is incorrect. The print job will not be canceled if the device fails; therefore, answer b is also incorrect. Priority levels have nothing to so with failed devices; therefore, answer c is wrong as well. If a physical print device in a printer pool fails in the middle of a print job, the print job is retained at that physical print device until the device is fixed. Therefore, choice d is correct. Any other print jobs sent to the printer pool will continue to print to other physical print devices in the printer pool.

Question 7

You want to configure a Windows NT computer to be the print server for an HP network interface print device. However, you are unable to locate the option to install a port for the printer. Why is this?

○ a. PostScript printing is enabled on the print device and must be disabled.

○ b. You didn't install the print driver on the print server.

○ c. The print processor is corrupt and must be fixed.

○ d. The DLC protocol is not installed on the print server.

PostScript printing has nothing to do with print device installation; therefore, answer a is incorrect. You can't install a print driver if NT can't recognize the print device; therefore, answer b is incorrect. The print processor is not involved in the installation of printers; therefore, answer c is also incorrect. For Windows NT to provide support for HP network interface print devices, you must install the DLC (Data Link Control) protocol; therefore, answer d is correct. You can't install a printer driver if Windows NT cannot recognize the print device.

Need To Know More?

 Heywood, Drew: *Inside Windows NT Server*. New Riders, Indianapolis, IN, 1995. ISBN 1-56205-472-4. Chapter 6, "Managing Print Services," details the issues relating to printing and printer permissions and management.

 Siyan, Karanjit S.: *Windows NT Server 4 Professional Reference*. New Riders, Indianapolis, IN, 1996. ISBN 1-56205-731-6. A nice discussion of using Windows NT print services is located in Chapter 17, "Windows NT Printing."

 Strebe, Matthew, Charles Perkins, and James Chellis: *MSCE: NT Server 4 Study Guide*. Sybex Network Press, San Francisco, CA, 1996. ISBN 0-7821-1972-7. Chapter 14 contains detailed information about creating and maintaining your printing environment.

 Search the TechNet CD (or its online version through www.microsoft.com) using the keywords "printing," "logical printers," "print management," and "print devices."

 The Windows NT Server Resource Kit contains a lot of useful information about printers and printer management. You can search the TechNet CD or the CD accompanying the *Resource Kit*, using keywords like "shares," "resource management," and "user management."

Windows NTBACKUP

9

Terms you'll need to understand:

√ Backup

√ Restoration

√ Tape drive

√ Differential backup

√ Incremental backup

√ Backup marker

√ Backup log

Techniques you'll need to master:

√ Installing, configuring, and implementing NTBACKUP.EXE

√ Assigning the right to back up the system

√ Establishing a backup plan

√ Scheduling backups

√ Using AT.EXE to perform scheduled backups

Backing up critical data is an important task for any network administrator. NT Server 4 ships with a program called NTBACK UP.EXE. Although it is automatically installed with NT Server, you must install drivers for your tape backup and have a good understanding of how the backup process works to successfully back up and restore important data. In this chapter, we explain the aspects of NTBACKUP that you must know to pass the Microsoft certification exam.

NTBACKUP Facts

NTBACKUP's advantages include:

➤ The program is free; you do not have to purchase a third-party back-up utility.

➤ Because it is a native NT program, the chances of the server running into stability problems are slim to none.

➤ It can back up from the two supported file systems, FAT and NTFS. It also can restore just as easily to either file system.

It also has disadvantages:

➤ The only acceptable media that NTBACKUP supports is a tape drive; you cannot back up to another hard drive, floppy, or even across the network to a network drive.

➤ There is no built-in scheduler program included with NTBACKUP; to accomplish an unattended backup, you must write a batch file (discussed later in this chapter).

➤ You cannot back up a remote Registry. (This task must be done locally. To back up the Registry of all the domain controllers, you must attach a tape drive physically to each one. You can, however, back up files both locally and remotely.)

➤ NTBACKUP only does a "file-by-file" backup and not a disk-image backup.

Who Has The Right?

Just like everything else in NT Server, a user must have the right to perform backups and restorations. All users can back up any files and folders with the read permission assigned to that user. This right must be granted to the user by selecting User Rights from the Policies menu in the User Manager For Domains tool. To restore files and folders, a user must have the Restore Files And Directories right, which is also granted in the User Manager For Domains. By default, members of the Backup Operators and Server Operators have these rights. Note: Throughout this book, we reference the backup utility with the term NTBACKUP; however, once the application is launched, it is only named Backup on the desktop.

Backup Types

Table 9.1 lists the different backup types in NTBACKUP.

Backup Markers

A backup marker, or mark, is an attribute of a file or folder set on certain types of backup to indicate that the file or folder has been backed up before by NT.

Examples Of Different Backup TypesAlert

Example 1: Monday is a normal backup and Tuesday through Friday are differential backups that do not set markers. Each differential backup backs up all the changes since Monday. If

Table 9.1 NTBACKUP's backup types.		
Type Of Backup	**Backs Up**	**Marked?**
Daily Copy	Files and folders that have changed during that day	No
Copy	All selected files and folders	No
Differential	Selected files and folders if they have changed since the last backup	No
Incremental	Selected files and folders if they have changed since the last backup	Yes

data is corrupted or bad on Friday, you only need to restore the Monday and Thursday backups. This strategy takes more time to back up, but less time to restore.

Example 2: Monday is a normal backup and Tuesday through Friday are incremental backups that do set markers. Each incremental backup only backs up changes since the previous day. If data becomes corrupted on Friday, you would need to restore all backups beginning with Monday. This strategy takes less time to back up, but more time to restore.

NTBACKUP.EXE

You launch NTBACKUP from Start|Programs|AdministrativeTools |NTBACKUP. When you start the program, you will see the screen shown in Figure 9.1.

If you have a blank tape in the tape drive, in the left pane you would see a tape icon with the words "blank tape" next to it. If there is something on tape, like in the preceding example, there is a tape icon and specific information about the tape itself. In the right pane is a list of the tape's contents.

The next step in NTBACKUP is to choose what drive, files, or folders are to be backed up. To accomplish this, choose Drives from the Window menu.

A list of available drives appears. If you want to back up an entire drive, place an X in the box next to the drive letter itself (see Figure 9.2). If

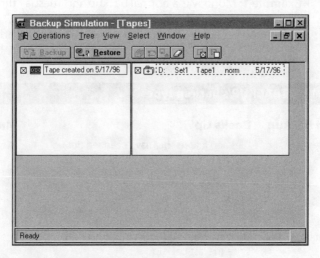

Figure 9.1 Windows NTBACKUP tape selection.

Figure 9.2   Select the drive to be backed up by placing an X next to it.

there are certain directories that you would like to back up, double-click the drive in the pane. If you decide to select certain directories, the screen will split into two panes. The left pane contains the drives, and the right pane contains the files in the directories written on the left pane, as shown in Figure 9.3.

Alternatively, you can select individual files by double-clicking the folders to show all files and placing an X next to the file. You have now selected the files that need to be backed up.

Figure 9.3   You can select files to be backed up along with other directories.

Here are a few items to remember when responding to exam questions on NTBACKUP:

➤ Do not back up temp files.

➤ Back up the Registry on both the PDC and all BDCs. The Registry contains the directory databases. Backing up on all domain controllers prevents the loss of all user accounts and security information.

Backup Options

Once you have selected which items to back up, next select different NTBACKUP options from the Backup Information dialog box (shown in Figure 9.4). These options include Tape Name, Verify After Backup, Backup Registry, and Restrict Access To Owner Or Administrator. To find the Options dialog box, click Backup in the Backup dialog box. Table 9.2 describes each option, along with the tape name.

After you select the options, type a meaningful description of the backup in the description box (for example: download server; drive C:). Finally, choose the backup type to be performed.

Figure 9.4 NTBACKUP's Backup Information dialog box.

Table 9.2   Vital statistics about NTBACKUP's tape options.

Option	Description
Operation: Append	Adds new backup set after the last backup set on the tape.
Operation: Replace	Overwrites all data on the tape.
Verify After Backup	Confirms files/folders were backed up.
Backup Registry	This option is available only if you have selected at least one other file. You *cannot* back up only the Registry.
Restrict Access To	Limits access to users with the correct permissions. When the Owner/Administrator is backing up the Registry, you always should choose this option.
Hardware Compression	If your tape drive supports data compression, select this option.

The last set of options to set is the Log Information. If you would like to create a backup log, simply put a path in the log file line of the backup information dialog box. The default is BACKUP.LOG in the \systemroot folder. The three options under Log Information are shown in Table 9.3. After the backup completes, you'll see a dialog box that provides details on the tape that was created, as shown in Figure 9.5.

Figure 9.5   Details on a successful backup.

Table 9.3	Vital statistics about Log Information options.
Option	**Description**
Full Detail	Logs all backup information, including the names of all of the files and folders backed up and skipped.
Summary Only	Logs only the major backup operations, such as loading and unloading the tape and starting backup.
Do Not Log	No log is created.

Scheduled Backup

There is not a scheduler inside the NTBACKUP program, but you can write a batch file to start the NT backup process. The syntax follows:

```
NTBACKUP.EXE BACKUP [pathname[options]]
```

Table 9.4 shows the options or switches that you can use with this command line process.

Table 9.4	Vital statistics about NTBACKUP options.
Option/Switch	**Description**
/a	This is not available for a blank tape. This appends the backup set to any existing backup set.
/b	Backs up the local Registry.
/d *text or description*	Allows for a backup description.
/e	Logs exceptions; similar to a summary log.
/l *file name*	Assigns a log file name.
/r	Limits the rights of the backup operation to Administrators, Backup Operators, or Owners.
/t{normal|copy |incremental| differential|daily}	Allows you to specify which type of backup to perform.
/v	Confirmation of backup.
/hc:{on|off}	Enables or disables hardware compression (if your tape drive will support it). The default is off.
Cmd /c net use x:	Connects to a remote share. Use this to connect to a remote machine.
Cmd /c net use x:/delete	Disconnects from remote shares.

| You *cannot* back up a remote Registry using NTBACKUP!

Using The AT Command

Once you have a batch file with the NTBACKUP link included, you can use AT.EXE to schedule the batch file to run at a specific time (see Table 9.5). AT.EXE schedules commands to be run by the scheduling service in Windows NT. The scheduling service must be running on the machine that will run the scheduled task. The syntax for the AT command follows:

```
AT [\\computername] [id] [/delete] time [interactive] [/every:
date[,...]| next; date[,...] "command"
```

Restoring With NTBACKUP

Restoring data with the NTBACKUP program is quite simple. You can restore data to the same system or a completely different system, which is a great advantage. (*Note:* A Registry cannot be restored remotely.)

 There are several steps to the restoration procedure:

1. Start NTBACKUP.EXE.

2. Load the tape to view the catalog, to see which files and folders are available for restoring. A catalog contains the

Table 9.5	Vital statistics about AT.EXE options.

Option	Description
computer name	Specifies a remote machine.
Id	Assigns ID number to a scheduled command.
/delete	Cancels a scheduled command. If this is omitted, all the scheduled commands are omitted.
Time	Expresses time in time:minute mode; runs from 00:00 through 23:59.
/interactive	Allows user to see network activity in real time.
/every: date[,...]	Specifies the days for the command to run.
/next:date[,....]	Specifies the next day of the month the command is to run.
"command"	Specifies the actual command to be run, e.g., NTBACKUP.

information on each backup set. This is useful if you have more than one backup set per tape. To create a catalog, simply view the Backup dialog box, and select Catalog under the Operations menu. This will create a catalog set (see Figure 9.6).

3. Once the cataloging is complete, select the files and folders to be restored.

   The dialog box shown in Figure 9.6 looks very similar to the Backup selection screen. You have the option to restore the entire backup set or individual files and folders. To select the files or folders to be restored, place an X in the checkbox next to the item you wish to restore. (*Note:* You can select more than one object at a time by holding down the Shift key.)

4. Once you have selected the files or folders to be restored, set the options for the restore procedure. You will see that the Restore Information dialog box (shown in Figure 9.7) looks very similar to the Backup Information dialog box.

   In the Restore Information dialog box, you will find useful information, including: Tape Name, Backup Set, Creation Date, Owner, a number of Restore options (detailed next), and Log Information. The Restore To Drive line provides the location where the program restores the data. Or, you may select an alternate location. If you are unsure of the alternate path, select the ... button to browse for your preferred restore location.

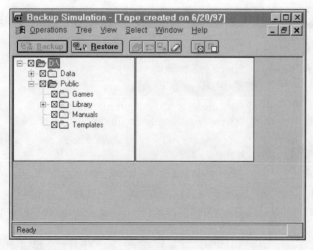

Figure 9.6 Select the files to be restored.

Figure 9.7   NTBACKUP's Restore Information dialog box.

5. Once the restore location is selected, you can choose additional options, as listed in Table 9.6.

6. After you have set restore options, set the Backup Log options. See Table 9.7 for an explanation of each option.

7. Once you select the options, click OK to start the backup process.

Next, you will see the Restore Status dialog box, shown in Figure 9.8. When the restore process is complete, you will see the following message: The operation was successfully completed.

Table 9.6   Vital statistics about restoration options and their descriptions.

Option	Description
Restore Local Registry	If you backed up the Registry, this option will restore the local Registry.
Restore File Permissions	Restores NTFS permissions. If this is not selected, the files and folders will follow the general rule of inheriting the new parent directory permissions.
Verify After Restore	Does a check of the tape against the files on the hard drive.

Table 9.7   Backup Log options and their descriptions.

Option	Description
Log File	The location of the restore text file. You can browse for the location.
Log Information: Full Detail	Logs everything, including names of all files and folders restored.
Log Information: Summary Only	Logs failures and major operations, such as the loading of the tape.
Log Information: Don't Log	No log is created.

Backup Tips

Here are a few items to keep in mind when backing up your NT system:

➤ Always back up the Registry on all domain controllers (PDCs and BDCs).

➤ Keep at least three copies of backup tapes. One should be located off site for safety.

➤ Create a backup log for each backup process.

➤ Have a weekly routine for performing a trial restore.

➤ Grant the appropriate rights to users who will perform the backup and restore procedure.

Figure 9.8   NTBACKUP Restore Status dialog box.

Exam Prep Questions

Question 1

> You want to use NTBACKUP.EXE to back up some local files. What type of media can the NTBACKUP Program use?
>
> ○   a. Floppy
>
> ○   b. Tape
>
> ○   c. Writable CDs
>
> ○   d. Across the network to another hard drive

The only backup media type that NTBACKUP.EXE supports is a tape drive; therefore, answer b is the only correct choice.

Question 2

> Where should you check to see if NTBACKUP ran successfully?
>
> ○   a. User Manager For Domains
>
> ○   b. Server Manager
>
> ○   c. Backup Log
>
> ○   d. The Registry

The User Manager For Domains is where most administration takes place for NT, such as adding users and changing their passwords. Backup is not affected directly by User Manager; therefore, answer a is incorrect. (You do, however, assign backup rights in User Manager.) Server Manager is for server administration as well. You can verify the remote users with Server Manager, but you cannot check if the backup was successful; therefore, answer b is incorrect. To find out whether a backup was successful, you must check the Backup Log in NTBACKUP; this means that answer c is correct. Although *everything* in NT lives in the Registry, you wouldn't look there for successful backup information; therefore, answer d is incorrect.

Question 3

> What files always should be backed up? [Check all correct answers]
>
> ❏   a. Temporary files
>
> ❏   b. Mission critical data
>
> ❏   c. Registries on all domain controllers
>
> ❏   d. The WinNT directory

Answers b and c are correct. Remember, do not waste your time on temp files. They simply take up space; therefore, answer a is incorrect. In case of a disaster, you always should have a copy of your data; therefore, answer b is correct. The Registry always should be backed up as well, so answer c also is correct. It is not necessary to back up the WinNT directory; therefore, choice d is incorrect.

Question 4

> You have 10 machines in one domain. Of these machines, one is a PDC, one is a BDC, and the rest are workstations. Your boss says he needs a backup of all the domain's files and folders, including the Registry of the domain controllers. You notice that there is one tape drive in the domain and it is installed on the BDC. What should you do to back up everything the boss wants on the PDC?
>
> ◯   a. Nothing. You can do a remote backup of everything on the PDC.
>
> ◯   b. Install a tape drive on the PDC to back up everything requested on the PDC, and use the tape drive on the BDC to back up everything requested on the BDC.
>
> ◯   c. Nothing. You cannot back up your domain controllers.

The Registry cannot be backed up remotely; therefore, answer a is incorrect. You must install a tape drive on each domain controller to back up the Registry; therefore, answer b is correct. You should always back up your domain controllers; therefore, answer c is incorrect.

Question 5

When you installed NT Server, you noticed that the backup utility was installed automatically. When you try to use your tape drive, nothing happens. What could be the cause of this?

○ a. Even though NT installs the NTBACKUP program, you still must install the drivers for the tape drive.

○ b. You have to shut down your server before you can run NTBACKUP.

○ c. You must have the RAS service running.

○ d. You must have CSNW installed.

When NT is installed, NTBACKUP is installed automatically. However, you must still install the drivers for the tape backup; therefore, answer a is correct. A server can be up during backup; therefore, answer b is incorrect. NT's Remote Access Service is a communications program and has nothing to do with backups; therefore, answer c is incorrect. The Client Services For NetWare is required for NetWare clients to communicate with an NT server; therefore, answer d also is wrong.

Question 6

Sheila is a member of the local group called Sales. She can back up files that she reads on a daily basis, but she cannot restore any files. What is the problem?

○ a. Sheila is not a member of Domain Admins, so she cannot see any files.

○ b. Sheila is not a member of the Backup Operators, Server Operators, or the Replicator group.

○ c. Sheila is not a member of the Backup Operators, Server Operators, or Administrator group.

Answer c is correct. You must be granted a right to restore data. Backup Operators, Server Operators, and the Administrator group all have the right to do this; therefore, answer c is the only correct answer. Remember, if users can read a file, they can back up the file, but to restore the file, they must have the Restore Files and Directories right.

Need To Know More?

 Chellis, Donald, Lisa, and James: *MSCE: NT Server 4 in the Enterprise Study Guide*. Sybex Network Press, San Francisco, CA, 1997. ISBN 0-7821-1970-0. Chapter 5, "Storage," contains an insightful discussion of the NTBACKUP program.

 Heywood, Drew: *Inside Windows NT Server*. New Riders, Indianapolis, IN, 1995. ISBN 1-56205-472-4. Chapter 11, "Backing Up Files," has a great discussion of backup and disaster recovery issues.

 Siyan, Karanjit S.: *Windows NT Server 4 Professional Reference*. New Riders, Indianapolis, IN, 1996. ISBN 1-56205-731-6. Chapter 20, "Data Protection in Windows NT Servers," contains a lengthy discussion of data protection.

 Search the TechNet CD (or its online version through www.microsoft.com) using the keywords "backup," "restore," "disaster recovery," and "tape backup devices."

 The *Windows NT Server Resource Kit* contains a lot of useful information about backing up your system. You can search the TechNet CD or the CD accompanying the *Resource Kit*, using keywords like "backup," "NTBACKUP," and "restore."

Windows NT Remote Access Service (RAS)

10

Terms you'll need to understand:

√ Remote Access Service (RAS)

√ RAS clients

√ Telephony Application Programming Interface (TAPI)

√ RAS Phonebook

√ Encryption

√ Autodial

√ Logging

√ Null modem

√ Name resolution

Techniques you'll need to master:

√ Installing and configuring RAS

√ Configuring the RAS Phonebook

√ Implementing RAS security measures

RAS (Remote Access Service) is a secure and reliable method of extending a network across communication links to remote computers. Modems and other communication devices act just like a network interface card (NIC) over a RAS connection. A remote RAS client can access and operate everything a standard network-attached client can. In this chapter, we provide the details you need to know to pass the RAS portion of the Microsoft certification exam.

NT RAS

RAS in Windows NT 4 is a significant improvement over the communications capabilities of version 3.51. Many of its advances were borrowed from Windows 95, including the ease of installation, process of configuration, and the look and feel. RAS is able to support 256 simultaneous connections; act as a firewall, a gateway, or a router; and maintain tight security.

The communication links through which RAS can connect include:

➤ Public Switched Telephone Network (PSTN)

➤ Integrated Services Digital Network (ISDN)

➤ X.25 packet switching network

Standard LAN protocols are used over the RAS connection. Thus, TCP/IP, IPX/SPX, or NetBEUI can be used for network communication over the link established by RAS. Because the actual network protocol is used, the remote RAS client acts just as if it were connected to the network locally. The only difference is that the speed of data transfer is slower over the RAS connection than it would be if the computer accessing the server were physically attached to the network. On the exam, there are questions that test your understanding of this. Always remember that a client is a client is a client, whether locally connected or using RAS.

RAS Clients

A RAS client is any machine that is able to dial in or connect to a RAS server and establish an authorized connection. Although optimized for the integration of Microsoft-based operating systems, other system types can gain access with the proper software, protocols, and configuration.

The links established between a client and a server using RAS are called Wide Area Network (WAN) links. Because RAS is most often used to connect a computer (or an entire LAN) to a centrally located network over a long distance, it is treated as a WAN link. The communication protocols used to establish a RAS connection are called WAN protocols. Windows NT supports two WAN protocols:

> ► **SLIP** The Serial Line Internet Protocol connection supports TCP/IP, but does not support IPX/SPX or NetBEUI. SLIP does not support DHCP; thus, every client must have an assigned IP address. SLIP does not support encrypted passwords, either. This protocol is provided only as a means for an NT server to act as a client when dialing into a Unix server; it cannot be used to accept inbound connections on NT.

> ► **PPP** The Point-to-Point Protocol supports several additional protocols, including AppleTalk, TCP/IP, IPX/SPX, and NetBEUI, and was designed as an improvement to SLIP. PPP supports DHCP and encrypted passwords. PPP is the most common and widely supported WAN protocol.

Windows NT Server can act as a RAS client whenever it dials out over a modem (or other communication link device) to establish a connection with another server or computer system. The most common situation in which NT is a client is when a LAN connects to the Internet.

RAS Servers

Windows NT Server can support up to 256 simultaneous incoming RAS connections. Important points to remember about NT as a RAS Server include:

> ► It only supports PPP clients—SLIP is not supported for dialup.

> ► A NetBIOS gateway is established between the server and PPP-attached RAS client to sustain standard NT network operations.

> ► RAS supports both IP and IPX routing.

> ➤ RAS supports NetBIOS and Windows Sockets applications.

> ➤ It supports Point-to-Point Tunneling Protocol (PPTP) connections, which makes it possible for Windows NT computers to communicate securely over the Internet. In addition, it also supports Multilink PPP (MP), where numerous connections can be aggregated.

Point-To-Point Tunneling Protocol (PPTP)

PPTP enables "tunneling" of IPX, NetBEUI, or TCP/IP inside PPP packets in such a way as to establish a secure link between a client and server over the Internet. PPTP connections are useful for establishing Virtual Private Networks (VPNs) in small companies that cannot afford expensive leased lines for network communications over long distances. PPTP enables users anywhere in the world to connect back to the home office's network. PPTP uses a powerful encryption security scheme that is more secure than standard communications over the network itself. Thus, all traffic over the Internet using PPTP is safe.

Like all other network protocols, PPTP must be installed through the Protocols tab of the Network applet.

Multilink PPP (MP)

Windows NT has the capability to combine the bandwidth of multiple physical links which increases the total bandwidth that could be used for a RAS connection. This aggregation of multiple communication links can be used as an inexpensive way to increase the overall bandwidth with the least amount of cost. MP must be supported by both the client and server systems. MP cannot be used with the callback security feature (discussed in detail later in this chapter).

The checkbox to enable MP is located on the Network Protocol Configuration dialog box (see Figure 10.1, later in the chapter).

Telephony API (TAPI) Properties And Phone Books

In Windows NT, the Telephony Application Programming Interface (TAPI) provides a standard method of controlling communications over voice, data, or fax. Although the hardware is not provided with NT, TAPI can be used to control many PBX systems and communications devices for automated activity.

When you install a modem or the RAS components of NT, TAPI automatically is installed. It is required to control any communications device. Each time a dial-out connection is attempted, TAPI controls the modem and moderates the connection. Once the connection is established, TAPI continues to oversee the operation of the communications link.

The Dialing Properties dialog box (reached through the Modem applet) controls how TAPI uses your modem to place calls. You can control long-distance dialing, calling card use, prefix numbers, and tone/pulse dialing. You can also define multiple configurations based on physical location. If you travel with an NT Server notebook, you can define a dialing property profile for each of the cities you visit regularly.

TAPI is also the controlling entity for the phonebook entries used to establish RAS connections. All of the functions and features of the modem and the communication types established over a modem are configured through a TAPI-controlled interface.

Installing RAS

RAS is installed through the Services tab of the Network applet. Installing RAS correctly does take some preparation and know-how. When performing the installation, you must remember the following:

1. Physically install or attach the modem first. During installation, if a modem has not been installed, you will be forced to install one.

2. Install RAS through the Services tab of the Network applet.

3. Select the communications port.

4. Add an installed modem as a RAS device.

5. Configure the port for one of the following:

    ➤ Dial out only

➤ Receive calls only

➤ Dial out and receive calls

6. Select the LAN network protocols (see Figure 10.1).

    ➤ If Dial out was selected, only the outbound protocols can be chosen.

    ➤ If Receive calls was selected, only the inbound protocols can be configured.

    ➤ If Dial out and receive calls was selected, then both outbound and inbound protocols can be configured.

7. Select protocol-specific configuration for each inbound protocol (see Figures 10.2 and 10.3).

Once RAS itself is installed, you need to check your port and modem configuration through the Port and Modem applets of the Control Panel.

If RAS is configured to receive calls, that port and modem cannot be used by any other application. RAS locks the port to maintain control to monitor for inbound calls.

Figure 10.1   The Network Configuration dialog box for RAS.

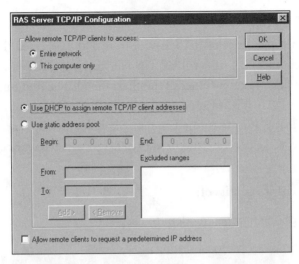

Figure 10.2 The RAS Server TCP/IP Configuration dialog box.

Figure 10.3 The RAS Server IPX Configuration dialog box.

RAS Routing, Gateway, Firewall

You can select whether to let RAS clients using network protocols access just the RAS server or the entire network. When you limit RAS clients to the RAS server, you are using RAS as a firewall; no network access of any kind through the RAS server is permitted. If you allow RAS clients to access the entire network, you are using RAS as a router. When NetBEUI is the only protocol in use, RAS acts as a gateway to enable the nonroutable protocol, NetBEUI, to access the network.

RAS Phonebook

The dial-out capabilities of RAS are controlled and accessed through the RAS Phonebook. This utility, Dial-Up Networking (DUN), is found in the Programs|Accessories folder of the Start menu. The first time DUN is launched, the RAS Wizard appears to help you create your first phonebook entry. Every time after that, the Phonebook dialog box appears. Through this interface, you can create and modify dial-up parameters for every RAS connection.

Phonebook entries consist of:

- ➤ Name, phone number, modem to use
- ➤ Server type and protocol settings
- ➤ Connection scripts
- ➤ Security settings
- ➤ X.25 settings (if applicable)

RAS Security

RAS has numerous levels and types of security that protect your network from unauthorized remote access. The following sections highlight these security features.

RAS Encryption

Windows NT can be configured to increase or decrease connection security through:

- ➤ The Security tab of a phonebook entry for outbound RAS links
- ➤ The Network Protocol Configuration dialog box for inbound RAS links (as shown in Figure 10.1)

The three settings available for RAS data encryption are:

1. **Accept any authentication, including clear text** This is the most permissive setting. It should be used when the user is not concerned about passwords. This option

allows a connection using any authentication provided by the server; therefore, it is useful when connecting to a non-Microsoft server.

2. **Accept only encrypted authentication** This option is beneficial when the transmission of clear text password is not desired and when you are connecting to a non-Microsoft server.

3. **Accept only Microsoft encrypted authentication** For this setting, the Microsoft Challenge Authentication Handshake Protocol (MS-CHAP) must be used; therefore, it is useful when calling a Microsoft Server. If the Require Data Encryption box is checked, all the data sent over the wire is encrypted. Data encryption is provided by Windows NT using the Rivest-Shamir-Adleman (RSA) Data Security Incorporated RC4 algorithm. If the data sent fails to encrypt correctly, the connection automatically is terminated.

RAS Callback

Callback is a security feature in which a RAS connection is established only after the server has disconnected the inbound call and then called the user back. Setting callback is performed via the User|Properties option in User Manager For Domains or the User|Properties command of the Remote Access Manger, by selecting from the following:

➤ **No Call Back** This is the default setting. It means that when a user is establishing a RAS connection, he or she will not be called back.

➤ **Set By Caller** Callback can be set by the user. This is a good way to save on long-distance charges, because the server calls the client back at the number set by the caller.

➤ **Preset To:** You can configure the call back for a preset number. This heightens security because the user must call from a predetermined phone number.

The RAS Logon Process

With Windows NT 4, you can log on to a domain via RAS at the Logon prompt by selecting the Connect Via Dial-In option and providing the proper domain. This allows you to establish a RAS connection to the remote network without requiring you to log on locally first.

 When you are using TCP/IP via a slow RAS connection, an LMHOSTS file might speed up network access and name resolution. Place an LMHOSTS file on the RAS client. Ensure that LMHOSTS entries have the #PRE tag so that the IP addresses will be cached.

Additional RAS Features

There is much more to RAS than what's covered in this chapter. You'll need to review the reference materials listed at the end of this chapter for more RAS information. However, we have included a short list of important features or options to RAS, and these are the most important to know for the exam.

AutoDial

AutoDial is the ability of NT to remember the location of resources accessed over a RAS connection. This is done by maintaining a map that correlates a network address to a phonebook entry. When that resource is referenced, RAS reestablishes the WAN connection to regain access to that resource without additional user interaction. AutoDial is enabled by default. AutoDial does not yet function over IPX/SPX, but it works with TCP/IP and NetBEUI.

Logging

Troubleshooting RAS difficulties is much simpler when the logging capabilities are employed. There are two logging features of NT that record RAS-related activities. The first is the MODEMLOG.TXT file that records the activities of the modem. This is enabled through a modem's properties in the Modem applet in the Advanced Connections Settings area. This file is placed in the NT root directory.

The second log file is DEVICE.LOG. This file only can be enabled through the Registry. The "Logging" value located in \HKEY_LOCAL_MACHINE \SYSTEM\CurrentControlSet\Services\RasMan\Parameters should be set to 1. The DEVICE.LOG file will be stored in the \%winntroot% \system32\ras directory.

The Event Viewer captures some RAS information that may be useful for troubleshooting and deciphering RAS. By default, all server errors, user connect attempts, disconnects, and so on, are logged in the System Log.

Null Modem

A null modem is a serial cable that enables two computers to connect without the need for a modem. These special cables are common peer-to-peer attachment devices, but they can be used by NT RAS to establish a standard NT network connection. A null modem can be installed through the Modem applet by selecting it from the standard modems. A cable is not actually required for the setup, and this offers you a way out when installing RAS if you don't already have the modem at hand. Once installed, a null-modem cable can be used just like a modem, which is itself used by RAS just as if it were a NIC—that is, a workstation attached via a null-modem cable can fully participate in a domain, but at a slower data transfer rate.

Multiple Protocols

A RAS link uses both a WAN protocol and a LAN protocol to enable network communications. Most often, the WAN protocol is PPP. The LAN protocol can be any of the protocols installed on your RAS server, which may or may not be the same set of protocols on your LAN. However, even if you use multiple protocols on your LAN, only a single LAN protocol is used over the RAS connection. The first common protocol identified between the client and server is used. Therefore, the proper binding order of protocols to the RAS dial-up adapters should be configured so that the most important protocol has the highest priority.

Name Resolution

In situations where static lookups occur, the configuration with optimal resolution speed and WAN link traffic is to store the HOSTS (DNS) and the LMHOSTS (WINS) files on the local hard drives of the RAS clients. This configuration makes it somewhat difficult to maintain the newest version of the files on multiple remote clients.

Exam Prep Questions

Question 1

> If no standards are in place for the operating system, protocol, or the method of access for your remote clients, what is the highest level of security you can implement and still allow your users to connect via RAS?
>
> O a. Allow Any Authentication Including Clear Text
>
> O b. Microsoft Encrypted Authentication
>
> O c. PGP Encryption
>
> O d. Require Encrypted Authentication

With nonstandardized configurations implementing any encryption security other than Allow Any Authentication Including Clear Text, some clients are restricted from accessing the network via RAS; therefore, only answer a is correct. Microsoft Encrypted Authentication and Require Encrypted Authentication are encryption security schemes that require special configuration or operating systems; therefore, answers b and d are incorrect. PGP Encryption is not a native NT option; therefore, answer c is incorrect.

Question 2

> Which of the following statements about PPP and SLIP are true? [Check all correct answers]
>
> ❑ a. PPP supports encrypted passwords; SLIP does not.
>
> ❑ b. SLIP supports NetBEUI, IPX/SPX, and TCP/IP; PPP only supports TCP/IP.
>
> ❑ c. PPP supports DHCP; SLIP does not.
>
> ❑ d. SLIP is used to access Unix servers.
>
> ❑ e. PPP is the most commonly used WAN protocol.

PPP supports encrypted passwords; SLIP does not. Therefore, answer a is correct. PPP supports NetBEUI, IPX/SPX, and TCP/IP, but SLIP only supports TCP/IP; therefore, answer b is incorrect. PPP supports DHCP; SLIP does not. Therefore, answer c is correct. SLIP is used to access Unix servers; therefore, answer d is correct. PPP is the most commonly used WAN protocol; therefore, answer e is also correct. Thus, answers a, c, d, and e are correct.

Question 3

Which of the following NT networking activities are supported by a PPP RAS connection? [Check all correct answers]

❑   a. Printer share access

❑   b. Named pipes

❑   c. WinSOCK API applications over TCP/IP

❑   d. InterProcess Communications (IPC)

❑   e. User logon authentication

Since a RAS connected client is no different from a direct connected client (other than in its speed of data transfer), all standard network activities still occur over the WAN link. Therefore, all five answers are correct.

Question 4

While connected to the office LAN, you create a shortcut on your desktop that points to a documents folder located on the LAN's file server. After working with a few files from this folder, you close your RAS session. Later, you attempt to reopen the files you edited earlier. What happens?

○   a. Access is denied because no link to the LAN exists.

○   b. The file is pulled from the network cache.

○   c. A file with a similar name on your local hard drive is accessed instead.

○   d. RAS AutoDial attempts to reconnect to the office LAN.

Only answer d is correct. RAS maintains a map list of the resources accessed over WAN links. When one of these resources is referenced, it will attempt to AutoDial to regain a connection to the server hosting the resource. Answer a would be the result if AutoDial was not enabled, but you always should assume the default configuration for computers in Microsoft exam questions unless otherwise indicated. Therefore, answer a is incorrect. Answers b and c are fictitious activities that do not occur; therefore, they are incorrect.

Question 5

Where can you find information related to RAS problems to aid in troubleshooting? [Check all correct answers]

❑ a. Event Viewer

❑ b. DEVICE.LOG

❑ c. Dr. Watson

❑ d. MODEMLOG.TXT

❑ e. NT Diagnostics

The Event Viewer, DEVICE.LOG, and MODEMLOG.TXT can be useful troubleshooting tools for RAS problems; therefore, answers a, b, and d are correct. Dr. Watson does not track RAS events; it focuses on applications. Therefore, answer c is incorrect. NT Diagnostics will not provide useful information related to RAS; therefore, answer e is incorrect.

Question 6

What is the best method for offering reliable and secure access to your network over the Internet for your remote users?

○ a. Internet Information Server

○ b. Serial Line Interface Protocol

○ c. Point-to-Point Tunneling Protocol

○ d. Require Encrypted Authentication

Internet Information Server will offer only WWW, FTP, and Gopher services—not access to the entire network, and without additional security. Therefore, answer a is incorrect. SLIP doesn't offer access over the Internet, it cannot be used to dial into an NT Server, and it does not support encryption; therefore, answer b is incorrect. PPTP offers a reliable and secure network connection over the Internet; therefore, answer c is correct. Require Encrypted Authentication is a mid-level security setting, but it does not directly offer connection over the Internet nor will it imply access to the network. Therefore, answer d is incorrect.

Question 7

You have a field technician who travels extensively around the country. Her schedule changes often, and she rarely visits the same places twice. It is important that she is able to connect to the office LAN periodically, but your organization's security policy requires callback security on all RAS connections. How can you configure her account so that she is able to gain access, while also supporting your organization's security?

○   a. Set the callback security to No Call Back only for her account.

○   b. Enable callback security with Set By Caller selected.

○   c. Set the callback security to Preset To with her home phone number.

○   d. Set the callback security to Roaming, and give her the page number to configure the callback number remotely.

○   e. Turn on the callback Caller ID capture.

Setting the No Call Back option will violate the organization's security policy; therefore, answer a is incorrect. Setting the Set By Caller option will allow her to input the callback number each time she needs to connect; therefore, answer b is correct. Setting the Preset To number will not allow her to gain access to the network because she never calls from the same location more than once; therefore, answer c is incorrect. There is not a Roaming callback setting; therefore, answer d is incorrect. NT does not have a Caller ID capture setting, but this can be obtained through third-party software; however it is not required for this situation, so answer e is incorrect.

Question 8

> Which protocols can be used over a RAS connection?
>
> ○　a. TCP/IP, NetBEUI, but not NWLink
>
> ○　b. TCP/IP, NWLink, but not NetBEUI
>
> ○　c. Only TCP/IP
>
> ○　d. TCP/IP, NetBEUI, and NWLink

TCP/IP, NetBEUI, but not NWLink, is the restriction for the AutoDial feature but not a limitation of RAS as a whole. Therefore, answer a is incorrect. TCP/IP, NWLink, but not NetBEUI, are the protocols that can be routed over RAS but not a limitation as to which protocols can be used. Therefore, answer b is also incorrect. Only TCP/IP can be used over SLIP, but RAS is not limited to SLIP. Therefore, answer c is incorrect. TCP/IP, NetBEUI, and NWLink can all be used over RAS; therefore, answer d is correct.

Question 9

> What are the possible uses of a null-modem cable?
> [Check all correct answers]
>
> ❏　a. Attach a workstation to a domain.
>
> ❏　b. Enable subnet routing.
>
> ❏　c. Test a RAS server locally.
>
> ❏　d. Establish a VPN over the Internet.
>
> ❏　e. Temporarily connect two LANs.

Attaching a workstation to a domain is a use for a null-modem cable; therefore, answer a is correct. Subnet routing can be implemented only when two NICs are installed on the same machine; therefore, answer b is incorrect. A RAS server can be tested using a null-modem cable to simulate a remote client; therefore, answer c is correct. A VPN over the Internet can be established only with PPTP and a connection to the Internet, requiring a modem. Therefore, answer d is incorrect. Two closely adjacent LANs can be connected over a null-modem cable; therefore, answer e is correct. Thus, answers a, c, and e are correct.

Question 10

> Your LAN uses both NetBEUI and NWLink protocols. Your RAS server supports NetBEUI and TCP/IP, bound in that order. A RAS client also uses both NetBEUI and TCP/IP, bound in that order. Which of the following activities cannot occur over a RAS connection made between the client and the server?
>
> ○ a. Accessing a directory list of NetBIOS share names
>
> ○ b. Accessing resources on the LAN
>
> ○ c. Accessing resources on the RAS server
>
> ○ d. Accessing WinSOCK applications

The binding order of the protocols on both the client and server determine what single LAN protocol is used over the RAS connection, resulting in a NetBEUI connection. WinSOCK applications based on the Windows TCP/IP API cannot be used, because TCP/IP is not a protocol being communicated over the link; therefore, answer d is correct. The other activities can occur using the NetBEUI protocol; therefore, answers a, b, and c are incorrect.

Question 11

> If static name resolution is used, what is the proper location of the HOSTS and LMHOSTS files to optimize the lookup time?
>
> ○ a. Both HOSTS and LMHOSTS should be stored on the RAS clients.
>
> ○ b. HOSTS should be stored on the RAS server, and LMHOSTS should be stored on the RAS clients.
>
> ○ c. Both HOSTS and LMHOSTS should be stored on the RAS server.
>
> ○ d. HOSTS should be stored on the RAS clients, and LMHOSTS should be stored on the RAS server.

The fastest lookup time will occur when the HOSTS and LMHOSTS files are stored on the local hard drive of each RAS client, because no WAN traffic need occur to resolve a resource location. Therefore, answer a is correct. All others answers are incorrect because they discuss storing these files somewhere other than on the client, which increases the lookup time.

Need To Know More?

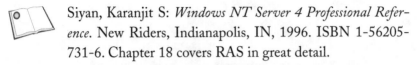 Heywood, Drew: *Inside Windows NT Server.* New Riders, Indianapolis, IN, 1995. ISBN 1-56205-472-4. The installation, configuration, and use of RAS are discussed in Chapter 14.

Siyan, Karanjit S: *Windows NT Server 4 Professional Reference.* New Riders, Indianapolis, IN, 1996. ISBN 1-56205-731-6. Chapter 18 covers RAS in great detail.

Strebe, Matthew, Charles Perkins, and James Chellis: *MSCE: NT Server 4 Study Guide.* Sybex Network Press, San Francisco, CA, 1996. ISBN 0-7821-1972-7. RAS is examined in Chapter 11.

Search the TechNet CD (or its online version through www.microsoft.com) using the keywords "RAS," "Remote Access," "PPP," and "modems."

The Windows NT Server Resource Kit contains some discussion of RAS—for example, Appendix E, "RAS Reference," in the *Networking Guide.*

Performance Monitor

. . . .

Terms you'll need to understand:

√ Performance Monitor

√ Server optimization

√ Objects

√ Counters

√ Baselining

√ Update interval

Techniques you'll need to master:

√ Using Performance Monitor

√ Key characteristics to monitor

√ Viewing network data in Chart, Alert, and Report views

√ Logging network statistics

√ Establishing a baseline

√ Setting administrative alerts

It's important to understand server optimization to pass the Windows NT Server 4 exam. Even though NT 4 installs quickly and easily, fine-tuning your system can be quite a task. There are many factors for administrators to consider when "tweaking" the server to achieve optimal performance.

Luckily, Microsoft has thrown in a wonderful tool called Performance Monitor (PerfMon). This server optimization tool comes with both NT Server and NT Workstation. Performance Monitor allows an administrator to observe almost every component within an NT server—both locally and remotely. In this chapter, we examine the details of Performance Monitor, to assist you in both maintaining optimal server performance and passing that portion of the Microsoft Certification exam.

How Performance Monitor Works

Performance Monitor treats system components as objects. This allows the system to track network performance trends to help establish a baseline against which you can make certain decisions regarding network optimization. Performance Monitor lets you examine important server characteristics, such as pages per second, processor usage, and even the number of available bytes. All of the data gathered can be viewed in different forms, including a chart view, alert view, and report view. Figure 11.1 shows the Performance Monitor interface.

Performance Monitor records the behavior of objects in the system by using counters. NT provides a specific set of counters for each server object. As in programming, these objects usually consist of code containing different properties and behavior patterns. The counters provide information on each object type. Some examples of objects in Performance Monitor include Processor, Server, System, and Thread. Figure 11.2 shows a list of these objects. Table 11.1 lists some of the most important objects, counters for those objects, and their significance.

Figure 11.1   The Performance Monitor interface, with nothing set to monitor.

Figure 11.2   Server objects that can be added to a chart for monitoring through Performance Monitor.

Table 11.1 **Performance Monitor's objects and counters, and their definitions and uses.**

Objects And Counters	Description	Significance
MEMORY:		
Available Bytes	The amount of virtual memory now available.	When the value falls below a threshold, NT gradually takes memory from running applications to maintain a minimum amount of virtual memory.
Pages/Second	The number of pages that had to be written to or read from the disk and placed in physical memory.	This indicates if you need more RAM. A value greater than 5 could indicate a bottleneck in your system.
Page Faults/Second	Number of faults in the processor.	This indicates that the data was not set in memory.
PAGING FILE:		
% Usage	Amount of the actual paging file that is in use by the system.	If this value is close to 100% you should increase your paging file size.
PHYSICAL DISK:		
Average Disk Sec/ Transfer	The amount of time a disk takes to fulfill requests.	A value greater than .3 can indicate that the disk controller is retrying the disk continuously, due to writing failures.
% Disk Time	The percentage of time that the disk is in use.	If this value is above 85%, consider upgrading the disk drive or controller.
SYSTEM:		
Processor Queue Length	The number of threads shown is an indicator of the system performance, because each thread requires a certain number of processor cycles.	If this value is greater than 2, you should consider a new processor.

(continued)

Table 11.1	Performance Monitor's objects and counters, and their definitions and uses (*continued*).	
Objects And Counters	**Description**	**Significance**
PROCESSOR:		
Interrupts/Second	Measures the rate of requests from I/O devices.	If there is a dramatic increase in this number with an increase in system activity, check your hardware.
% Processor Time	Shows how busy a processor is.	Anything over 80% means the processor might be the problem.

Which View Do I Want?

Performance Monitor has several views available. Once Performance Monitor is open, you can determine which is best suited for your needs. To choose a view, select the View menu. Your options include Chart, Alert, Log, and Report. Table 11.2 lists all the views and their individual purposes.

Creating A Chart

The Chart view displays counter information in the form of a graph or histogram. Each counter is represented by a separate, different-colored line for every entry, along with a legend at the bottom of the graph that explains each counter's purpose.

Once you have decided on the view, you must then decide what to monitor.

Table 11.2	Performance Monitor's views and their purposes.
View	**Purpose**
Chart	Displays collected data as a line graph or histogram.
Alert	Defines and monitors alert conditions based on criteria set by the Administrator (for example, notifying the administrator if disk space is low).
Log	Allows you to save performance data in a log file on disk.
Report	Lists counters and their current values.

What Gets Monitored?

The first decision is to determine on which computer Performance Monitor will be run. Remember that Performance Monitor is run locally by default, but you also can select a computer on the network to be monitored. To select a remote machine, simply type in the computer name in the dialog box or click on the ellipsis button to get a browse list of the systems available on the network.

Which Object Should I Select?

Once you have determined which computer needs monitoring, you must then select the objects to be monitored. Depending on your hardware and software, you may encounter objects that other machines might not have. For instance, if you have NWLink installed, you might see a counter called NWLink IPX for monitoring IPX traffic on the network.

Which Counter Should I Select?

Each object in Performance Monitor has specific counters associated with it; for example, the Server object's counters include Bytes Total/Second, Files Open, and Errors Logon. To add a counter to the chart window, click the plus sign (+) on the toolbar or select Add To Chart from the Edit menu. If you are unsure about what a counter does, hit the Explain button to get a detailed description of the counter (see Figure 11.3).

Figure 11.3 Performance Monitor with counter definitions enabled.

What If I Have More Than One Object?

If you want to monitor more than one object, you can select an instance to determine which object to monitor. For example, if you have more than one processor and you want to monitor all of them, the first processor would be instance zero, the second processor would be instance one, and so on. Once you have selected all of the necessary data, select Add, and the Chart will display lines for each selected processor.

Setting Chart Options

All four views in Performance Monitor have options that will affect only that particular view. The chart options allow you to change general preferences, such as the minimum and maximum value for the vertical axis and the type of chart you want to see. To choose the options, go to the Options menu and select Chart. When you need to monitor trends over time, you should use the line chart (see Figure 11.4). When you want to compare counters to other counters, you should consider the histogram. Figure 11.5

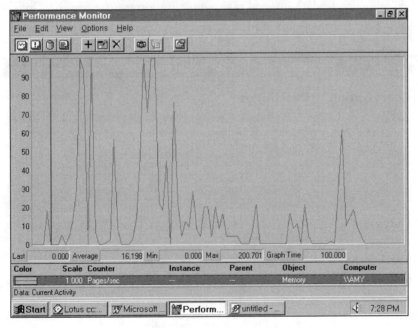

Figure 11.4   Performance Monitor charting memory usage.

Figure 11.5 The Chart Options dialog box in Performance Monitor.

shows the Chart Options dialog box. All of the chart options and their descriptions are listed in Table 11.3.

Adjusting The Update Interval

Adjusting the update interval is the most important item in the Options dialog box. It is very important that you select the correct interval for your

Table 11.3 Performance Monitor's chart options.	
Chart Option	**Description**
Legend	If this option is selected, the legend for each chart line appears at the bottom of Performance Monitor.
Value Bar	The value bar shows the values of Last, Average, Min, Max, and Graph Time.
Gallery	This allows you to choose what type of graph you want displayed.
Update Time	There are two options: Periodic Update (most commonly used) and Manual Update.
Vertical Grid	This displays gridlines on the vertical axis.
Horizontal Grid	This displays gridlines on the horizontal axis.
Vertical Labels	This displays a label for the y-axis.
Vertical Maximum	This sets the maximum value for the vertical axis.

data retrieval. If you sample too frequently, you could cause your system overhead to soar and slow the network; if you do not sample often enough, you could lose important data.

Starting A Performance Monitor Chart

To create a chart in Performance Monitor, follow these steps:

1. From the Start menu, select Programs|Administrative Tools|Performance Monitor.

2. From the View menu, select Chart.

3. From the Edit menu, select Add To Chart.

4. In the Add To Chart dialog box, select the computer to be monitored, the object (or objects) on that computer to be monitored, and which counters are to be observed.

5. Set different counter options, such as frequency, alert interval, etc.

6. Save your configuration in a file.

7. Analyze the data you have collected.

Creating A Report

The Report view in Performance Monitor displays a simple list of counters and their values. The values are updated at each set interval. (*Note:* There is no chart associated with the Report view.) Start Performance Monitor and select Report on the View menu. In Chart view, the more counters you add, the harder it becomes to read the data, so Report view is a definite plus. In Figure 11.6, there are so many counters added to the report that Chart view would be very hard to read.

Choosing Counters

Each view has its own set of counters, and these counters will not appear in any other window. To add counters, click on the plus sign (+) on the toolbar

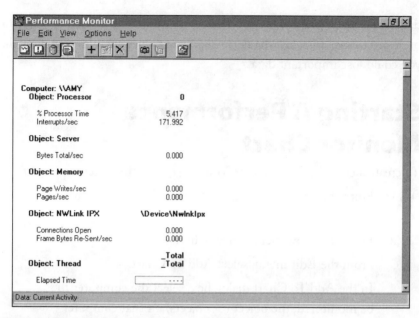

Figure 11.6 Monitoring objects through the Report view in Performance Monitor.

or select Add To Report from the Edit menu. The only real difference between adding chart counters and adding report counters is that report counters show up as numeric values rather than as a line on a chart.

Report Options

The Report view has only one useful option (unlike the Chart view, which has several): the update interval value. The default value is to update every five seconds. To change this interval, select Report from the Options menu, as shown in Figure 11.7.

So You Want To Save This Data For Later?

When you add a counter to the Report or Chart view, you will soon notice that data is displayed based on the current activity. There is no way to save the data being collected in the chart or report for later use. The Log view allows you to do that; you can specify the objects that you want to observe

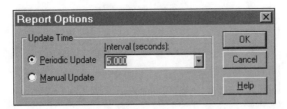

Figure 11.7 Selecting the interval update time on the Report Options dialog box in Performance Monitor.

and the interval at which to record the data. You even have the option of recording data from both local and remote machines in one log file. After the data is captured to a specific location, you can view this data in any other view. Figure 11.8 illustrates a log file that has been set to monitor three objects.

Setting Log Options

Once you have selected the counters to be monitored, you must select where you want Performance Monitor to place the log file. Select Log from the Options menu. This brings up the Log Options dialog box (see Figure

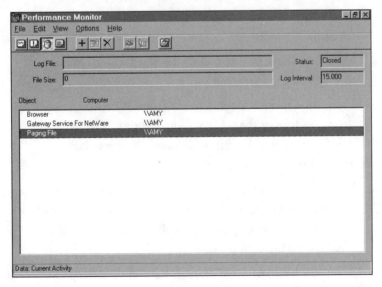

Figure 11.8 The Performance Monitor Log view, set to capture information on the Browser, Gateway Service For NetWare, and Paging File.

Figure 11.9   Selecting the location for the log to be stored in Performance Monitor.

Browse through the directories in the Save In window until you locate the directory where you want the log files to be stored. There is also an Update Time section in the Log Options dialog box.

Here are the steps to follow to log data to a file:

1. From the Add To Log window, highlight the objects you want to monitor, and click the Add button for each.

2. When you have selected all of the objects to be monitored, click the Done button.

3. From the Options menu, choose Log. At this point, the Log Options dialog box should appear. This is where you should specify a file name, location, and update interval for the log.

4. Once you have selected all the important information in the Log Options dialog box, click on Start Log. The log will start building, and you will notice the size of the file growing in the File Size field.

5. After you have collected enough data, choose Stop Log from the Options|Log menu.

Viewing Logged Data

Following are the steps to follow to view logged data. This process is the same for every view you choose:

1. Open Performance Monitor in the window or view of your choice.

2. From the Options menu, choose Data From.

3. Select the Log File bullet box, and type the path and name of the log file to view, or click the ellipsis (…) button to browse for the file (see Figure 11.10).

4. Click OK to close the Data From dialog box.

Setting Alerts In Performance Monitor

The Alert view usually is the favorite view among administrators. If you need to monitor many servers at a time, the last thing you want to do is sit in front of the monitor and wait for something to happen. With the Alert view, you do not have to be strapped to one machine all day; the alert will monitor any counter and will carry out a specific task when the counter exceeds or falls below a predetermined threshold. You can have Performance Monitor notify you when an event occurs. You can even specify a command line that you want to run after the alert is sent out. In Table 11.4, the common threshold values for alert counters are defined.

Figure 11.10 Selecting the location from which to view saved data in Performance Monitor.

Table 11.4	Performance Monitor's counters and their threshold values.

Object: Counter	Threshold
Processor: % Processor Time	>90
System: Processor Queue Length	>2
Physical Disk: % Disk Time	>70
Logical Disk: Free Space	<10
Memory: Pages/Second	>30
Memory: Available Bytes	<4 MB

You can use the Alert view to monitor a critical resource such as free disk space: You will be notified when the system falls below a certain level.

Getting Started In Alert View

To add a new alert, follow these steps:

1. Start Performance Monitor.

2. Select Alert from the View menu.

3. Select Add To Alert from the Edit menu, or click the plus sign (+) on the toolbar. The Add To Alert dialog box will appear (see Figure 11.11).

4. Select the computer you wish to monitor. Remember, the local machine is the default.

5. In the Object field, select from the drop-down list the object you wish to monitor.

6. Next, select the counters that fall in line with the object. Do not forget about the Explain button; it provides a brief explanation of each counter.

7. Select the instance you wish to monitor. The counting of the physical hardware begins with zero.

8. Select the color of the alert. This is very helpful if you have set more than one instance of an alert.

Figure 11.11   Adding alerts in Performance Monitor.

9. Enter a number in the Alert If Over/Under box (refer to Table 11.4 for important values).

10. If an application is supposed to run when something triggers an alert, specify in the Run Program On Alert dialog box both the application name and whether the program is to run every time the alert is triggered or only the first time the alert is triggered.

Setting Alert Options

As with charts, alerts can be customized with a variety of options. To set alert options, select Alert from the Options menu. The Alert Options dialog box will appear (see Figure 11.12). The options provided in the Alert Options dialog box, along with their descriptions, are listed in Table 11.5.

Figure 11.12   The Alert Options dialog box in Performance Monitor.

Table 11.5	Performance Monitor's alert options and their descriptions.
Alert Option	**Description**
Switch To Alert View	Performance Monitor switches to Alert view when an alert is triggered.
Log Event In Application Log	You can view an event in the Application Log in Event Viewer.
Send Network Message	Performance Monitor sends a message to the machine specified in the text box.
Update Time	Two options are available here: Periodic Update, which tells Performance Monitor when to read new data; and Manual Update, in which the user must tell Performance Monitor to update the data.

It is highly recommended that you add at least one computer name to the Send Network Message box in the Alert Options dialog box. This ensures that someone will be notified in case of emergency.

Exam Prep Questions

Question 1

> When you are running a graphics-intensive program, you notice
> your hard drive is very active. You do not know what to do next.
> What object and counter can you monitor to see if you need to
> add more RAM to your machine?
>
> ○   a. Memory: Pages/Thread
>
> ○   b. Memory: Pages/Second
>
> ○   c. Processor: % Processor Time
>
> ○   d. None of the above

There is no such thing as Pages/Thread; therefore, answer a is incorrect. To
find out how overloaded your system memory is, you would look at Memory:
Pages/Second to decide whether you need more RAM; therefore, answer b
is correct. If you want to find out the percentage of elapsed time that a
processor is busy, you would look at % Processor Time; therefore, answer c
is incorrect. Because b is the correct answer, d is incorrect.

Question 2

> You decide that Alert view is the best option for your group. When
> you are monitoring resources, you notice that just running Per-
> formance Monitor itself causes a performance hit. What can you
> do to fix this problem?
>
> ○   a. Increase the interval of time that Performance Monitor
> will obtain data.
>
> ○   b. Turn off Performance Monitor, because it does nothing
> useful anyway.
>
> ○   c. Decrease the interval of time that Performance Monitor
> will obtain data.
>
> ○   d. Use User Manager For Domains to monitor your
> resources.

Increasing the interval gives the server more time between data gathering sessions, rather than retrieving data every five seconds; therefore, answer a is the correct choice. Decreasing the interval only makes the server work much harder; therefore, answer c is incorrect. User Manager For Domains doesn't allow you to monitor server resources—it's where accounts are created and maintained. Therefore, answer d is incorrect.

Question 3

Your boss called you and said he was confused about certain counters in Performance Monitor. Where can you tell him to look for information? [Check all correct answers]

❑   a. Tell him to look in the Registry.

❑   b. Tell him to click on the counter itself and click the Explain button.

❑   c. Tell him to select Search For Help On... from the Help menu.

❑   d. Tell him to change the view to Report.

You should *never* go to the Registry to "look up" information; therefore, answer a is incorrect. In Performance Monitor, you can click on the counter itself and hit the Explain button to get a better explanation of the objects and counters; therefore, answer b is correct. Although it would be more difficult, you can search for help on this topic from the Help menu; therefore, answer c is also correct. Unless you know what each counter does, the report view won't clarify things; therefore, answer d is incorrect. Thus, b and c are the correct answers.

Question 4

Which feature of Performance Monitor can you use to have the system notify you when a certain threshold is reached?

○   a. The Log view

○   b. The Registry view

○   c. The Chart view

○   d. The Alert option

The correct answer is d. The Log view allows you to save data for perusal at a later date; therefore, answer a is incorrect. There is no such thing as the Registry view; therefore, answer b is also incorrect. The Chart view allows you to view current activity, but not to schedule notification at certain threshold levels; therefore, answer c is incorrect.

Question 5

What counter and object would you look at if you wanted to see how busy your processor was?

- ○ a. System: Interrupts/Second
- ○ b. Memory: Pages/Second
- ○ c. Processor: % Processor Time
- ○ d. None of the above

System: Interrupts/Second doesn't provide information about the CPU; therefore, answer a is incorrect. Checking Memory: Pages/Second allows you to verify if the amount of RAM in your system is adequate; therefore, answer b is incorrect. Processor: % Processor Time is used to see how busy the processor is; therefore, answer c is correct. Anything over 80% might mean you need to replace the processor or add additional ones. Because answer c is correct, answer d is incorrect.

Question 6

Which option allows you to save the server data for later viewing?

- ○ a. Log
- ○ b. Alert
- ○ c. Chart
- ○ d. Disk

The Log option allows you to collect data to a file to be viewed later; therefore, answer a is the correct choice. The Alert option notifies administrators when certain system thresholds are reached; therefore, answer b is incorrect. The Chart option allows you to view current system data; therefore, answer c is incorrect. There is no Disk option in Performance Monitor; therefore, answer d is also incorrect.

Question 7

In the past, you have only monitored one object at a time. You realize that you should monitor at least ten objects at any given time. You really like the Chart view, but realize it looks messy. What can you do to solve your problem?

- ○ a. Switch the Performance Monitor to Report view.
- ○ b. Do nothing. You cannot monitor ten objects at a time.
- ○ c. Switch to Alert view.
- ○ d. Use Windows NT diagnostics to view the data.

Report view is much easier to look at when you are monitoring many objects at a time; therefore, answer a is the correct response. You cannot get a graph from Report view, but you can see more things on the screen at one time. It is possible to view many more than ten objects at a time; therefore, answer b is incorrect. Because the Alert view sends network messages to the Administrators when something goes wrong, answer c also is incorrect. NT diagnostics will not allow you to view counters and objects; therefore, answer d is incorrect.

Need To Know More?

 Chellis, Donald, Lisa, and James: *MSCE: NT Server 4 in the Enterprise Study Guide.* Sybex Network Press, San Francisco, CA, 1997. ISBN 0-7821-1970-0. Chapter 15 contains information on Performance Monitor, Task Manager, and Server service Optimizations.

 Heywood, Drew: *Inside Windows NT Server.* New Riders, Indianapolis, IN, 1995. ISBN 1-6205-472-4. The Performance Monitor is discussed in Chapter 13, on pages 561-576.

 Siyan, Karanjit S.: *Windows NT Server 4 Professional Reference.* New Riders, Indianapolis, IN, 1996. ISBN 1-56205-731-6. Chapter 21 contains a lengthy discussion of the Performance Monitor, Task Manager, process priority settings, and Server service Optimizations.

 The Windows NT Server 4 manuals cover planning, configuration, and installation issues quite well. The *Concepts and Planning Manual* contains useful documentation on the Performance Monitor in Chapter 8, "Monitoring Performance."

 The *Windows NT Server Resource Kit Supplement #1* contains many discussions on using Performance Monitor to investigate all aspects of a network.

The Windows NT Boot Process

Terms you'll need to understand:

√ Boot, boot up, bootstrap, bootstrap loader

√ ARC names, ARC pathnames

√ MBR (Master Boot Record)

√ BOOT.INI, NTLDR, NTDETECT.COM, NTBOOTDD.SYS

√ Boot partition or boot drive

√ System partition or system drive

Techniques you'll need to master:

√ How to edit the BOOT.INI file

√ How to interpret and construct Advanced RISC
  Computer (ARC) device names and pathnames

√ How to troubleshoot the Windows NT boot sequence

Starting up a computer from scratch involves a lot more work, and many more pieces and parts, than might immediately meet the eye. Because a computer that won't boot is essentially a dead computer, it's important to understand the Windows NT boot process, and where that process can go awry.

In this chapter, we walk you through the Windows NT boot process, explain the important pieces and parts, and explore some of the things that can derail this process. Along the way, you'll get to know more about how computers work in general, and what's involved in fully completing Windows NT's intricate boot process for the purposes of passing that section of the Microsoft Certification exam.

Bootstrapping A Computer

When you boot a computer that has Windows NT installed as one of its operating systems, the machine goes through a number of steps before an operating system (OS) can be selected. Then, if Windows NT is selected as the OS to boot, a number of additional steps follow before the login prompt dialog ever appears.

The initial phase, called "the bootstrap process," covers the steps necessary to turn a computer from a lump of inert metal and plastic into a device that is ready to accept and react to input. For ordinary PCs, this consists of the following steps:

1. **Power on the computer, or initiate startup**
    This one's easy—it requires only that the computer be plugged in and that you turn the power switch to On. For Windows NT, the startup process also may be initiated when you click Restart the Computer in the Shut Down Windows dialog box (Start|Shut Down), or when you select the Shut Down button, followed by Shutdown and Restart, through the Windows NT Security Dialog box that's always available by entering Ctrl+Alt+Del at any time while Windows NT is running.

2. **Power on Self Test (POST) processing**

    Once the computer begins its startup process, it per-
    forms a number of built-in diagnostics and hardware
    tests to make sure all of its components are working
    properly. This is driven by firmware on the mother-
    board through the BIOS, and may involve other
    BIOSs (like those typically found on graphics adapters)
    once the onboard BIOS completes its checks. This
    activity produces all the messages and status informa-
    tion that flashes by on your screen while the computer
    is going through the hardware check stages of startup.
    POST also determines how much RAM is available on
    the machine, and checks to make sure essential periph-
    erals (like keyboard, mouse, and so on) are present and
    connected.

3. **Initial startup process**

    Once the hardware has been checked out, this exhausts
    the onboard diagnostics and self-check capabilities of
    most computers. At this point, it's time to read some
    real software from disk to continue the boot process,
    which requires that an operating system to establish a
    runtime environment for the computer be loaded.
    If booting from a floppy, the first sector on the disk
    contains the Partition Boot sector; if booting from a
    hard disk, the first sector contains the Master Boot
    Record (MBR) and the Partition Table. These records
    contain the information that points the computer in
    the right direction to obtain boot information; they
    also provide a map for how the disk (or floppy) is
    physically arranged. The MBR is probably the most
    important record on any hard disk; it contains the
    Partition Table that describes a disk's physical layout
    and arrangement, and includes a small program whose
    job is to examine the Partition Table and identify the
    system partition. The program then locates the system

partition's starting address on disk (sector 0), and loads a copy of the Partition Boot Sector into memory. Once this step is complete, the program transfers execution to another program, usually an operating system loader from code included in the Partition Boot Sector just loaded. This Partition is identified in the Partition Table by being marked as the "active partition," which indicates that it is the partition to which control should next be passed during the boot process.

Warning! For reasons too arcane to explain fully here, it's essential to recognize that the files that reside in the system partition on a drive are the files needed to boot a computer and some operating system, while the files that reside in what Microsoft calls the boot partition on a drive are those files needed to run Windows NT itself. Thus, the boot files—that is, NTLDR, BOOT.INI, NTDETECT.COM, and so on—reside in the system partition, while the Windows NT OS files—including NTOSKRNL.EXE, the Windows NT kernel—reside on the boot partition. It's bass-ackwards. Get it?

4. **Boot loader process**
   When the Partition Boot Sector code is loaded, a program designed to bring up a designated operating system—or, as with Windows NT's NTLDR program, to provide a menu of load choices—runs. This starts an execution sequence for full-blown programs from files on disk (as opposed to code embedded in the MBR or a Partition Boot Sector), ultimately resulting in complete loading of an operating system, after which the computer will be ready to run applications or services on demand.

Windows NT Server also runs on RISC CPUs, as well as on generic PCs. The boot process differs for RISC machines to some degree. We'll point out these differences in Tips as we step through the rest of this process. The primary difference as far as the bootstrap process is concerned is that once a RISC computer completes its POST routines, built-in firmware selects a startup disk by reading a boot precedence table from nonvolatile RAM on the machine. This identifies the system partition (where the boot files reside) and indicates if a floppy may be used as an alternate boot selection. The information in nonvolatile RAM also indicates where the OSLOADER.EXE program resides and names the folder that contains the OS to be booted.

At this point, the bootstrap process is complete, and the activities specific to the operating system to be booted begin. Once NTLDR is loaded into memory, it becomes possible to choose an operating system (or multiple versions of the same operating system), one of which is definitely Windows NT. The steps that follow next assume that Windows NT is selected as the operating system to boot.

5. **Selecting the OS**

When NTLDR executes, it reads another important Windows NT boot file, BOOT.INI, which we discuss in detail later in this chapter. BOOT.INI provides information about what choices of operating system to offer, defines their locations on disk, and assigns some important default characteristics for the load process. These make it possible to boot a Windows NT machine without requiring human intervention, so that keyboard input is not strictly required to start up a Windows NT machine. We now will choose a version of Windows NT in the loader menu, to begin the process of loading Windows NT itself.

At this point in the process for RISC machines, the program that loads is called OSLOADER.EXE. It performs all of the functions that are supplied for PCs by NTLDR, NTDETECT.COM, and BOOTSECT.DOS.

6. **Detecting hardware**

   Now the Windows NT program named NTDETECT.COM executes. This is a hardware recognition program that collects a list of currently installed components and returns the information to NTLDR. NTDETECT will not run, however, unless you select a version of Windows NT on the boot loader screen (or the default selection is Windows NT, and the timer times out). During this phase, the following message appears on screen:

   ```
   NTDETECT V1.0 Checking Hardware . . .
   ```

7. **Choosing a load configuration**

   Once NTDETECT finishes its job, the boot loader resumes control, and the following message appears:

   ```
   OS Loader V4.0

   Press spacebar now to invoke Hardware Profile/Last
   Known Good menu.
   ```

   The boot loader waits several seconds to give you time to press the spacebar. If it isn't pressed and there's only one hardware profile defined for the computer (which is completely typical, except for laptops), the boot loader loads Windows NT's default configuration. Otherwise, you can elect to use an alternate hardware profile here (for laptops, this usually means selected Networked or Detached hardware profiles), or switch to the Last Known Good Configuration menu, which permits you to boot Windows NT using the Registry values defined the last time the machine booted successfully.

8. **Loading the Windows NT kernel**

   The next phase, once the configuration or Registry versions have been identified (or chosen by default as is most often the case), is to load the operating system kernel for Windows NT. At this point, a sequence of periods appears on screen, as the boot loader loads NTOSKRNL.EXE and the hardware abstraction layer (HAL.DLL) into memory.

On RISC machines, OSLOADER.EXE handles everything through this step. It concludes its job by loading the appropriate version of NTOSKRNL.EXE and HAL.DLL for the CPU in use.

The remaining steps are identical whether the machine is a PC clone or a RISC computer.

9. **Initializing the kernel**

When the PC's screen turns blue and displays a message like the following

```
Microsoft (R) Windows NT (TM) Version 4.0 (Build 1381)
1 System Processor (64 MB Memory)
```

this indicates that the kernel has initialized properly and that it has taken control; at this point, Windows NT may be said to be running the computer. During kernel initialization, the following tasks are completed:

➤ Initializing low-level device drives loaded along with the kernel in the preceding step

➤ Loading and initializing other device drivers, as needed

➤ Running diagnostic or setup programs, such as CHKDSK, before loading services

➤ Loading and initializing all services identified with automatic startup in the OS configuration

➤ Creating the paging file for temporary storage and swap space

➤ Starting all subsystems needed for Windows NT (such as the Win32 subsystem, security subsystem, and possibly the OS/2 or POSIX subsystems)

10. **Logging on**

When kernel initialization is complete, the Begin Logon dialog box appears (this contains the message "Press Ctrl+Alt+Delete to log on"). Once a successful logon occurs, Windows writes the values in the Registry to a special backup file that will provide the data needed to invoke the Last Known Good Configuration boot option the next time the machine starts up (a successful login is required to make this change, since numerous Registry values will not be updated until the first actual logon occurs).

The Windows NT Boot Components

The most important components of the Windows NT boot process are worth memorizing:

➤ **BOOT.INI** This is the PC information file that describes Windows NT boot defaults, plus operating system locations, settings, and menu selections. This file resides in the root directory of the system partition.

➤ **BOOTSECT.DOS** This MS-DOS boot sector file is used if NTLDR offers the option to boot to some other Microsoft (or near-equivalent) operating system such as DOS or Windows 95. This file resides in the root directory of the system partition.

➤ **NTDETECT.COM** This is the PC hardware detection program that gathers equipment and configuration information prior to booting Windows NT (to make sure the stored configuration agrees with the detected one). This file resides in the root directory of the system partition.

➤ **NTLDR** This is the PC operating system loader program, which can load Windows NT, or another designated operating system, and then relinquish control once the loading is complete. This file resides in the root directory of the system partition.

> **NTOSKRNL.EXE** This is the executable file for the Windows NT operating system that includes all the basic capabilities and components necessary to establish a working runtime environment. This file resides in the \Winnt_root\system32 directory on the boot partition.

> **OSLOADER.EXE** This is the OS loader program for RISC computers, which provides all of the services and information provided by BOOTSECT.DOS, NTDETECT.COM, and NTLDR on PCs. This file resides in a nonvolatile memory area that's always available when the machine boots.

 There's one other PC-based Windows NT boot file that sometimes crops up in test questions. It is named NTBOOTDD.SYS, and must be present when a SCSI drive, with its onboard BIOS disabled, is used either as the system partition or the boot partition on a Windows NT system. This file replaces the functions that the onboard BIOS would normally provide with a software-based driver. Like the other boot files, NTBOOTDD.SYS resides in the root directory of the system partition.

ARC Names And Attached Hard Drives

To fully understand the ins and outs of the BOOT.INI file that drives much of NTLDR's behavior during the Windows NT boot process, it is essential to understand what Microsoft calls Advanced RISC Computer (ARC) names (and sometimes, ARC pathnames). ARC represents a common naming convention used within disk controller software to specify the unique combination of disk controller, disk drive, and disk partition that identifies the boot partitions for Windows NT. These names appear in the BOOT.INI file and must sometimes be edited by hand, particularly when recovering from failure of the primary member of a mirrored or duplexed drive pair.

ARC names not only provide a method to specify the type and location of the disk controllers, drives, and partitions in use, but also include pointers to files and directories. Such names typically take one of two forms:

```
scsi(0)disk(0)rdisk(0)partition(1)\path
multi(0)disk(0)rdisk(0)partition(1)\path
```

Here's a breakdown of the terms involved:

➤ **scsi(*) or multi(*)** Normally, most ARC names will begin with multi(*); scsi(*) appears only when a SCSI controller with its onboard BIOS disabled is in use. Multi(*) is used for other hard disks of all kinds, including IDE, EIDE, ESDI, and SCSI (where the onboard BIOS is enabled, as is most often the case). The (*) indicates the address of the hardware adapter from which to boot, numbered ordinally, beginning with zero. Controller numbers begin at zero, starting with the controller that is seated closest to slot 0 on the PC's motherboard.

➤ **disk(*)** Applies only to SCSI devices that do not use BIOS translation. If the drive is SCSI without BIOS translation, it takes the logical unit number (LUN) that the device is set for. If the drive is non-SCSI or SCSI with BIOS translation, the value will always be zero.

➤ **rdisk(*)** Applies to all drives except SCSI drives with BIOS translation disabled. Numbering begins with zero, so the first drive in the chain is named rdisk (Ø), the second rdisk (1), and so forth. If the drive is SCSI without BIOS translation, the rdisk setting will always be zero.

➤ **partition(*)** This portion of the name indicates the disk partition that contains the designated files. Unlike the other numbering schemes in ARC names, partition numbers begin with one, so that the first partition is partition(1), the second partition(2), and so on.

Please note that for PCs, a maximum of four partitions per drive is allowed. But one of those partitions can be something called an *extended partition*, which simply means that more than one logical drive can be created within that partition. The other three (or four, if no extended partition exists) are called primary partitions and can have only one logical drive per partition.

Here are two important things to remember about primary and extended partitions: (1) only a primary partition can be a system partition (where boot files reside and initial boot phases occur), but Windows NT system files (the boot partition) can reside on a logical drive within an extended partition; and (2) on a drive with primary and extended partitions, the extended partition is always numbered the highest. If a test question indicates that NT files reside on an extended partition and that a new primary has been defined, this means the partition number for the extended partition increases by one as a result of that new definition.

➤ **\path** Indicates the directory (or subdirectory) on the partition where the operating system files may be found. The default path for Windows NT is \winnt.

Working with ARC names requires understanding the rules by which they're to be applied or interpreted. Remember that scsi(*) appears only for SCSI controllers with their onboard BIOSs disabled, and that numbering for scsi(*), multi(*), disk(*), and rdisk(*) starts with zero, but that numbering for partition(*) starts with one. Remember also that when multi(*) appears, disk(0) is the only valid value, and that when scsi(*) appears, rdisk(0) is likewise the only valid value. These three rules, properly applied, will see you through the ARC name questions.

Managing The BOOT.INI File

You can make changes to BOOT.INI from the Control Panel, using a text editor. In case problems occur as a result of these changes, always make a backup copy of the file to a floppy to keep around. Here's an exhibit of a typical BOOT.INI file (sans most of the many possible bells and whistles):

```
[boot loader]
timeout=30
default=multi(0)disk(0)rdisk(0)partition(3)\WINNT
[operating systems]
multi(0)disk(0)rdisk(0)partition(3)\WINNT="Windows
NT Server Version 4.00"
multi(0)disk(0)rdisk(0)partition(3)\WINNT="Windows
NT Server Version 4.00 [VGA mode]" /basevideo /sos
C:\ = "MS-DOS"
```

Note that this file is divided into two sections, labeled [boot loader] and [operating systems]. The [boot loader] section supplies the timeout interval after which the default operating system to load (defined in the following default= line) will load automatically. The [operating systems] section supplies the complete menu of operating system choices that NTLDR displays right after the program loads. You can disable the timer before it elapses by striking any arrow or letter key on the keyboard. Then, you can wait as long as you like to make your menu selection.

Using The Control Panel

Using the System applet Control Panel to change BOOT.INI is definitely the safest method, but it doesn't expose everything you may sometimes need to access. The System applet includes a Startup/Shutdown tab that permits you to choose a default boot selection, and to set the interval for the delay before the default boot selection is automatically invoked. This delay time corresponds to the timeout value in the [boot loader] section of the file shown previously. Also, the value assigned to the default= statement in that section defines the ARC name for the default OS to be loaded.

Using A Text Editor

BOOT.INI is a plain, pure-ASCII file that should be edited with a plain text editor like Notepad or some other equivalent program. As with any initialization file, be careful when editing. Anything between quotation marks in the [operating systems] section of the file is fair game, but it is vital to be careful if you must edit an ARC name by hand. If you configure the BOOT.INI file incorrectly, Windows NT may not boot. That's why you should always create an Emergency Repair Disk before making any changes to BOOT.INI, and be sure to have a set of Windows NT boot disks on hand.

BOOT.INI has the following DOS attributes: read-only, system, and hidden. You will need to turn off the read-only attribute to make changes to the file, and you'll probably want to turn off the hidden attribute as well. It's necessary to restore the file to read-only after editing, so be sure to remember this step before you try to reboot.

Troubleshooting The Windows NT Boot Process

There are lots of ways that things can break down and interfere with the Windows NT Boot process. Here, we recount those problems—and their fixes—that you're most likely to encounter when dealing with boot problems. While you're troubleshooting, remember that hardware problems are always possible (if vexing and unpleasant), and that sometimes the computer won't boot because a component has failed, not because of the kinds of software and configuration difficulties we recount here.

That's why our first step with a PC that won't boot Windows NT is to insert a DOS boot disk. If the machine will boot DOS, it's pretty easy to run DOS-based diagnostics to check out the hardware. This eliminates many of the potential avenues for problems from further consideration. Our next step is to boot the system from a set of Windows NT boot floppies—if that works, it illustrates that the machine itself will still boot Windows NT, no matter how badly the current configuration may be mangled or disturbed.

The next step is to try to boot using the Last Known Good Configuration boot option. If this works, it indicates the problem lies in changes made to the system since the last time it booted successfully. This should narrow the field considerably, and let you focus on the most likely causes of problems. If you can't get to this point, you'll have to get the hardware working before you can proceed any further.

Common Boot-Related Problems, Causes, And Fixes

Here's a litany of potential woes, with possible causes, and definite fixes.

I/O Error Accessing Boot Sector File

These types of errors can occur when a power failure or fluctuation interrupts file system activity or software installation. Sometimes, these errors occur when installing another operating system over an existing Windows NT installation. The symptom will be some kind of BIOS-level error message from the computer that indicates that the boot sectors are damaged or that the drive is unavailable. The only way to repair this problem is to boot the PC from a DOS floppy, and run the FDISK/MBR command to rebuild the MBR.

Corrupted Partition Tables

This generally won't happen unless you attempt to use some operating system other than Windows NT, or other operating systems incompatible with the IBM/Microsoft partitioning scheme, to create or manipulate partitions on a drive. For obvious reasons, Unix can be a culprit here. If this happens, a backup is your best bet—you'll have to reformat the drive, reestablish the partitions, and then restore the data. If no data was written to the drives following their partition changes, it may be possible to restore the partition table to its prior state and attempt to carry on from there. But this can be an unbelievable exercise in frustration.

BOOT: Couldn't Find NTLDR

When this error message appears, it indicates that NTLDR is corrupt or missing. This may sometimes pop up if the wrong partition has been made active in Disk Administrator, but is usually remedied by copying a good copy of NTLDR onto the root of the errant drive.

NTDETECT V1.0 Checking Hardware...

If this message appears repeatedly on your PC, it means that NTDETECT.COM is corrupted or missing. In most cases, a fresh copy of the program onto the root of the errant system partition will do the trick.

Windows NT Could Not Start Because The Following File Is Missing Or Corrupt: \<winnt root>\system32\ntoskrnl.exe

This may indicate any number of problems, but it generally means that NTLDR couldn't find the NT operating system kernel file needed to complete the OS load. The most frequent cause of this problem is that allocation of free space on a Windows NT drive results in a change to the partition number for the boot partition where the Windows NT system files reside. Proper assignment of the partition number for the boot partition will usually fix this problem.

Could Not Read From The Selected Boot Disk...

This is your clue that something is amiss with the boot partition. It could be that there is a missing or malfunctioning drive (unlikely, but possible). Otherwise, it might be that the disk partition specified in an ARC name does not contain a file system that's recognizable to the NTLDR program. In that case you'll want to check to see if partition allocations have changed lately, or if someone has been tinkering with BOOT.INI. Restoring the malfunctioning drive or correcting the ARC name should fix the problem.

STOP: 0x000007E: Inaccessible Boot Device

A STOP error is as fatal as it gets; Windows NT won't go any further until you fix the problem. This error occurs most frequently when a SCSI controller that fails to adhere completely to the SCSI standard is installed in a Windows NT machine. It can also occur if you add a SCSI controller to an NT machine that boots from an IDE hard disk: In that case, make sure that no SCSI device is set to SCSI ID 0 (or otherwise disable booting from the SCSI drive(s)). This prevents the SCSI controller from attempting to boot the disk, and will also stop NTDETECT.COM from assigning the SCSI adapter a bus number equal to zero, which may cause BOOT.INI to point to the wrong partition.

Exam Prep Questions

Question 1

> A Windows NT Server PC is configured with two 2.2 GB EIDE hard drives, with both drives attached to a controller built into the motherboard. Each disk contains a single primary partition; the Windows NT system files reside on Disk 1, and the boot files reside on Disk 2. Which of the following ARC names correctly identifies the system disk?
>
> ○ a. multi(1)disk(1)rdisk(0)partition(0)
>
> ○ b. multi(0)disk(1)rdisk(0)partition(1)
>
> ○ c. multi(0)disk(0)rdisk(0)partition(0)
>
> ○ d. multi(1)disk(0)rdisk(0)partition(0)
>
> ○ e. multi(0)disk(0)rdisk(1)partition(1)

The options for the first element in an ARC name are either scsi or multi, but scsi applies only to a genuine SCSI drive whose onboard BIOS has been disabled. Since multi(*) appears at the start of all five choices, all of them are correct to that point. The number that follows multi within the parentheses is the ordinal number of the disk controller to which the drive (or drives) is attached. Ordinal numbers start with 0. There is only one controller mentioned in the question, which immediately rules out answers a and d because they allude to a second controller (as denoted by multi(1)) to which neither drive in the preceding question is attached.

The disk(*) element in an ARC name designates the SCSI bus number for a SCSI drive with its BIOS disabled, and is always zero for a non-SCSI disk. This eliminates answer b from further consideration.

The rdisk(*) element in an ARC name indicates the SCSI logical unit number (LUN) or the drive that contains the operating system. rdisk(*) is always set to zero when an ARC name starts with "scsi". Because this one starts with "multi", it indicates the position in the order in which drives are attached to the controller. Further, the question indicates that the NT system files are on the first disk, and boot files on the second disk. Knowing that rdisk numbers begin with zero, this means that the NT system files live on the drive named multi(0)disk(0)rdisk(0) partition(1), and that the boot files live on the drive named multi(0)disk(0)rdisk(1)partition(1).

One small trick to ARC names is that although scsi, multi, disk, and rdisk all number ordinally, starting with 0, partition numbers start with 1. Thus, any valid ARC name will not ever have zero as a value for partition(*). Because each of the partitions mentioned in this question is the one and only on its drive, it must be partition(1).

Here's the real trick in this question: Boot files reside on the system partition on an NT Server. This means that the correct answer is the ARC name for the drive that contains the boot files, or answer e. Note that the correct ARC name for the first disk, where the Windows NT system files reside, does not appear as an option in the list of answers on the question.

Question 2

Jane has just installed a new device driver for her UPS on her Windows NT Server, and now the machine will not boot properly. What is the easiest way to get the system to boot, so that the driver problem can be fixed?

○ a. Add the /NoSerialMice option to the BOOT.INI file.

○ b. Run the emergency repair process to restore the Windows NT Registry.

○ c. Boot Windows NT from the Emergency Repair Disk (ERD).

○ d. Select the Last Known Good Configuration option when it appears during the next reboot.

First, we dispense with a couple of red herrings: Answer a has nothing to do with getting an unbootable Windows NT machine running for trouble-shooting purposes (even if it may be the fix that's finally enacted for a UPS that resets a PC when its serial port is probed). And because it's impossible to boot from the ERD, answer c is completely bogus.

Answer b sounds tempting, but it raises interesting questions about how the emergency repair process knows what to fix in the Registry and how it can change the behavior of possibly damaged or mismatched driver software. Answer b, too, is bogus.

Answer d is the only option that really makes sense, because it reverts the Windows NT Server to the working configuration that held the last time it booted successfully. Since this cheerfully ignores anything changed since then—such as the errant UPS driver that may (or may not) be causing the problem—it brings the Server back up so that Jane can try again from a relatively pristine state.

Question 3

> Which ARC name listed below correctly identifies that Windows NT boot files reside on the fourth partition on a SCSI disk drive whose onboard BIOS is disabled, with a SCSI Bus ID of 1 on the first SCSI controller on the Server machine?
>
> ○ a. scsi(0)disk(0)rdisk(0)partition(3)
>
> ○ b. scsi(0)disk(1)rdisk(0)partition(4)
>
> ○ c. scsi(0)disk(1)rdisk(1)partition(4)
>
> ○ d. multi(0)disk(0)rdisk(0)partition(4)

The secret to answering this question lies in knowing how to "unpack" its contents, and what values to assign based on the information it contains. Partitions are numbered ordinally, starting from one, so any correct answer must end in partition(4). This automatically disqualifies answer a.

Any SCSI hard disk with its onboard BIOS disabled must begin with the string scsi(*). This automatically disqualifies answer d. Likewise, if the scsi keyword begins an ARC name, the value for rdisk will always be zero; this disqualifies answer c.

By process of elimination, this means that b must be the right answer. By unpacking the question, we discover that:

➤ The first SCSI controller with BIOS disabled translates into scsi(0).

➤ The SCSI Bus ID provides the value for disk(*), whenever the BIOS is disabled, which translates into disk(1).

➤ Because the BIOS is disabled, rdisk(*) is always rdisk(0).

➤ The value for partition equals its number on the drive, so partition(*) translates into partition(4).

Once again, only b matches the entire string.

Question 4

> XYZ Corp.'s newest Windows NT Server uses disk mirroring for its system partition. What is the best way to create an emergency boot disk that points to the mirror partition to permit the Server to boot should the primary partition fail?
>
> ○ a. Choose Emergency Repair Disk from the Fault Tolerance menu in Disk Administrator.
>
> ○ b. Format a blank floppy using the server. Copy NTLDR, NTDETECT.COM, and BOOT.INI from the system partition to the floppy. Manually edit BOOT.INI to specify the ARC pathname for the mirror partition.
>
> ○ c. Choose Emergency Repair Disk from the Tools menu in Disk Administrator.
>
> ○ d. In the System applet in Control Panel, choose the Recovery tab, and check the Create Emergency Repair Disk option.

A strong working foundation with Windows NT makes this question trivial. The only way to boot from the mirror partition on a Windows NT Server is for the boot process to point at the controller, drive, and partition where the boot files reside. This only can be done by hand, because none of the administrative utilities mentioned in the preceding answers know how to construct such an emergency boot disk automatically. This means that answers a, c, and d are completely fanciful (and reflect nonexistent options in all three cases), and that only answer b is correct.

Question 5

> Both system and boot partitions are not working on the PDC, but disk mirroring means that the mirror may still be intact. How should you modify the BOOT.INI file on an emergency boot floppy to boot the system from the mirrored copy? [Check all correct answers]
>
> ❑ a. Do nothing; the BOOT.INI file will handle this automatically.
>
> ❑ b. Modify the ARC name specifications in the [operating systems] section of the file.
>
> ❑ c. Modify the ARC name specification in the default= line of the [boot loader] section of the file.
>
> ❑ d. Add an /m switch to the appropriate lines in the [operating systems] section of the file.

Windows NT boots from the ARC name specified in the [operating system] section of the BOOT.INI file if a deliberate OS selection is made, but most commonly, it boots from the default line in the [boot loader] section. Therefore, changes to the ARC names in both parts of BOOT.INI will be required; as we've already explained, these changes must be entered by hand to point to the mirror copy in a mirrored set of drives. Thus, answers b and c are correct.

Answer a is false because BOOT.INI does not handle mirrored sets automatically. Answer d is false because there is no /m switch defined among the available Windows NT boot options.

Question 6

> When the System Administrator at XYZ Corp. tries to boot into
> DOS on a dual-boot Windows NT machine, she gets an error mes-
> sage that reads:
>
> ```
> I/O Error accessing boot sector file
> multi(0)disk(0)rdisk(0)partition(2):
> \bootsect.dos
> ```
>
> What is the most expedient way to fix this problem?
>
> ○ a. Boot from the Last Known Good Configuration.
>
> ○ b. Start the computer from the Windows NT boot disks and
>   copy BOOTSECT.DOS from another server.
>
> ○ c. Boot the computer from the Emergency Repair Disk and
>   follow the prompts.
>
> ○ d. Start the computer from the Windows NT boot disks and
>   insert the Emergency Repair Disk when prompted.

Here, full-blown repair is needed, because BOOTSECT.DOS stores partition information entirely specific to the computer where it is generated.
Any copy of this file from another machine is useless; this disqualifies
answer b. Since the machine won't boot completely, the Last Known Good
Configuration option never appears; this eliminates answer a. Because
the ERD is not bootable, answer c is bogus. This leaves only answer d,
where the NT boot disks permit the system to boot completely and the
ERD then can regenerate a new BOOTSECT.DOS.

Question 7

> On a Windows NT Server computer, there are two duplexed SCSI
> drives. The boot partition is on the drive that is connected to the
> primary SCSI controller, the mirror on the drive connected to the
> secondary SCSI controller. If the primary controller fails, how must
> you modify the BOOT.INI file so that the system will now boot
> from the mirror?
>
> ○ a. Change scsi(0) to scsi(1) on the appropriate lines.
>
> ○ b. Change scsi(1) to scsi(2) on the appropriate lines.
>
> ○ c. Change multi(0) to multi(1) on the appropriate lines.
>
> ○ d. Change multi(1) to multi(2) on the appropriate lines.

As with Question 3, the key is knowing how to "unpack" ARC names. Unless the BIOS is disabled on a SCSI controller, the initial keyword in an ARC name is always multi. Since there's no mention of BIOS in the question, this eliminates answers a and b immediately. The rest of the answer hinges on understanding that SCSI controllers are numbered ordinally, starting with zero. Since the primary must therefore be multi(0), this must change to multi(1); this makes c the only correct answer.

Question 8

XYZ Corp. has just added a new IDE hard drive and controller to a Windows NT Server. The machine continues to boot from its SCSI drive, which has its BIOS disabled. Each drive has only a single primary partition. Of the following options, which is the correct ARC name for the machine's boot partition?

○ a. scsi(0)disk(0)rdisk(0)partition(1)

○ b. scsi(0)disk(1)rdisk(0)partition(0)

○ c. scsi(1)disk(0)rdisk(0)partition(1)

○ d. scsi(1)disk(1)rdisk(0)partition(1)

○ e. scsi(0)disk(0)rdisk(1)partition(1)

Once again, a working knowledge of ARC name construction comes in handy. Because the drive in question is SCSI, but its onboard BIOS is disabled, the ARC name must begin with scsi(*). Because there is only one SCSI controller, and numbering begins with zero, it must begin with scsi(0); this disqualifies answers c and d immediately.

For ARC names that begin with scsi(*), only the disk(*) keyword is significant; in such cases rdisk(*) is always rdisk(0); this disqualifies answer e. Here again, disks are numbered by their SCSI bus number, starting with zero. By default, disk(0) is the correct value (since no replacement bus number was specified); this disqualifies answer b (and d).

By process of elimination, this leaves answer a, which may be constructed as follows:

➤ scsi(*) becomes scsi(0) because the BIOS is disabled, and it is the first and only SCSI controller.

➤ disk(*) becomes disk(0) because that's the default assignment and no overriding values were supplied.

➤ rdisk(*) must be rdisk(0) because the BIOS is disabled on a SCSI controller, and this value is therefore ignored.

➤ partition(*) becomes partition (1) because it is the first and only partition on the drive, and partition numbering begins with 1.

Question 9

After modifying the Registry, a Windows NT Server machine will no longer boot. What is the easiest way to get the machine to boot?

❍   a. Start the computer from the Windows NT boot disks and restore the Registry from a backup.

❍   b. Start the computer from the Windows NT boot disks and select the Emergency Repair option.

❍   c. Start the computer from the Emergency Repair Disk and follow the prompts.

❍   d. Choose the Last Known Good Configuration option when it appears during bootup.

The easiest approach to this kind of problem, be it caused by untoward edits to the Registry or installation of drivers or new system components, is to choose the Last Known Good Configuration option during bootup. Answers a and b may produce the same results eventually, but they're nowhere near as easy (and perhaps not as up-to-date as the Last Known Good Configuration). Answer c is flat wrong, because you can't boot from the ERD.

Question 10

> While booting a Windows NT Server, the following error message appears right after the Last Known Good Configuration prompt:
>
> ```
> Windows NT could not start because the follow-
> ing file is missing or corrupt:
>   \Winnt_root\system32\ntoskrnl.exe.
> Please reinstall a copy of the above file.
> ```
>
> You're certain that this file is present, even though the boot process cannot locate it. What's the most likely cause of this error message?
>
> ○ a. Missing NTLDR
>
> ○ b. Missing BOOTSECT.DOS
>
> ○ c. Missing NTDETECT.COM
>
> ○ d. Missing BOOT.INI

The most common cause of this error is setting an invalid partition as active in Disk Administrator—that is, one that does not include any of the requisite Windows NT boot files. When this happens, none of these files is actually present on the designated boot partition, but it's really the absence of BOOT.INI that makes the difference, because it's the file that indicates where the other files are located. Thus, the correct answer to this question is d. This message also will appear if the ARC name for the NTOSKRNL.EXE file is incorrect in BOOT.INI (which is sometimes specified as the default= entry in the [boot loader] section, and always in at least two entries in the [operating systems] section).

Question 11

> Which of the following files must appear in the system partition of
> an Intel PC-based Windows NT machine, if that machine uses one
> or more SCSI drives with their onboard BIOSs disabled?
> [Choose all correct answers]
>
> ❑ a. BOOT.INI
>
> ❑ b. NTLDR
>
> ❑ c. NTOSKRNL.EXE
>
> ❑ d. NTBOOTDD.SYS
>
> ❑ e. OSLOADER.EXE
>
> ❑ f. BOOTSECT.DOS

The files that always appear in the system partition on a PC running Windows NT are: BOOT.INI, NTDETECT.COM, and NTLDR. When a drive with its onboard BIOS disabled is used as the boot or system partition, an additional file, NTBOOTDD.SYS, also is required. Thus answers a, b, and d are correct. Answer e applies only to RISC machines (that is, non-Intel CPUs) running Windows NT; answer c names a file that appears in the default directory where the Windows NT system files reside (usually specified as winnt_root\system32, or as the common default: winnt\system32). Answer f applies only to a multiboot machine with DOS or Windows 95 as a bootable OS. Because it's not required for NT per se, it's not a correct answer to this question.

Question 12

> Of the choices listed below, what is the most likely cause of the
> following Windows NT error message at boot time?
>
> ```
> Boot: Couldn't find NTLDR
> Please insert another disk
> ```
>
> ○ a. An incorrect hard disk partition is set active.
>
> ○ b. NTLDR is missing or corrupt.
>
> ○ c. An unbootable floppy was left in the A: drive.
>
> ○ d. The designated system disk is damaged or inaccessible.

Trick!
question

The most common cause of this error message, by far, is powering down a Windows NT machine with a nonbootable floppy in the floppy drive. Because many PCs' BIOSs try to boot from any floppy inserted during bootup, this error occurs whenever you forget to remove a floppy before the machine is powered back up. Thus, answer c is by far the most likely. Answers a, b, and d are possible, but nowhere near as likely to provoke this error message. When you see it, look for (and remove) a floppy and try again.

Need To Know More?

 Heywood, Drew: *Inside Windows NT Server*. New Riders, Indianapolis, IN, 1995. ISBN 1-56205-472-4. Chapter 1 includes a useful overview section entitled, "Customizing the Boot Process" (pp. 66 through 72), covering most of the high points of this subject.

 Strebe, Matthew, Charles Perkins, and James Chellis: *MSCE: NT Server 4 Study Guide*. Sybex Network Press, San Francisco, CA, 1996. ISBN 0-7821-1972-7. The section of Chapter 17 that deals with boot issues, "Troubleshooting the Windows NT Boot Process" (pp. 634 through 638), provides some useful "if you get this error message, here's the likely cause" examples and fixes.

 Search the TechNet CD (or its online version through www.microsoft.com) using the keywords "Windows NT boot," "BOOT.INI" (or other important boot file names), and related topics. The Knowledge Base, in particular, contains lots of good troubleshooting tips and configuration details.

 The *Windows NT Server Resource Kit* is the most detailed of all available resources on boot-related topics. You can search the TechNet CD or the CD accompanying the *Resource Kit*, using the same keywords mentioned in the preceding paragraph. Useful boot-related information appears in the *Resource Guide* volume, especially on pages 83 through 113.

Troubleshooting

Terms you'll need to understand:

√ Troubleshooting

√ Boot failures

√ NTLDR

√ NTOSKRNL

√ BOOT.INI

√ BOOTSECT.DOS

√ NTDETECT.COM

√ Event Viewer

√ Last Known Good Configuration (LKGC)

√ Registry

√ Emergency Repair Disk (ERD)

√ Dr. Watson

√ Kernel debugger

Techniques you'll need to master:

√ Understanding the troubleshooting process

√ Troubleshooting media errors, domain controller communication difficulties, stop message errors or halt on blue screen, hardware problems, and dependency failures

√ Recognizing installation failures

√ Troubleshooting boot failures

√ Using NT's built-in repair tools

Troubleshooting a Windows NT-based network can be both extensive and difficult. There is much more troubleshooting material than we could ever sift down into a single chapter. So, we've focused on the troubleshooting issues that appear on the Microsoft certification test for NT Server.

The Troubleshooting Process

Troubleshooting is more often an art than a science. Thus, there is rarely a single action that will fix the same problem each time it occurs. However, you can streamline your problem-solving techniques with a few simple rules:

➤ Have patience.

➤ Understand your system.

➤ Attempt to isolate and repeat the fault.

➤ Suspect the most recent change or addition.

➤ Inspect the most common points of failure.

➤ Peruse your problem's history.

➤ Attempt easy fixes first.

➤ Let the problem guide your solution.

➤ Make a single alteration or fix at a time.

➤ Dissect a multisided problem into numerous single issues.

➤ Maintain a log of problems, attempts, and solutions.

Keep these troubleshooting principles in mind as you read the sections that follow.

Installation Failures

Five common types of errors can occur during the initial installation of NT:

➤ Media errors

➤ Domain controller communication difficulties

➤ Stop message errors or halt on blue screen

> Hardware problems
> Dependency failures

Media errors are problems with the distribution CD-ROM itself, the copy of the CD-ROM hosted on a network drive, or the communication between the installation and the distribution files. The only ways to resolve media errors are to attempt to switch media, such as from one server's CD-ROM to another, or to copy the CD-ROM files to a network drive. If media errors are encountered, always start the installation process over from the beginning.

Not being able to communicate with the existing domain controller prevents the current installation from joining the domain. This is especially a problem when installing a BDC. This is often due to a mistyped name, a network failure, or the domain controller being offline. Verify the viability of the domain controller directly and with other workstations (if present).

Stop messages and halting on the blue screen during installation are usually caused by the wrong driver for a controller card. If any information is presented to you about the error, try to determine if the proper driver is installed. If not or if you can't tell, double-check your hardware and the drivers required to operate them under NT.

Hardware problems should occur only if you failed to verify with the HCL (Hardware Computability List) or a physical defect has surfaced in previously operational devices. In such cases, replacing the device is the only solution. However, it is not uncommon for a device to be improperly configured or installed. Always double-check the setup of your hardware before purchasing a replacement. One common error is the failure of the NT setup to recognize a second SCSI drive during initial setup. In such cases, select the S option when prompted to identify additional devices before continuing with the installation, or use the Devices applet to add them after the installation is complete.

Dependency failures occur when one or more dependent services fail due to the absence of an underlying service, hardware, or driver. An example of a dependency failure is when server and workstation services fail because the NIC fails to initialize properly. If NT boots with such errors, check the Event Log.

Boot Failures

Boot failures are problems during the startup of NT after a successful installation has completed. Some of the more common boot failures are covered in the sections that follow.

NTLDR Error Message

If a floppy is in Drive a: or if the NTLDR executable is missing, this error message will be displayed:

```
BOOT: Couldn't find NTLDR. Please insert another disk.
```

If there is a floppy in the drive, eject it and continue the boot process. If the NTLDR is damaged or missing, you must use the Emergency Repair Disk (ERD) to repair or replace it (this process is explained in detail later in this chapter).

NTOSKRNL Missing Error Message

If the NTOSKRNL (NT Operating System Kernel) is corrupt, missing, or the BOOT.INI points to the wrong partition, this error message will appear:

```
Windows NT could not start because the following file is missing
or corrupt:
\winnt root\system32\ntoskrnl.exe
Please re-install a copy of the above file.
```

This can be resolved by repairing the NTOSKRNL file using the ERD repair process. Or, if the BOOT.INI is wrong, by editing it and correcting the problem.

BOOT.INI Missing Error Message

If no BOOT.INI is present, the NTLDR will attempt to load NT from the default \winnt directory of the current partition. If this fails, an error message appears:

```
BOOT: Couldn't find NTLDR. Please insert another disk.
```

To alleviate this problem, replace the BOOT.INI file from a backup or use the ERD to repair.

BOOTSECT.DOS Missing Error Message

If the BOOTSECT.DOS file is not present to boot to MS-DOS or another operating system (not NT), an error message appears:

```
I/O Error accessing boot sector file
multi(0)disk(0)rdisk(0)partition(1):\bootsect.dos
```

This indicates that the BOOT.INI file has been changed, the partition numbering has changed, or the partition is missing, inactive, or inaccessible. To attempt repair/replace of the BOOTSECT.DOS file, use the ERD repair procedure.

NTDETECT.COM Missing Error Message

If the NTDETECT.COM file is not present, an error message appears:

```
NTDETECT V1.0 Checking Hardware...
NTDETECT failed
```

This error must be repaired with the ERD repair process.

Repair Tools

Fortunately, NT does not leave you high and dry when you encounter errors. A handful of valuable tools can be used to repair and correct operational difficulties. These tools are examined in detail in the sections that follow.

Event Viewer

The Event Viewer, located in Start|Programs|Administrative Tools, is used to inspect the three logs automatically created by NT. These logs are:

➤ **System** Records information and alerts about NT's internal processes.

➤ **Security** Records security-related events.

➤ **Application** Records NT application events, alerts, and system messages.

Each log records a different type of information, but all collect the same information about each event: date, time, source, category, event, user ID, and computer. Plus, each event recorded has at worst an error code number or at best a detailed description with a memory HEX buffer capture.

Most system errors, including stop errors that result in the blue screen, are recorded in the System log. This allows you to review the time and circumstances around a system failure.

Last Known Good Configuration

The Last Known Good Configuration (LKGC) is a recording made by NT of all the Registry settings that existed the last time a user successfully logged in to the server. Every time a login completes, NT records a new LKGC. If a system error occurs or the Registry becomes corrupted so that booting or logging in is not possible, the LKGC can be used to return to a previously operational state. The LKGC is accessed during bootup when this message displays: "Press the spacebar now to boot with the Last Known Good Configuration." A menu then appears where you can select to load using the LKGC (by pressing L) or other stored configurations.

The Registry

Editing the Registry by hand should be the last resort, only to be attempted when all other possible avenues of repair have been exhausted. A single improperly configured Registry entry can render an installation of NT DOA. There are two Registry editing utilities—REGEDIT and REGEDT32. Both of these must be launched from the Run command or a DOS prompt. REGEDIT displays all five hives of the Registry in a single display window, and the entire Registry can be searched at one time. REGEDT32 displays each of the five hives in a separate display window, but it offers more security and control related functions.

It is a good idea to regularly back up your Registry. This can be done using:

➤ NTBACKUP

➤ Disk Administrator (SYSTEM key only)

➤ Either of the Registry editing tools (REGEDIT or REGEDT32)

➤ The REGBACK utility from the Resource Kit

The best times to make a backup are just before and just after any significant change to your system, such as hardware installation, software installation, or service pack application. If NT fails to operate properly but does boot, you can attempt a repair by restoring the Registry from a backup.

There are a few things you should note about working with the Registry. When you edit the Registry, you are working with it in memory, so changes will go into effect as soon as they are made. However, in some cases a reboot is required to correct memory settings and launched applications to fully comply with the changes. It is always a good idea to reboot after editing the Registry. Also, when a key of the Registry is saved (or backed up), you capture all of the subcontents of that key. This is important to remember when restoring portions of the Registry from backup. All of the subkeys below the point at which restoration occurs also will be overwritten by the saved version. Any and all changes made since the backup will be lost in the restored sections.

Emergency Repair Disk

The ERD is the miniature first aid kit for NT. This single floppy contains all the files needed to repair the system partition and many boot partition-related problems. The ERD is most often used to repair or replace files that are critical to the boot process of NT. An ERD usually is created during the installation of NT, but additional and updated ERDs can be created using the RDISK.EXE utility. At the Run command, RDISK /S forces NT to save to disk all current Registry settings in memory to \Winnt\System32 \Config, followed by a prompt for a preformatted disk. The ERD contains the following files:

➤ SYSTEM. _HKEY_LOCAL_MACHINE\SYSTEM compressed

➤ SOFTWARE._HKEY_LOCAL_MACHINE\SOFTWARE compressed

➤ SECURITY._HKEY_LOCAL_MACHINE\SECURITY compressed

➤ SAM. _HKEY_LOCAL_MACHINE\SAM compressed

➤ NTUSER.DA_Default profile, compressed

➤ AUTOEXEC.NT %winntroot%\system32\autoexec.nt

➤ CONFIG.NT %winntroot%\system32\config.nt

➤ SETUP.LOG a list of installed files and their checksums

➤ DEFAULT. _KHET_USERS\DEFAULT compressed

The ERD does not contain the entire Registry, but just enough to fix the most common errors.

To use the ERD to make repairs, you need the three setup floppies that are used to install NT. The repair process is as follows:

1. Reboot the computer using Windows NT Setup disks 1 and 2.

2. Select R for Repair. A menu appears containing the following options:

   ➤ Inspect Registry files

   ➤ Inspect startup environment

   ➤ Verify Windows NT system files

   ➤ Inspect boot sector

3. Deselect any items you do not wish to perform, then press Continue.

4. Insert disk 3 and the ERD when prompted.

Reinstalling Windows NT

If you have tried every troubleshooting path you can think of, consider reinstalling Windows NT. Multiple configuration problems can be corrected at once by reinstallation. However, reinstallation can cause new problems. All existing applications may need to be reinstalled and reconfigured. Most configuration and setup changes made to NT will be lost, including installation of specialized drivers, additional services, and protocols.

There are two types of reinstallation possible with NT: full and upgrade. A full reinstallation overwrites everything, just as if NT was installed on a new system for the first time. No data from the previous configuration is saved, not even the Security ID (SID). Thus, a full reinstall causes the computer to have a new identity within the domain.

An upgrade reinstall retains most of the configuration of the current installation, while repairing and restoring areas of NT that are damaged. An upgrade reinstall also retains the SID so the machine will not change identities. It is recommended to use an upgrade install to repair a PDC or BDC before attempting a full reinstall.

Remember, no matter what type of reinstall is performed, always protect mission-critical files by performing a backup before reinstalling the NOS. The reinstallation process does not guarantee the integrity of any data residing on the system.

Printing Solutions

When working with printers, there seem to be an infinite number of issues to resolve before normal operation is restored. Many printer problems are either simple or obvious, so take these measures before moving on to the more complicated solutions:

> ➤ Always check the physical aspects of the printer—cable, power, paper, toner, etc.

> ➤ Check the logical printer on both the client and server.

> ➤ Check the print queue for stalled jobs.

> ➤ Make sure the printer driver has not become corrupted by reinstalling it.

> ➤ Attempt to print from a different application or a different client.

> ➤ Print using Administrator access.

> ➤ Stop and restart the spooler using the Services applet.

> ➤ Check the status and CPU usage of the SPOOLSS.EXE using the Task Manager.

➤ Check the free space on the drive hosting the spooler file, and change its destination.

For additional information on print troubleshooting, see Chapter 8.

Remote Access Service

There are many things that can go wrong with RAS—everything from the configuration of the computers on both ends, to the modem settings, to the condition of the communications line. There is no ultimate RAS trouble-shooting guide, but here are some solid steps in the right direction:

➤ Check all physical connections.

➤ Check the communication line itself, with a phone if appropriate.

➤ Verify the RAS installation, the port configurations, and the modem setup.

➤ Check that both the client and the server dialup configurations match— including speed, protocol, and security.

➤ Verify that the user account has RAS privileges.

➤ Inspect the RAS-related logs—DEVICE.LOG and MODEMLOG. TXT (see Chapter 10).

The key to troubleshooting RAS is knowing the possible configuration options available to you. Most RAS problems are related to configuration (unless there is damage to the communication line)—either something was set incorrectly or someone made an alteration.

Miscellaneous

The following sections cover a handful of great troubleshooting topics that just don't fit well into any of the other sections.

Permissions Problems

If a permissions problem is suspected, perform the action using the Administrator account or temporarily add the user account to the Admin-istrators group. Double-check group memberships for conflicting access levels, especially No Access. Check the Access Control List (ACL) on the object in question for group and No Access assignments. Check the permissions on the share if appropriate. Check user, group, or computer policies for access restrictions. You may also attempt to take ownership to see if that changes the account's ability to access resources. Permission problems almost always are linked to multiple group memberships that include a No Access setting.

You should also remember that any changes made to a user's access permissions, especially those of group members, will not have an effect on that user until the next time they log on to the network. The Access Token used by the security system of NT is created at the time of logon and is not altered during a session. The only way to take advantage of new settings is to log off and log back on so the Access Token is re-created using the new data.

A related issue to permissions is that of logging in after an account has expired. Accounts expire after 11:59 PM on their expiration date. Once an account expires, that user is unable to establish any new network connections; however, he or she can continue to use any existing connections. Watch out for exam questions that indicate the time a login failure occurs—local or over RAS—even when everything else about the situation seems to indicate the problem should not be occurring.

UPS

A UPS (Uninterruptible Power Supply) can be configured to use a serial port to communicate with NT. This enables the UPS to inform NT when a power failure occurs and when to power down. There are numerous configurations possible for a UPS; most are dependent on the manufacturer, but all are controlled through the UPS applet.

Some of the most common problems with UPSs are:

➤ Failure to add the /NOSERIALMOUSE parameter to the BOOT.INI file to prevent NT from polling the UPS port for a mouse. This often causes the computer to power off, and thus, it never can boot.

➤ Failure to properly define the interface voltages for the control features. If the UPS sends a positive signal when NT expects a negative signal, NT will not respond. Once the battery in the UPS is drained, the computer will lose power and data in memory will be lost.

➤ Improper time settings for battery life and recharge time. Conservative numbers should be used to give a margin of error.

➤ Missing or wrong cable. UPS interfaces require a special UPS cable, not a standard RS-232 serial cable.

A UPS functions well if, and only if, NT is properly configured to understand its communications.

Re-creating The Setup Disks

If you need a new set of installation floppies, run the WINNT.EXE (or WINNT32.EXE) program from the installation CD with the /OX parameter. This creates the three floppies without initializing the actual installation process. However, you must preformat the disks beforehand.

Master Boot Record

If the Master Boot Record (MBR) fails on the system partition—the section of the disk that contains BOOT.INI, NTLOADER, and NTDETECT—the ERD will not help with its restoration. Instead, you'll need to use the first disk from DOS 6.0 (or higher). Executing FDISK /MBR re-creates the MBR and allows the system to boot.

Dr. Watson

Dr. Watson is NT's application error debugger. It detects application errors, diagnoses the errors, and logs the diagnostic information. Most of the information gathered by Dr. Watson is useful only when working with a Microsoft technical professional to diagnose an application error. Data captured by Dr. Watson is stored in the DRWTSN32.LOG log file. Dr. Watson also can be used to create a binary crash dump file of the memory where the failing application operates.

Dr. Watson launches itself automatically whenever an application error occurs. However, to configure Dr. Watson, you can launch it by executing DRWTSN32 at the command prompt or in the Run dialog box. The configuration options of Dr. Watson are fairly obvious. The only two that may cause some confusion are:

➤ **Dump Symbol Table** Adds the corresponding symbol data to the dump file, greatly increasing its size.

➤ **Dump All Thread Contexts** Forces a dump file to be created for all active threads, not just those owned by the failed application.

BOOT.INI Switches

To improve the troubleshooting abilities of the bootup, you can use one of the following switches after each OS line in the BOOT.INI file (remember, those are the ones with the ARC name followed by the displayable name in quotes):

➤ **/BASEVIDEO** Boots using the standard VGA video driver.

➤ **/BAUDRATE=**n Sets the debugging communication baud rate when using the Kernel Debugger. Default is 9600 for a modem and 19200 for a null-modem cable.

➤ **/CRASHDEBUG** Loads the debugger into memory. It remains inactive unless a Kernel error occurs.

➤ **/DEBUG** Loads the debugger into memory to be activated by a host debugger connected to the computer (see Kernel Debugger, under Advanced Troubleshooting later in this chapter.)

➤ **/DEBUGPORT=** COMx Sets the debugging COM port.

➤ **/MAXMEM:n** Sets the maximum amount of RAM that Windows NT can use.

➤ **/NODEBUG** No debugging information is being used.

➤ **/NOSERIALMICE=[**COMx | COMx,y,z...**]** Disables serial mouse detection of the specified COM port(s).

➤ **/SOS** Each driver name is displayed when it is loaded.

VGA Mode

If you set your video driver to something that prevents a readable display, you can select VGA Mode from the boot menu to boot with the standard VGA driver loaded. Then, you can modify the display drivers to correct the problem.

NTDETECT Debugged

If NTDETECT fails to detect the proper hardware, it may be corrupted or damaged, or your hardware may not be functioning properly. A debugged or checked version of NTDETECT is stored on the CD in the Support\Debug\I386 directory. First, rename NTDETECT.COM to NTDETECT.BAK, then copy the file named NTDETECT.CHK to the system partition and rename it to NTDETECT.COM. Then you can reboot; this version of NTDETECT will give a verbose display of all detection activities to help isolate the problem. NTDETECT.COM has the attributes of Hidden, System, and Read Only set. You need to deselect these attributes before renaming the file, and reset them after. Once you've solved the hardware detection problem, return the original NTDETECT from NTDETECT.BAK or an ERD.

ESDI Hard Drives

Some ESDI hard drives are not supported by NT. ESDI are pre-IDE type storage devices that have the ability of being low-level formatted with varying numbers of sectors per track. Due to special formatting geometry and drive controllers, NT may be able to access cylinders beyond 1,024. If NT has direct access to the cylinders above 1,024, only NT—not DOS—can access these areas. If the controller can handle the translation so that it is transparent, both NT and DOS can access cylinder areas above 1,023.

The determination of whether NT can even use an ESDI disk cannot be made until an installation is attempted. If NT fails to install properly on an ESDI disk, after NTLDR starts, a Fatal System Error:0x0000006b message will be displayed. When this occurs, you can deduce that the ESDI drive is not supported by NT.

Advanced Troubleshooting

In addition to the tools and utilities listed previously in this chapter, there are three more troubleshooting mechanisms that require a professional support engineer to interpret. We list them here only for your general understanding.

Blue Screen

No matter what "they" tell you, NT has General Protection Faults (GPFs), but they aren't called that. When a GPF occurs under NT, the "blue screen of death" appears. This is a test display of the stop message error. There are lots of details included on this screen, such as the location of the error, type of error, and whether or not a memory dump is created. Unfortunately, most of the data is in hex or a strange acronym shorthand that you won't be able to read.

Kernel Debugger

The Kernel Debugger records the activity of NT during bootup and when a stop error occurs. To employ the Kernel Debugger, two computers with the same version of NT connected by a null-modem cable or RAS must be used. One is designated as the host, the other the target. The host machine must have the symbol files installed from the NT CD-ROM (or the version associated with the installed Service Pack). The debugging software is located on the CD in the \support\debug\platform directory. This must be copied onto the host machine as well.

Memory Dump

A memory dump is the act of writing the entire contents of memory to a file when a stop error occurs. The contents of this file can be inspected to determine the cause of the failure. Memory dumps are configured on the Startup/Shutdown tab of the System applet. The options are:

➤ Write the error even to the System log

➤ Send an Administrative alert

➤ Write a dump file

➤ Automatically reboot

The default location and name of the memory dump file on a Windows NT server is %winntroot%\ Memory.dmp. The DUMPEXAM.EXE utility can be used to view the contents of a memory dump file; however, most of the contents require a Microsoft technical professional to interpret.

Exam Prep Questions

Question 1

> Which of the following can be corrected by the repair process using the three installation disks and a recent Emergency Repair Disk? [Check all correct answers]
>
> ❏ a. Boot sector corruption
>
> ❏ b. Inability to locate Master Boot Record
>
> ❏ c. NTLDR not found
>
> ❏ d. Corrupt NTOSKRNL

The ERD repair process often can correct boot sector problems, replace the NTLDR, and repair the NTOSKRNL; therefore, answers a, c, and d are correct. The MBR cannot be repaired with the ERD or the installation floppies—that requires a DOS setup disk. Therefore, answer b is incorrect.

Question 2

> A UPS is attached to your NT Server. You have configured NT's UPS utility to wait five seconds before sending an initial warning message after a power failure. The UPS is fully charged and has five minutes of battery life. You are using the correct UPS cable to attach the device to the serial port of the NT machine. To test your setup, you unplug the device from the wall. No warning message ever appears and the computer loses power after five minutes. Why?
>
> ○ a. The Expected Battery Life setting is less than the actual battery life of the UPS.
>
> ○ b. The UPS Interface Voltage for the power failure signal is set incorrectly.
>
> ○ c. The UPS service was not installed through the Network applet.
>
> ○ d. The Delay Between Warning Message setting is greater than 300 seconds (five minutes).

If the Expected Battery Life setting was less than the actual battery life of the UPS, the computer would power down before the UPS ran out of juice. In this situation, the computer never understood the communications from the UPS; therefore, answer a is incorrect. The UPS Interface Voltage for the power failure signal is set incorrectly: If the UPS sends a positive signal when NT is expecting a negative signal, NT will not respond, because it won't understand the communication from the UPS. Answer b, therefore, is correct. There is no UPS service to install: The UPS applet is a default utility of NT, so answer c is incorrect. The Delay Between Warning Message setting cannot be greater than 300 seconds (five minutes), because the situation stated it was set to five seconds. Therefore, answer d is incorrect.

Question 3

Which two parameter switches are present by default on the VGA Mode selection ARC name line in the BOOT.INI file? [Check two answers]

❑　a. /NODEBUG

❑　b. /BASEVIDEO

❑　c. /NOSERIALMICE

❑　d. /SOS

❑　e. /VGAVIDEO

/NODEBUG and /NOSERIALMICE are not present on the VGA Mode line by default; therefore, answers a and c are incorrect. /BASEVIDEO and /SOS are present on the VGA Mode line by default; therefore, answers b and d are correct. /VGAVIDEO is not a valid parameter; therefore, answer e is incorrect.

Question 4

> The SYSTEM Registry key contains errors. You do not have a re-
> cent ERD, but you do have a floppy copy of the SYSTEM key itself.
> Which of the following programs should you use to restore the
> SYSTEM key from the floppy?
>
> O   a. Disk Administrator
>
> O   b. System applet
>
> O   c. Network Client Administrator
>
> O   d. Server Manager

The Disk Administrator is the correct utility to use to restore the SYS-
TEM key if you have a stored copy, so answer a is correct. The other three
utilities do not offer Registry restoration options; therefore, answers b, c,
and d are incorrect.

Question 5

> Your NT Server has been experiencing numerous stop errors
> recently. Where should you configure NT so that a memory
> dump will occur before the system reboots to help pinpoint
> the problem?
>
> O   a. The server properties within Server Manager
>
> O   b. The recovery option in Dr. Watson
>
> O   c. The tracking tab of the Task Manager
>
> O   d. On the Startup/Shutdown tab of the System applet

The Server Manager does not offer memory dump configuration options,
so answer a is incorrect. Dr. Watson is used to perform memory dumps on
application faults, not for NT Server itself; therefore, answer b is incorrect.
The Task Manager does not have a tracking tab nor does it offer memory
dump options; this means that answer c also is incorrect. The Startup/Shut-
down tab of the System applet is the location of the memory dump options
for NT, so answer d is correct.

Question 6

> After installing a new SCSI driver, NT will not boot successfully. No other changes have been made to the system. What is the easiest way to return the system to a state where it will boot properly?
>
> ○ a. Use the repair process with the ERD.
>
> ○ b. Use the Last Known Good Configuration.
>
> ○ c. Launch the Kernel Debugger.
>
> ○ d. Boot to DOS and run the setup utility to change the installed drivers.

The LKGC is the fastest way to return to a bootable configuration, especially since only a single change was made to the system; therefore, answer b is correct. The ERD repair process will restore the system so it can boot; however, this requires a recent ERD and all three installation diskettes, and this process can take upwards of 30 minutes. So answer a is incorrect. The Kernel Debugger will not help this situation, especially since it was not preconfigured to watch the boot process before the new driver was installed; therefore, answer c is incorrect. There is no DOS setup utility—that only was available for Windows 3.1; so answer d is incorrect.

Question 7

> During the boot process, you receive an error message after the Last Known Good Configuration prompt:
>
> ```
> Windows NT could not start because the
> following file is missing or corrupt: \winnt
> root\system32\ntoskrnl.exe. Please reinstall
> a copy of the above file.
> ```
>
> What are the possible explanations for this error?
> [Check all correct answers]
>
> ❏ a. The NTOSKRNL.EXE file is missing.
>
> ❏ b. The BOOT.INI file points to the wrong partition.
>
> ❏ c. The NTOSKRNL.EXE file is corrupt.
>
> ❏ d. The BOOT.INI file is missing.

All of these explanations can result in the given error message; therefore, all four answers are correct. When the boot process cannot find NTOSKRNL.EXE, it does not indicate if the problem is with the file itself, its location, or the pointers to it.

Question 8

Which of the files on the ERD lists the files installed during setup and the checksums of each of these files?

O   a. INSTALLED.DAT

O   b. CONFIG.NT

O   c. DEFAULT._

O   d. SOFTWARE._

O   e. SETUP.LOG

INSTALLED.DAT is not a file present on an ERD; therefore, answer a is incorrect. CONFIG.NT, DEFAULT._, and SOFTWARE._ are all files on an ERD, but they do not contain installed file and checksum information; so answers b, c, and d are incorrect. SETUP.LOG is the only file on the ERD that lists the files installed during setup and their corresponding checksums; therefore, answer e is correct.

Question 9

Your NT Server experiences yet another stop error. Fortunately you enabled the memory dump option through the System applet. What utility can you use to view the contents of the .DMP file?

O   a. Event Viewer

O   b. Debug Inspector

O   c. DUMPEXAM.EXE

O   d. NT Diagnostics

The Event Viewer and NT Diagnostics are not able to view the contents of a memory dump file, so answers a and d are incorrect. There is not a Debug Inspector, so answer b is incorrect. Only DUMPEXAM.EXE can be used to view the contents of .DMP files; therefore, answer c is correct.

Question 10

Which of the following are valid ways to make full or partial backups of the Registry? [Check all correct answers]

❑ a. Create an ERD using the RDISK /S command.

❑ b. Use NTBACKUP.

❑ c. Copy all of the contents of the \Winnt\System32\Config directory.

❑ d. Use the Disk Administrator.

❑ e. Use REGEDT32.

All of these methods are valid ways to create full or partial backups of the NT Registry, so all five answers are correct. However, it should be noted that the files stored in \Winnt\System32\Config (answer c) are only as current as the last reboot or execution of RDISK /S.

Question 11

Bob, one of your users, tries to access a new project data file stored in the shared Account directory. Bob is not currently a member of the Accounts group, which has exclusive access to this directory. You add Bob to the Accounts group. Bob still is unable to access the directory, but he can access other resources. Why?

○ a. Bob did not use the Network Neighborhood to access the share.

○ b. Bob did not log off and log back in.

○ c. Bob is logged in remotely.

○ d. Bob typed in the wrong password.

The Network Neighborhood does not have to be used to access a share; a mapped drive or a UNC name can be used to access a share, so answer a is incorrect. By not relogging in to the system, Bob's Access Token was not rebuilt using the new group membership, so he effectively was not a member of the Account group; therefore, answer b is correct. The method of Bob's access is not relevant—a local and a remote logon have the same abilities under NT. So answer c is incorrect. If Bob failed to use the correct password, he would not be logged in and thus would be unable to access any resources; therefore, answer d is incorrect.

Need To Know More?

 Heywood, Drew: *Inside Windows NT Server*. New Riders, Indianapolis, IN, 1995. ISBN 1-56205-472-4. This book does not have a chapter focused on troubleshooting; however, tips and tricks about resolving problems are scattered throughout the text.

 Siyan, Karanjit S.: *Windows NT Server 4 Professional Reference*. New Riders, Indianapolis, IN, 1996. ISBN 1-56205-731-6. This book also fails to include a focused chapter on resolving problems, but troubleshooting information is present in some chapters.

 Strebe, Matthew, Charles Perkins, and James Chellis: *MSCE: NT Server 4 Study Guide*. Sybex Network Press, San Francisco, CA, 1996. ISBN 0-7821-1972-7. Chapter 17 contains lots of great troubleshooting information. Other tips and tricks are scattered through the rest of the text as well.

 Searching the TechNet CD (or its online version through www.microsoft.com) and the *Windows NT Server Resource Kit* using the keyword "troubleshooting" will result in numerous hits on relevant materials. However, for more focused searching, use keywords associated with the topic or subject in question, such as "boot," "installation," "printing," "Emergency Repair Disk," or "Registry."

Sample Test

The sections that follow provide numerous pointers for development of a successful test-taking strategy, including how to choose proper answers, how to decode ambiguity, how to work within the Microsoft framework, how to decide what to memorize, and how to prepare for the test. Finally, we provide a number of questions that cover subject matter likely to appear on the Microsoft Windows NT Server 4 exam. Good luck!

Questions, Questions, Questions

There should be no doubt in your mind that you are facing a test full of questions. Each exam comprises 55 to 75 questions. You are allotted 90 minutes to complete the exam. Remember, questions are of four basic types:

➤ Multiple choice with a single answer

➤ Multiple choice with multiple answers

➤ Multipart with a single answer

➤ Picking the spot on the graphic

Always take the time to read a question twice before selecting an answer. Also, be sure to look for an Exhibit button. The Exhibit button brings up graphics and charts used to help explain the question, provide additional data, or illustrate layout. You'll find it difficult to answer this type of question if you fail to look at the exhibits.

It is easy to assume that a question demands only a single answer. However, there are lots of questions that require more than one answer. In fact, there are even some questions for which all the answers should be marked. Read the question carefully enough to decipher how many answers are needed, and look for additional instructions on marking your answers. These instructions are usually in brackets.

Picking Proper Answers

It should be obvious that the only way to pass an exam is to select the correct answers. But the Microsoft exams are not standardized like SAT and GRE exams—they are much more diabolical and convoluted. In some cases, questions are so poorly worded that deciphering them is nearly impossible. In those cases, you may need to rely upon answer elimination skills. There is almost always at least one answer out of four that can be immediately eliminated because:

➤ The answer doesn't apply to the situation

➤ The answer describes a nonexistent issue

➤ The answer is already eliminated by the question text

Once obviously wrong answers are eliminated, you must rely on your retained knowledge to eliminate further answers. Look for items that sound correct but refer to actions, commands, or features not present or not available in the described situation.

If, after these phases of elimination, you still are faced with a blind guess between two or more answers, reread the question. Try to picture in your mind's eye the situation and how each of the possible remaining answers would alter that situation.

After you have exhausted your ability to eliminate answers and are still unclear about which of the remaining possible answers is the correct one—guess! An unanswered question offers you no points, but a guessed question gives you a chance of getting the question right. But don't be too hasty in making a blind guess. Wait until the last round of reviewing marked questions before you start to guess. Guessing should be a last resort.

Decoding Ambiguity

Microsoft exams have a reputation for including questions that are difficult to interpret, confusing, and ambiguous. In our experience with numerous exams, we can fully understand why the reputation is so pronounced. The Microsoft exams are difficult. They are designed specifically to limit the number of passing grades to around 30 percent of all who take the test. In other words, Microsoft wants 70 percent of test takers to fail.

The only way to beat Microsoft at its own game is to be prepared. You'll discover that many exam questions test your knowledge of things not directly related to the issue raised by the question. This means that the answers offered to you, even the incorrect ones, are just as much part of the skill assessment as the question. If you don't know about all aspects of NT cold, you may not be able to eliminate answers that are obviously wrong because they relate to a different area of NT than the one addressed by the question itself.

Questions often give away the answer, but you have to be better than Sherlock Holmes to see the clues. Often, subtle hints are included in the text in such a way that they seem like irrelevant information. You must realize that each question is a test in and of itself, and you need to inspect and successfully navigate each question to pass the exam. Look for small clues such as the mentioning of times, group names, configuration settings, and even local or remote access methods. Little items such as these can point out the right answer; if missed, they can leave you facing a blind guess.

Another common difficulty with the certification exams is that of vocabulary. Microsoft has an uncanny ability to name utilities and features very obviously on some occasions and completely inanely in others. Especially in the area of printing and remote access, be sure to brush up on the terms presented in those chapters. You may also want to review the Glossary before approaching the test.

Working Within The Framework

The test questions are presented to you in a random order. Plus, many of the same elements or issues are repeated in multiple questions. It is not uncommon to find that the correct answer to one question is the wrong answer of another. Take the time to read each answer, even if you know the correct one immediately. The incorrect answers may spark a memory that helps you on another question.

You can revisit any question as many times as you like. If you are uncertain of the answer to a question, make a mark in the box provided, so that you can come back to it later. Also, mark questions you think may offer data you can use to solve other questions. We've marked 25 to 50 percent of the questions on exams we've taken. The testing software is designed to help you mark an answer for every question, so use its framework to your advantage. Everything you want to see again should be marked; the software will help you return to marked items.

Deciding What To Memorize

The amount of memorization you must do for the exams depends on your ability to remember what you've read and interacted with. If you are a visual learner and can see the drop-down menus and the dialog boxes in your head, you won't need to memorize as much as if you can't. The tests will stretch your recollection skills through selection of commands and location of features of the utilities of NT.

The important types of information to memorize are:

> ➤ The order of steps in setup or configuration

> ➤ Features or commands found in pull-down menus and configuration dialog boxes

> ➤ Applications found by default in the Start menu

> ➤ Applets in the Control Panel

> ➤ Names and functions of the five main Registry keys

If you work your way through this book while sitting at an NT Server machine, you should have little or no problem interacting with most of these important items.

Preparing For The Test

The best way to prepare for the test—after you've studied—is to take at least one practice exam. We've included a practice exam in this chapter. The test questions are located in the section that follows. You should give yourself 90 minutes to take the test. Keep yourself on the honor system, and don't cheat by looking at the text earlier in the book. Once your time is up or you finish, you can check your answers in the Answer Key To Sample Test, which follows this chapter.

If you want additional practice exams, visit the Microsoft Training and Certification site (http://www.microsoft.com/train_cert/), and download the Self-Assessment Practice Exam utility.

Taking The Test

Relax. Once you are sitting in front of the testing computer, there is nothing more you can do to increase your knowledge or preparation. Take a deep breath, stretch, and attack the first question.

Don't rush; there is plenty of time to complete each question and to return to skipped questions. If you read a question twice and are clueless, mark it and move on. Easy and hard questions are dispersed throughout the test in a random order. Don't cheat yourself by spending too much time on a difficult question early on that prevents you from answering numerous easy questions positioned near the end. Move through the entire test. Then, before returning to the skipped questions, evaluate your time in light of the number of skipped questions. As you answer questions, remove the mark. Continue to review the remaining marked questions until your time expires or you complete the test.

That's it for pointers. Following are several questions for you to practice on.

Sample Test

Question 1

A Windows NT Server PC is configured with two 1 GB SCSI hard drives. Both drives are attached to the same SCSI drive controller with an operating onboard BIOS. Each disk contains a single primary partition; the Windows NT system files reside on Disk 1, and the boot files reside on Disk 2. Which of the following ARC names correctly identifies the boot partition that appears in the BOOT.INI?

○ a. multi(0)disk(0)rdisk(0)partition(1)

○ b. multi(0)disk(1)rdisk(0)partition(1)

○ c. multi(0)disk(0)rdisk(0)partition(0)

○ d. multi(1)disk(0)rdisk(0)partition(0)

○ e. multi(0)disk(0)rdisk(1)partition(1)

Question 2

You perform a daily backup on all the files you have access to, but you are unable to restore these files from the backup tape. You are a member only of the Marketing group. What is preventing the restoration?

○ a. You are not a member of the Administrators group, so you should not even be able to make backups.

○ b. You are not a member of the Domain Users, Print Operators, or Replicator group.

○ c. You are not a member of the Backup Operators, Server Operators, or Administrator group.

○ d. You failed to check the Enable Restore option when you performed the backups.

Question 3

> Which of the following statements are true about PPP and SLIP?
> [Check all correct answers]
>
> ❑   a. PPP supports DHCP; SLIP does not.
>
> ❑   b. SLIP supports NetBEUI, IPX/SPX, and TCP/IP; PPP
>   supports only TCP/IP.
>
> ❑   c. SLIP is the most commonly used WAN protocol.
>
> ❑   d. SLIP is used to access Unix servers.
>
> ❑   e. SLIP supports encrypted passwords; PPP does not.

Question 4

> After failed attempts to print several documents, you inspect the
> print queue. You discover that all of your print jobs are listed in
> the display window and that you are unable to delete any of them.
> What is the best course of action to resolve this problem?
>
> ○   a. Turn off the Pause Printing command from the Printer
>   window.
>
> ○   b. Delete the printer from the print server, and create a new
>   printer.
>
> ○   c. Delete all files from the spool folder on the print server.
>
> ○   d. Stop the spooler service, and then restart it.

Question 5

> You add four new drives to your Windows NT Server computer,
> sized 900 MB, 700 MB, 500 MB, and 350 MB. You wish to estab-
> lish a disk stripe set with parity. What is the total size of the larg-
> est set you can create using any or all of these drives?
>
> ○   a. 1200 MB
>
> ○   b. 1000 MB
>
> ○   c. 900 MB
>
> ○   d. 1500 MB

Question 6

Your BDC experiences a power surge that results in the destruction of the primary drive. The primary drive was comprised of two partitions—one used for the boot files and the other for the system files. Fortunately, you implemented a disk mirror on both partitions using a duplicate drive. How should you modify the BOOT.INI file on an emergency boot floppy to boot the system from the mirrored copy? [Check all correct answers]

❑ a. Add an /m switch to the appropriate lines in the
     [operating systems] section of the file.

❑ b. Modify the ARC name specification in the default= line of
     the [boot loader] section of the file.

❑ c. Modify the ARC name specifications in the [operating
     systems] section of the file.

❑ d. Do nothing; the BOOT.INI file will handle this
     automatically.

Question 7

Where should updated logon scripts be placed, and how should the replication service be configured so they will be distributed throughout the network automatically?

○ a. In the Scripts subdirectory of \Winnt\System32\
     Repl\Export on the PDC, replicate to all other domain
     controllers.

○ b. In the \Winnt\System32\Repl\Export directory on the
     PDC, replicate to each domain workstation.

○ c. In the Scripts subdirectory of \Winnt\System32\Repl\
     Export on the PDC, replicate to each domain workstation.

○ d. In the \Winnt\System32\Repl\Export directory on the
     PDC, replicate to all other domain controllers.

Question 8

If you performed a directory listing on your Intel-based Windows NT Server machine, the one with a SCSI controller card without an onboard BIOS, which of the following files would appear in the system partition? [Choose all correct answers]

❏ a. BOOT.INI

❏ b. NTLDR

❏ c. NTOSKRNL.EXE

❏ d. NTBOOTDD.SYS

❏ e. OSLOADER.EXE

❏ f. BOOTSECT.DOS

Question 9

While performing normal daily activities, you notice that your server's hard drive is extremely active. You suspect your physical RAM needs to be increased. What Performance Monitor object and counter should you monitor to determine if the drive thrashing is due to a memory shortage?

○ a. Memory: Pages/Thread

○ b. Memory: Pages/Second

○ c. Processor: % Processor Time

○ d. LogicalDisk: Avg. Disk Bytes/Transfer

Question 10

Within a single domain, you have two NT Server machines—a PDC and a BDC—plus fourteen NT Workstation machines. You need to perform a backup of the domain data and the Registry for both of the domain controllers. You have a tape backup installed only on the BDC machine. Using NTBACKUP as your backup software, what should you do to ensure you capture all of the data necessary?

- ○   a. Nothing. You can do a remote backup of everything on the PDC.

- ○   b. Install a second tape drive on the PDC.

- ○   c. Nothing. You cannot back up your domain controllers.

- ○   d. Create an ERD for the PDC.

Question 11

While connected to the office LAN remotely, you interact with numerous documents stored on a machine hosted by the LAN via a shortcut added to your desktop. After closing your RAS connection, you attempt to access another document through your desktop shortcut. What happens?

- ○   a. Access is denied because no link to the LAN exists.

- ○   b. The file is pulled from the network cache.

- ○   c. A file with a similar name on your local hard drive will be accessed instead.

- ○   d. RAS AutoDial attempts to reconnect to the office LAN.

Question 12

Which items below describe disk striping without parity?
[Check all correct answers]

❏ a. Requires three physical drives

❏ b. Can be implemented with FAT

❏ c. Provides fault tolerance

❏ d. Has faster read-write performance than disk mirroring

❏ e. Cannot recover data if a single drive within the set fails

Question 13

What is the best method for offering full network capabilities to remote users without compromising security over the Internet?

○ a. Internet Information Server

○ b. Serial Line Interface Protocol

○ c. Point-to-Point Tunneling Protocol

○ d. Require Encrypted Authentication

Question 14

You need to watch numerous counters simultaneously, but you find the Chart view of Performance Monitor very difficult to follow. What can you do to solve your problem?

○ a. Switch the Performance Monitor to Report view.

○ b. Do nothing. You cannot monitor multiple objects at a time.

○ c. Switch to Alert view.

○ d. Use Windows NT diagnostics to view the data.

Question 15

How do you demote a BDC to a file server without domain controller capabilities?

○ a. Choose the Network option in Control Panel, select the
    BDC, and click Demote.

○ b. Highlight the BDC in the Server Manager, and select
    Demote on the Computer menu.

○ c. Reinstall Windows NT Server.

○ d. Restart the BDC, and choose Member Server at the
    startup screen.

Question 16

Which of the following is the best application to use to create a
new shared directory on a domain server from your Windows NT
Workstation computer? (Assume you have remote tools installed
on the Workstation from the NT Server CD.)

○ a. User Manager

○ b. Server Manager

○ c. Windows Explorer

○ d. Network Client Administrator

Question 17

On an NWLink-based network using a star topology, one of the
workstations is not able to establish a network connection. None
of the other clients on the system is having communication difficulties. Of the following possibilities, which is the most likely to
be the cause of this problem?

○ a. Faulty NIC on the server

○ b. A protocol mismatch

○ c. A PC memory conflict

○ d. An incorrect IPX frame type

Question 18

You have two SCSI hard drives on a single drive controller in your Windows NT Server computer. There is only one partition on each of the two drives. The first drive's partition is formatted with FAT, and the second drive's partition is formatted with NTFS. The drive controller has onboard BIOS. The boot files are located on the second drive. What is the ARC name for the system partition?

○　a. multi(0)disk(1)rdisk(0)partition(1)

○　b. multi(0)disk(0)rdisk(1)partition(1)

○　c. multi(1)disk(0)rdisk(1)partition(1)

○　d. multi(0)disk(0)rdisk(1)partition(0)

○　e. multi(1)disk(0)rdisk(0)partition(1)

Question 19

A Windows NT server is added to a NetWare network. The NetWare-based network is comprised of various versions of NetWare—from very old to the latest release. The NT server is configured to autodetect the IPX frame types in use. What kinds of frame types can a Windows NT server detect successfully?

○　a. 802.2 frame type

○　b. 802.3 frame type

○　c. 802.3 frame type with SNAP header

○　d. 802.5 frame type

○　e. 802.5 frame type with SNAP header

Question 20

To track the level of processor use, what Performance Monitor object and counter should you watch?

○　a. System: Interrupts/Second

○　b. Memory: Pages/Second

○　c. Processor: % Processor Time

○　d. Processor: Interrupts/Second

Question 21

A user is a member of the following groups with the indicated access privileges to a share named ProjectA:

- Sales: Change
- Department12: Full Control
- DomainUsers: Read

The user is the leader of the team responsible for the data in ProjectA, so his user account has been assigned Change permissions on the directory hosted on an NTFS volume pointed to by this share. What is the resultant access privilege for this share for this user?

- ○ a. No Access
- ○ b. Read
- ○ c. Change
- ○ d. Full Control

Question 22

The Springfield Homeless Shelter operates its network on donated equipment. The network is based on Windows NT Server 4. Recently, a NetWare server was donated. The existing Windows for Workgroups machines now need access to resources on the NetWare server. How can these client machines access the new server without adding any additional software?

- ○ a. Install Gateway Service For NetWare on the Windows NT server, and make those users members of an NTGATEWAY group on that server.
- ○ b. Install NWLink and File And Print Services For NetWare on the Windows NT server.
- ○ c. Install Gateway Service For NetWare on the Windows NT server, and make those users members of an NTGATEWAY group on the NetWare server.
- ○ d. Install Gateway Service For NetWare on the NetWare server, and NWLink on the Windows NT server.

Question 23

In an attempt to customize the activity of Windows NT, you modify numerous entries in the Registry. You perform a reboot to force your changes to take effect; however, the Windows NT Server machine will no longer boot. What is the easiest way to return the machine to an operating configuration?

○   a. Start the computer from the Windows NT boot disks, and restore the Registry from a backup.

○   b. Start the computer from the Windows NT boot disks, and select the Emergency Repair option.

○   c. Start the computer from the Emergency Repair Disk, and follow the prompts.

○   d. Choose the Last Known Good Configuration option when it appears during bootup.

Question 24

What component of NT can be used to verify that NTBACKUP completed a batch file automated backup successfully?

○   a. User Manager For Domains

○   b. Server Manager

○   c. Backup log

○   d. The Registry

Question 25

You are training a new system administrator. You want to reduce the level of instruction you give and encourage the new
recruit to learn through direct interaction. While working with
the Performance Monitor, what is the fastest method to train the
new system admin about the counters that appear there? [Check
all correct answers]

❑   a. Working with the Registry

❑   b. Clicking on the counter itself and clicking the Explain
      button

❑   c. Reading the documentation from the Help menu

❑   d. Changing the view to Report

Question 26

Which of the following components are required for a Windows
NT workstation running Client Service For NetWare to access
NetWare-based resources successfully? [Choose all correct
answers]

❑   a. Gateway Service For NetWare

❑   b. File And Print Services For NetWare

❑   c. NWLink

❑   d. A valid account on a NetWare server

❑   e. Membership in the NTGATEWAY group on the NetWare
      server to which Gateway Service For NetWare is connected

Question 27

To improve the printing speed of your office, you decide to establish a printer pool using five printers. Which of the following conditions are required to create a printer pool? [Choose all correct answers]

❏ a. All print devices must be identical.

❏ b. All physical print devices must be connected to the same logical printer.

❏ c. All print devices must use the same printer port.

❏ d. All print devices must be located in the same room.

Question 28

Your Ethernet network consists of a Windows NT 4 server, several NT Workstation clients, a NetWare 3.12 client, and one NetWare 4.1 client. NWLink is running on the network. Each of the NetWare clients is using different frame types. How would you configure the NWLink IPX/SPX Properties dialog box on the Windows NT 4 server to enable the server to recognize both NetWare clients?

○ a. By enabling Auto Frame Type Detection

○ b. By selecting the Manual Frame Type Detection option and adding a NetWare client's network number and frame type to the frame type configuration list

○ c. By selecting the Auto Frame Type Detection option and adding both NetWare clients' network numbers and frame types to the frame type configuration list

○ d. By selecting the Manual Frame Type Detection option and adding each of the NetWare clients' network numbers and frame types to the frame type configuration list

Question 29

Your programmer has been hired away by a competitor. You hire a replacement. What is the best way to give the new user the same access to network resources as the previous programmer?

○   a. Create a new account, and manually duplicate all of the settings and group memberships of the old account. Then delete the old account.

○   b. Rename the old account, and change the password in User Manager For Domains.

○   c. Rename the old account, and change the password in Server Manager.

○   d. Copy the old account, make any needed alterations to the copy, and disable the old account.

Question 30

You purchase a new HP network interface device for your printer. You want to attach the printer to the network directly instead of through a parallel cable to a server. During the install, you are unable to locate the option to install a new port. Why?

○   a. PostScript printing is enabled on the print device and must be disabled.

○   b. You didn't install the print driver on the print server.

○   c. The print processor is corrupt and must be fixed.

○   d. The DLC protocol is not installed on the print server.

Question 31

Due to a change in your organization, users must now move from one computer station to another depending on the project in which they are currently involved. What must you do so that users can maintain the look and feel of their desktops no matter what machine they log in to?

○ a. Create a single network profile on the PDC in the \Winnt\Profiles directory, followed by the .DAT suffix. Have all user accounts load this profile.

○ b. Rename all current profiles from NTUSER.DAT to NTUSER.MAN.

○ c. Using the Copy Profile To box from the System option in Control Panel, copy all current profiles from the workstations to a shared network path. Delete the current profile from the workstations.

○ d. Copy each user's workstation profile to a shared network path using the Copy Profile To box. Change the type of profile to roaming. Then, type the network path in the User Profile Path box for each user account.

Question 32

You want to enable your NT Workstation and Windows 95 clients to access a NetWare server without installing NetWare client software on those machines. How can this objective be met most effectively?

○ a. Install Gateway Service For NetWare on a Windows NT server on the same network.

○ b. Install NWLink on the NT Workstation and Windows 95 computers.

○ c. Install Gateway Service For NetWare on the NetWare server.

○ d. Install File And Print Services For NetWare on a Windows NT server on the same network.

Question 33

Your company employs numerous independent consultants who operate throughout the United States. They regularly dial into the central Windows NT Server-based LAN to upload new orders and download the latest product descriptions. Each user purchased his or her own equipment and operating system. In this situation, what is the highest level of security you can implement and still allow your users to connect via RAS?

- ○ a. Allow Any Authentication Including Clear Text
- ○ b. Require Microsoft Encrypted Authentication
- ○ c. PGP Encryption
- ○ d. Require Encrypted Authentication

Question 34

After upgrading a Windows NT 3.51 Server to version 4, you discover one of the storage drives is formatted with HPFS. You can convert this to NTFS using the CONVERT utility bundled with NT 4?

- ○ a. True
- ○ b. False

Question 35

Your Windows NT boot drive resides on the fourth partition of a SCSI disk drive, the onboard BIOS of which is disabled. It is attached to a drive controller with a Bus ID of 1. What is the ARC name listed in the BOOT.INI file that points to the system files?

- ○ a. scsi(0)disk(0)rdisk(0)partition(3)
- ○ b. scsi(0)disk(1)rdisk(0)partition(4)
- ○ c. scsi(0)disk(1)rdisk(1)partition(4)
- ○ d. multi(0)disk(0)rdisk(0)partition(4)

Question 36

What are the RAS restrictions for protocols used over a remote connection?

○ a. TCP/IP, NetBEUI, but not NWLink

○ b. TCP/IP, NWLink, but not NetBEUI

○ c. Only TCP/IP

○ d. TCP/IP, NetBEUI, and NWLink

Question 37

Your organization wants to migrate users from a NetWare server to an NT 4 server to terminate the process of maintaining user accounts on two different types of servers. What must be installed on the Windows NT server to provide clients with access to the NetWare resources after this migration is complete? [Check all correct answers]

❏ a. Gateway Service For NetWare

❏ b. The NWLink protocol

❏ c. Client Service For NetWare

❏ d. SAP Agent

Question 38

The Sales department of your organization has asked that its print jobs be handled in priority over those from the Research department. Since you only have a single printer on your network, and this will improve overall work performance, you agree to make this change. How is it performed?

○   a. Create a separate logical printer, assign rights to the Sales group, and set the printer priority to 1.

○   b. Create a separate logical printer, assign rights to the Sales group, and set the printer priority to 99.

○   c. Create a separate logical printer for the Sales group, and configure the printer to start printing immediately.

○   d. Create a separate logical printer for the Sales group, and configure the printer to print directly to the physical print device.

Question 39

The system and boot partitions can participate in which of the following drive sets supported by Windows NT Server? [Check all correct answers]

❏   a. Disk mirroring

❏   b. Disk striping without parity

❏   c. Volume set

❏   d. Disk duplexing

Question 40

On a Windows NT Server, a disk mirror is implemented. During a thunderstorm, the original disk of the mirror fails. The mirror did not contain the system or boot partitions. What are the steps required to restore the mirror set?

○   a. Replace the failed disk, reformat both drives, re-create a mirror set, and restore the data from a backup tape.

○   b. Replace the failed disk; Windows NT Server will automatically restore the mirror set.

○   c. Replace the failed disk, break the mirror set, and re-create the mirror set.

○   d. Replace the failed disk, select the mirror set and the replaced drive, and select Regenerate from the Fault Tolerance menu.

Question 41

There are 25 Windows 95 machines on your network. You want to upgrade them to Windows NT Workstation with a minimum of effort. The installation files reside in a shared directory named \\Server5\Wks4. What is the best way to handle the installation across the network?

○   a. Attach to the shared directory and run WINNT.EXE across the network.

○   b. Attach to the shared directory and run SETUP.EXE across the network.

○   c. Install the Windows NT Workstation client using Network Client Administrator.

○   d. Use Network Client Administrator to create a DOS Installation Startup Disk, attach to the shared directory, and run SETUP.EXE across the network.

Question 42

> You want to install Windows NT Server 4 on an old Pentium machine. The machine was purchased in November 1995. What tools can be used to determine if the system can support the operation of NT? [Check all correct answers]
>
> ❑   a. Microsoft Windows NT Diagnostics
>
> ❑   b. System Sleuth
>
> ❑   c. NTHQ disk
>
> ❑   d. A current copy of the Hardware Compatibility List—to check every system component and be sure it appears therein

Question 43

> You have a machine with an IDE CD-ROM drive. You had no difficulty installing Windows 95 on the machine, but the CD-ROM is not supported by Windows NT Server 4. How can you install Windows NT Server 4 on that machine anyway? [Choose all the correct answers]
>
> ❑   a. Create a set of installation disks from another Windows NT Server machine, and use the disks to perform the install.
>
> ❑   b. Use the XCOPY command to copy the files from the \i386 directory onto the Windows 95 machine's hard disk, and run WINNT.EXE from there.
>
> ❑   c. While running Windows 95, change to the \i386 directory on the NT CD, and run WINNT32.EXE.
>
> ❑   d. Copy the installation files from \i386 to a server, map a drive from the Windows 95 machine to that directory, and run WINNT.EXE from there.

Question 44

> After recent data loss due to hardware failures and a power brown-out, you want to protect your data. You decide to use Windows NT Server's built-in fault tolerance schemes to offer you the protection you need. Which of the following techniques will provide you with some type of fault tolerance? [Check all correct answers]
>
> ❑ a. RAID 1
>
> ❑ b. Disk duplexing
>
> ❑ c. Volume set
>
> ❑ d. Disk striping without parity
>
> ❑ e. RAID 5

Question 45

> A remote user wants to connect to the central LAN. The user's notebook computer is using NetBEUI and TCP/IP protocols, and these protocols are bound to the dial-up adapter in that order. The LAN uses NetBEUI and NWLink protocols, and these protocols are bound in that order. Which of the following activities will the remote user not be able to perform?
>
> ○ a. Accessing a directory list of NetBIOS share names
>
> ○ b. Accessing resources on the LAN
>
> ○ c. Accessing resources on the RAS server
>
> ○ d. Accessing WinSOCK applications

Question 46

You have a 50 MB partition you wish to use as a share for users to store document files. What is the best file system type to format this partition with?

○   a. FAT

○   b. CDFS

○   c. NTFS

○   d. HPFS

Question 47

If you need to maximize the storage space on a Windows NT server without care for fault tolerance, what is the best drive configuration to use?

○   a. Disk mirroring

○   b. Disk striping without parity

○   c. Volume set

○   d. Disk stacking

Question 48

You need to install Windows NT Server across a network onto a computer that currently runs Windows 95. Which of the following procedures will perform this activity?

○   a. Connect to the network directory that contains the Windows NT installation files, and run WINNT32.EXE.

○   b. Connect to the network directory that contains the Windows NT installation files, and run WINNT.EXE.

○   c. Connect to the network directory that contains the Windows NT installation files, and run SETUP.EXE.

○   d. Create a client installation disk using Network Client Administrator, boot the machine with that disk, and run NETWORK.EXE.

Question 49

The primary SCSI drive controller fails on your Windows NT Server computer. That controller hosted the system files. Fortunately, you had a second drive controller that hosted a duplicate hard drive, which participated with the first drive in a mirror set. How should you modify the BOOT.INI file so the system can start up using the mirror drive?

○　a. Change scsi(0) to scsi(1) on the appropriate lines.

○　b. Change scsi(1) to scsi(2) on the appropriate lines.

○　c. Change multi(0) to multi(1) on the appropriate lines.

○　d. Change multi(1) to multi(2) on the appropriate lines.

Question 50

To upgrade a Windows for Workgroup computer to a Windows NT Server 4 machine, which of the following steps should be performed?

○　a. Install Windows NT in a separate directory, and reinstall all applications.

○　b. Install Windows NT in a separate directory, and import WIN.INI and SYSTEM.INI into the registry.

○　c. Run WINNT32.EXE and install Windows NT into WfW's home directory, c:\windows.

○　d. Run WINNT.EXE and install Windows NT into WfW's home directory, c:\windows.

Question 51

If you place data on a VFAT formatted partition, users can access that data provided that: [Check all correct answers]

- ❏   a. users can log on across the network to the machine hosting the partition.
- ❏   b. a share is defined for the partition.
- ❏   c. users have READ or better permission to the share.
- ❏   d. users have READ or better file permissions.

Question 52

When operating over a PPP RAS connection, which of the following NT networking activities can occur? [Check all correct answers]

- ❏   a. Printer share access
- ❏   b. Named pipes
- ❏   c. WinSOCK API applications over TCP/IP
- ❏   d. InterProcess Communications (IPC)
- ❏   e. User logon authentication

Question 53

You want to access resources on a NetWare server from a Windows NT workstation that is running Client Service For NetWare. Which of the following are required to enable such access? [Select all that apply]

- ❏   a. A group on the NetWare server, called NTGATEWAY, containing the Windows NT workstation's user account
- ❏   b. Gateway Services For NetWare
- ❏   c. A user account on the NetWare server
- ❏   d. The NWLink protocol

Question 54

You want to implement Directory Replication to distribute security files across the network. Which of the following computer types can be used as export servers? [Check all correct answers]

❏ a. Windows NT servers that are configured as domain controllers

❏ b. Windows NT member servers

❏ c. Windows NT workstations

❏ d. Windows 95 clients

Question 55

You print a document using your normal word processor. When you get to the printer to retrieve your work, all you find is pages of nonsensical lines of seemingly random characters. You remember that this printer was recently added. What is likely to be the cause of the print problem?

○ a. The DLC protocol is not installed.

○ b. The print spooler is corrupt.

○ c. An incorrect printer driver has been installed.

○ d. There is not enough hard disk space for spooling.

15

Answer Key
To Sample Test

Here are the answers to the questions presented in the sample test in Chapter 14.

Question 1

The options for the first element in an ARC name are either scsi or multi, but scsi applies only to a genuine SCSI drive whose onboard BIOS has been disabled. Since multi(*) appears at the start of all five choices, all of them are correct to that point. The number that follows multi within the parentheses is the ordinal number of the disk controller to which the drive (or drives) is attached. Ordinal numbers start with 0; because there's only one controller mentioned in the question, that immediately rules out answer d, because it alludes to a second controller (as denoted by multi(1)) to which neither drive in the preceding question is attached.

The disk(*) element in an ARC name designates the SCSI bus number for a SCSI drive with its BIOS disabled, and is always zero for a non-SCSI disk. This eliminates answer b from further consideration.

The rdisk(*) element in an ARC name indicates the SCSI logical unit number (LUN) or the drive that contains the operating system. RDISK(*) always is set to zero when an ARC name starts with "scsi"—because this one starts with "multi", it indicates the position in the order in which drives are attached to the controller. Further, the question indicates that the NT system files are on the first disk, and boot files on the second disk. Knowing that rdisk numbers ordinally (beginning with zero), we know that the NT system files live on the drive named multi(0)disk(0)rdisk(0)partition(1), and that the boot files live on the drive named multi(0)disk(0)rdisk(1) partition(1). Therefore, answer a is correct.

One small trick to remembering about ARC names is that whereas scsi, multi, disk, and rdisk all number ordinally, starting with 0, partitions number cardinally, starting with 1. Thus, no valid ARC name will ever have zero as a value for partition(*). Therefore, answer c is incorrect. Because each of the partitions mentioned in this question is the only one on its drive, it must be partition(1).

Here's the real trick in this question: Boot files reside on the system partition on an NT Server. This means that the correct answer is the ARC name for the drive that contains the boot files, or answer e.

Question 2

Any user can back up a file if he or she can read it, but only users with the Restore Files And Directories right can pull data from backups; therefore, answer a is incorrect. These groups do not have settings that affect the ability of their members to operate NTBACKUP, making answer b incorrect. You must be granted the User Right to restore data. By default, the Backup Operators, Server Operators, and Administrator groups all have the right to do this; therefore, answer c is the only correct answer. There is no such option as Enable Restore for a backup; restoration is a right granted to select groups and specific users, so answer d is incorrect.

Question 3

PPP supports DHCP; SLIP does not. Therefore, answer a is correct. PPP supports NetBEUI, IPX/SPX, and TCP/IP; SLIP only supports TCP/IP. Therefore, answer b is incorrect. PPP is the most commonly used WAN protocol; therefore, answer c is incorrect. SLIP is used to access Unix servers; therefore, answer d is correct. PPP supports encrypted passwords, SLIP does not; therefore, answer e is incorrect. Thus, only answers a and d are correct.

Question 4

Even if the printer is paused, that would not prevent you from deleting print jobs; therefore, answer a is incorrect. Deleting and re-creating the logical printer will force you to resend your documents; in addition, this is not the best solution. Therefore, answer b is incorrect. Deleting all the files from the print spool folder will remove the print jobs from the queue, but it does not address why the printer is not printing, so answer c is incorrect. The spooler service is most likely the cause of the problem. By restarting the spooler service, it will pull all print jobs from the spool and print them; therefore, answer d is correct.

Question 5

1200 MB would be the size of the set if you used all four drives and 300 MB on each drive. This is not the largest possible configuration using this set of drives, so answer a is incorrect. 1000 MB is the amount of data that could be stored on the largest set created from these drives, but the question asked for the total size of the set, so answer b is incorrect. 900 MB is the size of the largest individual drive; you must use three devices to create a disk stripe set with parity, so answer c is incorrect. 1500 MB is the total size of the largest set created from these drives, using only the 900, 700, and 500 MB drives; therefore, answer d is correct.

Question 6

Answer a is incorrect because there is no /m switch defined among the available Windows NT boot options. Windows NT boots from the ARC name specified in the [operating system] section of the BOOT.INI file if a deliberate OS selection is made, but most commonly, it boots from the default line in the [boot loader] section. Therefore, changes to the ARC names in both parts of BOOT.INI will be required; these changes must be entered by hand to point to the mirror copy in a mirrored set of drives. Thus, answers b and c are correct. Answer d is incorrect because BOOT.INI does not handle mirrored sets automatically.

Question 7

The NETLOGON share is where all user accounts pull logon scripts. This share corresponds to the SCRIPTS subdirectory of \Winnt\System32\ Repl\Export, making answers b and d incorrect. Logon scripts should be exported from the PDC to all BDCs responsible for authenticating logons on the network; therefore, answer a is correct. Replication of logon scripts should not occur with workstations but should remain on domain controllers, so answer c is incorrect.

Question 8

The files appearing in a PC system partition are: BOOT.INI, NTDETECT.COM, and NTLDR. When a BIOS-disabled SCSI drive is used as the boot or system partition, an additional file, NTBOOTDD.SYS, also is required. Thus, answers a, b, and d are correct. Answer e applies only to RISC machines (that is, non-Intel CPUs) running Windows NT; answer c names a file that appears in the default Windows NT system32 directory; answer f names the file that appears in the system partition only on a multiboot machine that numbers DOS, Windows, Windows 95, or some other near DOS-equivalent among the list of boot options in BOOT.INI.

Question 9

There is no counter named Pages/Thread; therefore, answer a is incorrect. The Memory Pages/Second counter should be watched to decide whether you need more RAM; therefore, answer b is correct. If you want to find out the percentage of elapsed time that a processor is busy, you would look at % Processor time; therefore, answer c is incorrect. The LogicalDisk: Avg. Disk Bytes/Transfer counter indicates the amount of bytes transferred to and from a disk, but does not relate to memory; therefore, answer d is incorrect.

Question 10

The Registry cannot be backed up remotely; therefore, answer a is incorrect. Adding a second tape drive to your network is the only solution for capturing the Registry on the PDC without switching backup software products, so answer b is correct. A domain controller can be protected by a backup, and all of its files can be backed up remotely, but the Registry can only be backed up locally, so answer c is incorrect. An ERD does not contain an entire copy of the Registry, so answer d is incorrect.

Question 11

Only answer d is correct. RAS maintains a map list of the resources accessed over WAN links. When one of these resources is referenced, it will attempt to AutoDial to regain a connection to the server hosting the resource. Answer a would be the result if AutoDial was not enabled, but you always should assume the default configuration for computers in the Microsoft exam questions unless indicated otherwise; therefore, answer a is incorrect. Answers b and c are fictitious activities that do not occur, so they are incorrect.

Question 12

Disk striping without parity requires only two physical drives to be implemented; therefore, answer a is incorrect. Disk striping without parity can host either NTFS or FAT, so answer b is correct. Disk striping without parity is not a fault tolerance storage method, so answer c is incorrect. Disk striping without parity does have better performance than disk mirroring, so answer d is correct. Disk striping without parity cannot be recovered without a full backup, so answer e is correct.

Question 13

IIS will offer only WWW, FTP, and Gopher services—not access to the entire network, and without additional security; therefore, answer a is incorrect. SLIP will not offer access over the Internet, it cannot be used to dial into an NT Server, and it does not support encryption; therefore, answer b is incorrect. PPTP offers a reliable and secure network connection over the Internet, so answer c is correct. Require Encrypted Authentication is a mid-level security setting, but it does not directly relate to establishing a connection over the Internet, nor does it imply access to the network, so answer d is incorrect.

Question 14

Report view is much easier to look at when you are monitoring many objects at a time; therefore, answer a is the correct response. You cannot get a graph from Report view, but you can easily monitor multiple counters at a time; therefore, answer b is incorrect. The Alert view sends network messages to the Administrators when something goes wrong; therefore, answer c also is incorrect. NT diagnostics will not allow you to view counters and objects; therefore, answer d is incorrect.

Question 15

The Network applet is not used in any way to work with domain controller status, so answer a is incorrect. The Demote command in the Server Manager menu will appear only when two PDCs are booted into the same domain, and the second PDC will remain inactive in security support until it is demoted to BDC status; therefore, answer b is incorrect. Although you promote a BDC to a PDC by using Server Manager, you need to reinstall Windows NT Server to change the role of the server from a domain controller to a member server, and vice versa; therefore, choice c is correct. For this particular scenario, you must reinstall Windows NT Server and select Stand-Alone or Member Server when the system asks for a role for the server. There is no such selection as Member Server on a BDC's startup screen or boot menu, so answer d is incorrect.

Question 16

The User Manager does not have the ability to modify shares, so answer a is incorrect. Server Manager allows users to create new shares on remote computers; therefore, choice b is correct. Windows Explorer cannot be used to create shares on other computers over the network; it is able only to access existing shares. Therefore, answer c is incorrect. NCA does not modify shares—it is used to create boot disks for installing new client machines; therefore, answer d is incorrect.

Question 17

If the other machines on the network were experiencing problems, the server's NIC could be suspect, but because the problem is limited to a single workstation, the server NIC probably is not the culprit. Therefore, answer a is incorrect. Because the only protocol in use is NWLink (or IPX/SPX, if you prefer), there is no possibility of protocol mismatch, so answer b is incorrect. Most memory conflicts will cause a machine to crash rather than simply rendering network access inoperative; therefore, answer c is incorrect. Since NWLink can use various frame types, the workstation easily could be misconfigured to use a different frame type than the rest of the network; therefore, answer d is correct.

Question 18

Answer a displays an improperly formatted ARC name: When multi is used, the disk(0) number must be zero, so answer a is incorrect. Answer b indicates the first partition of the second hard drive on the first multi type drive controller. This is the location of the system partition (the location of the boot files) for this question; therefore, answer b is correct. Answer c points to a second drive controller that doesn't exist for this example; therefore, answer c is incorrect. Answer d uses an incorrect number for the partition element—this number never can be zero, as the first partition is defined by using the number one. Therefore, answer d is wrong. Answer e indicates a second drive controller that doesn't exist—the first drive on that controller, the system partition in this example, is on the first and only existing controller and on the second hard drive, so answer e is incorrect.

Question 19

The secret to this question is understanding that Auto Detect is aimed at newer versions of NetWare (3.12 and higher), which support only 802.2 headers by default, in keeping with common practice for most networks. Auto Detect will not be able to detect anything but 802.2, which means that the only correct answer to this question is answer a. The 802.3 and 802.5 frame types are used by older versions of NetWare (pre-3.12) and are not detected by NT, making answers b, c, d, and e incorrect.

Question 20

System: Interrupts/Second doesn't provide information about the CPU; therefore, answer a is incorrect. Checking the pages per second allows you to verify if the amount of RAM in your system is adequate; therefore, answer b is incorrect. Processor: % Processor Time is used to see how busy the processor is; therefore, answer c is correct. Anything over 80 percent might mean you need to replace the processor and add additional ones. The Processor: Interrupts/Second indicates the level of hardware interrupts occurring, not the use level of the CPU; therefore, answer d is incorrect.

Question 21

To calculate share and NTFS permissions combined, take the most permissive of each kind and then the least permissive of the remaining share and NTFS permissions. If No Access appears anywhere, the resulting permission always will be No Access. Of the three share permissions that pertain to the ProjectA share, Full Control is the most permissive, so that becomes his share permission. The NTFS permission is Change. The less permissive of Change and Full Control is Change, so the effective permission is Change; therefore, answer c is correct.

Question 22

The key to answering this question is to understand GSNW and what must happen on the NetWare side of a connection that uses GSNW. In essence, GSNW provides a way to "translate" ordinary Microsoft Network client traffic bound for a Windows NT server into a usable kind of NetWare equivalent. This prevents administrators from having to add software to network clients that need access to NetWare resources, which is especially useful on older machines (for example, those running Windows for Workgroups at the shelter) where memory and system resources already are at a premium. The correct answer to this question requires you to recognize that GSNW does the job, but it also requires you to know that it is necessary to set up a group account on the NetWare server to handle GSNW requests from the Windows NT server. This means that c is the only correct answer.

Answer a is incorrect because it places the NetWare group on the Windows NT server. Answer b is incorrect because it provides a way to make Windows NT services available to NetWare clients, not vice versa. Finally, answer d is incorrect because it puts the gateway on the NetWare server (a highly unlikely place to run a Windows NT service).

Question 23

The easiest approach to this kind of problem, be it caused by untoward edits to the Registry or installation of drivers or new system components, is to choose the LKGC (Last Known Good Configuration) option during bootup. Therefore, answer d is correct. Answers a and b may produce the same results eventually, but they're nowhere near as easy (and perhaps not as up-to-date as the LKGC). Answer c is flat wrong, because you can't boot from the ERD.

Question 24

The User Manager For Domains is where most administration—such as adding users and changing their passwords—takes place for NT. Backup is not affected directly by User Manager; therefore, answer a is incorrect. Server Manager is for server administration, but you cannot check if a backup was successful; therefore, answer b is incorrect. To find out whether a backup was successful, you must check the Backup log in NTBACKUP; this means that answer c is correct. Although *everything* in NT lives in the Registry, you wouldn't look there for successful backup information; therefore, answer d is incorrect.

Question 25

You *never* should go to the Registry to "look up" information; therefore, answer a is incorrect. In Performance Monitor, you can click on the counter itself and hit the Explain button, which gives a better explanation of the objects and counters; therefore, answer b is correct. Although it is much more difficult, you can search for help on counters through the Help menu; therefore, answer c also is correct. The Report view will not offer any additional information about counters, because it simply displays an updated instant snapshot of counters in text form. Therefore, answer d is incorrect.

Question 26

This may seem like an irrelevant question on a Windows NT Server test. But the complete name for the gateway appears as Gateway (and Client) Service For NetWare in the Services applet in Control Panel under Windows NT Server. This means that CSNW is a subset of GSNW, strictly for use by the server where GSNW is installed. Whether CSNW is explicitly supplied on a Windows NT workstation or implied in the contents of GSNW on a Windows NT server, the answers to this question are the same: None of the gateway or access services is required to use CSNW capabilities. This automatically eliminates answers a, b, and e.

Both of the remaining elements—that is, answers c (NWLink) and d (a valid account on a NetWare server)—are necessary to make successful use of CSNW. NWLink supplies the necessary protocol to communicate from client to server; a valid account on a NetWare server provides the necessary permission to access the NetWare server once communication commences.

Question 27

All print devices must be identical; therefore, answer a is correct. To create a printer pool, all print devices must be connected to the same print server; therefore, answer b also is correct. Answers c and d are both incorrect—you don't have to use the same port for multiple printer devices, and printers don't have to be in the same room.

Question 28

If frame types other than 802.2 are being used on a network, Manual Frame Type Detection must be enabled. Frame types belonging to each client must be added to the frame type configuration list on the NWLink IPX/SPX Properties dialog box. Therefore, answer d is correct.

Question 29

Creating a new account manually is both time-consuming and tedious; because answer a is inefficient, it's clearly not the best way to do this. Answer b makes the switch with the simple change of a name and a password; it's fast and simple, which is why Microsoft recommends this approach. Answer c is a nice try, but you must use User Manager for Domains, not Server Manager, to make this change. Answer d will work and leaves the old account around in case the old programmer ever comes back. While this process leaves the old account around for security auditing, it is Microsoft's current position that it is best to rename the account instead of keeping it around.

Question 30

PostScript printing has nothing to do with print device installation; therefore, answer a is incorrect. You can't install a print driver if NT can't recognize the print device; therefore, answer b is incorrect. The print processor is not involved in the installation of printers; therefore, answer c is also incorrect. For Windows NT to provide support for HP network interface print devices, you must install the DLC (Data Link Control) protocol to create a network attached port; therefore, answer d is correct. You can't install a printer driver if Windows NT cannot recognize the print device through a specified port.

Question 31

A single network profile that retains the .DAT suffix will not give each user a familiar desktop setting; instead, it will cause desktop chaos because each user's changes will be saved. Therefore, answer a is incorrect. Changing all profiles from custom to mandatory will not establish roaming profiles and will prevent users from making any future changes to their profiles; therefore, answer b is incorrect. Moving the profiles from the workstations to a server without changing them to roaming or editing the user accounts will not accomplish the goal, because accounts will not be pulled from the server and they will not be present on the workstations; therefore, answer c is incorrect. By moving the profiles to a server, changing them to roaming, and configuring the user accounts to access the new storage location, the goal with be accomplished. Therefore, answer d is correct.

Question 32

The whole point of a gateway is to permit clients to access services that their current configurations otherwise would make inaccessible. For that reason, answer a is the only correct answer because it opens a gateway for the Windows NT and Windows 95 workstations to access NetWare resources with no change to their current configurations.

Answer b is incorrect, because by adding NWLink to the workstations, it not only violates the requirement that no NetWare client software be added to those machines, but it does not do the complete job (additional software would be necessary to make it possible for these machines to communicate with a NetWare server). Answer c mentions the right software product, but puts it on a NetWare server rather than on a Windows NT server, where it was designed to be run. And finally, File and Print Services For NetWare let native NetWare clients access Windows NT, not native Microsoft Networking clients access NetWare (thus completely missing the point of the question). Therefore, answer d is incorrect.

Question 33

With nonstandardized configurations implementing any encryption security other than Allow Any Authentication Including Clear Text, some clients are restricted from accessing the network via RAS. Therefore, only answer a is correct. Microsoft Encrypted Authentication and Require Encrypted Authentication are encryption security schemes that require special configuration or operating systems; therefore, answers b and d are incorrect. PGP Encryption is not a native option of NT; therefore, answer c is incorrect.

Question 34

The correct answer is b, False. Since Windows NT 4 no longer supports HPFS, you'll have to obtain the ACLCONV utility from Microsoft to convert the HPFS partition into NTFS. For NT 4, you can convert only FAT partitions into NTFS partitions. Since NT 3.51 convert will switch HPFS to NTFS, it might be even better to convert HPFS to NTFS before installing the upgrade to 4.

Question 35

The secret to answering this question lies in knowing how to "unpack" its contents and what values to assign based on the information it contains. Partitions are numbered ordinally, starting from one, so any correct answer must end in partition(4). This automatically disqualifies answer a.

Any SCSI hard disk with its onboard BIOS disabled must begin with the string scsi(*). This automatically disqualifies answer d. Likewise, if the scsi keyword begins an ARC name, the value for rdisk will always be zero; this disqualifies answer c.

By process of elimination, this means that b must be the right answer. When we unpack the question, we see that:

➤ the first SCSI controller with BIOS disabled translates into scsi(0)

➤ the SCSI Bus ID provides the value for disk(*) whenever the BIOS is disabled, which translates into disk(1)

➤ because the BIOS is disabled, rdisk(*) is always rdisk(0)

➤ the value for partition equals its number on the drive, so partition(*) translates into partition(4)

Only answer b matches the entire string.

Question 36

TCP/IP and NetBEUI, but not NWLink, is the restriction for the AutoDial feature, but not a limitation of RAS as a whole. Therefore, answer a is incorrect. TCP/IP and NWLink, but not NetBEUI, are the protocols that can be routed over RAS, but not a limitation as to which protocols can be used. Therefore, answer b is incorrect. Only TCP/IP can be used over SLIP, but RAS is not limited to SLIP; therefore, answer c is incorrect. TCP/IP, NetBEUI, and NWLink can all be used over RAS; therefore, answer d is correct.

Question 37

Gateway Service For NetWare must be installed on the Windows server; therefore, answer a is correct. For the Windows NT server to communicate with the NetWare server, the NWLink protocol must be installed on the

Windows NT server; therefore, answer b also is correct. CSNW is not used because there are no longer individual user accounts on the NetWare server; therefore, answer c is incorrect. The SAP Agent is not used when providing clients access to NetWare resources through NT; therefore, answer d is incorrect.

Question 38

It is possible to set priorities between groups of documents by creating different logical printers for the same physical print device and setting different priority levels on the printers. To set printer priority, select the Scheduling tab in the Printer Properties dialog box. The lowest priority is 1; therefore, answer a is incorrect. The highest priority is 99; therefore, b is the correct answer. There is no Start Printing Immediately option; therefore, answer c is incorrect. Any NT printer automatically prints to the print device; therefore, answer d is incorrect.

Question 39

Disk mirroring can contain the same system and/or boot partitions as the original disk; therefore, answer a is correct. Disk striping without parity cannot contain the system or boot partitions, so answer b is incorrect. A volume set cannot contain the system or boot partitions, so answer c is incorrect. Disk duplexing can contain the system and/or boot partitions as the original disk; therefore, answer d is also correct.

Question 40

The steps in answer a cause you to perform many long and unnecessary steps—neither formatting the two drives nor restoring from tape backup is required, so answer a is incorrect. Windows NT will not restore a mirror set automatically; therefore, answer b is incorrect. The steps in answer c will restore the mirror set properly, with the roles of the drives reversed, making answer c correct. The steps in answer d are used to repair a stripe set with parity; therefore, answer d is incorrect.

Question 41

To perform a network installation of Windows NT on a computer running Windows 95, it is necessary to obtain access to and run the WINNT.EXE program. Thus, a is the only possible correct answer. Both answers b and d refer to SETUP.EXE, which is the install program for Windows 3.x and Windows 95, not for Windows NT (you must choose WINNT.EXE because it is the only version of the NT installation program that works on non-Windows NT systems). Answer c is incorrect because it assumes that NCA includes support for installing Windows NT Workstation; because this is not the case, the answer is wrong.

Question 42

Windows NT Diagnostics aren't available until Windows NT is installed successfully on a machine, nor does the program perform hardware checking on its own; rather, it reports the contents of the registry written by the NTDETECT.EXE program that runs at bootup. This means answer a is incorrect. System Sleuth is an old PC diagnostics program that doesn't perform Windows NT hardware compatibility checks of any kind, which makes answer b incorrect as well. The Windows NT Hardware Qualifier disk may be constructed by running the MAKEDISK.BAT program in the \Support\Hqtool directory on the Windows NT CD-ROM. Because NTHQ checks the machine against a built-in version of the HCL, it will do the job (except on machines with hardware newer than August 1996, which the software may not recognize). But because the machine is older than NTHQ, NTHQ should work correctly. This makes answer c correct. Finally, the HCL is indeed the source of the latest information on what works with Windows NT, even though checking by hand is more work than using NTHQ. This will produce a correct assessment of the machine, making answer d correct as well.

Question 43

Because the machine can recognize and use the CD-ROM while it's still running Windows 95, the easiest approach is to copy the files from the \i386 directory to a directory on the machine's hard disk. But this will work only if the drive is formatted to permit creation of another partition for NTFS or if the FAT partition where the files are deposited may be converted to NTFS later (see Chapter 3 for a discussion of FAT and NTFS). That's why b is correct. Answer d also is correct, because if the drives on the machine need to be reformatted completely—as often will be the case when upgrading from Windows 95 to Windows NT—it might be smarter to copy the installation files to a server and perform a network install. This leaves the drives on the machine free to be reformatted completely but will require a boot disk (that you might build using the Network Client Administrator).

Answer a is incorrect because the install disks alone don't convey all the Windows NT installation files; there's still a need to gain access to the CD-ROM or a copy of its contents. Answer c is incorrect because the 16-bit installation program, WINNT.EXE, works with Windows 95; WINNT32.EXE works only with versions of Windows NT 3.5 and higher.

Question 44

RAID 1 is disk mirroring that provides some fault tolerance; therefore, answer a is correct. Disk duplexing is a fault-tolerant storage method; therefore, answer b also is correct. A volume set is not fault tolerant; therefore, answer c is incorrect. Disk striping without parity is not fault tolerant, so answer d is incorrect. RAID 5 is disk striping with parity that provides fault tolerance; therefore, answer e is also correct.

Question 45

The binding order of the protocols on both the client and server determines what single LAN protocol is used over the RAS connection. This situation will result in a NetBEUI connection. Thus, WinSOCK applications (those based on the Windows TCP/IP API) cannot be used, because TCP/IP is not a protocol being communicated over the link. Therefore, answer d is correct. The other activities can occur using the NetBEUI protocol; therefore, answers a, b, and c are incorrect.

Question 46

FAT is the best choice because it requires much less overhead than NTFS, and Microsoft does not recommend NTFS on partitions smaller than 400 MB. Therefore, answer a is correct. CDFS is not a file system type that can be used to format a hard drive; it is the format of a CD-ROM. Therefore, answer b is incorrect. NTFS has too much overhead for a partition of this size. Therefore, answer c is incorrect. HPFS is not supported by NT 4.0. Therefore, answer d is incorrect.

Question 47

Disk mirroring will cut your storage capacity in half to implement fault tolerance, so answer a is incorrect. Disk striping with parity will reduce your storage capacity by one full drive to implement fault tolerance; therefore, answer b is incorrect. A volume set will maximize your storage capacity and allow you to add additional space as needed; therefore, answer c is correct. Disk stacking is not a valid storage method for NT, so answer d is incorrect.

Question 48

WINNT32.EXE works only with Windows NT, not with Windows 95; this disqualifies answer a. Answer b accurately describes a network install scenario and cites the correct version of the install program, so it is correct. SETUP.EXE is not the name of a program used to install Windows NT, so answer c is incorrect. Likewise, d fails because NETWORK.EXE will not perform a networked Windows NT installation.

Question 49

As with Question 35, the key is knowing how to "unpack" ARC names. Unless the BIOS is disabled on a SCSI controller, the initial keyword in an ARC name always is multi. Since there's no mention of BIOS in the question, this eliminates answers a and b immediately. The rest of the answer hinges on understanding that SCSI controllers are numbered ordinally, starting with zero. Since the primary must therefore be multi(0), this must change to multi(1); this makes c the only correct answer.

Question 50

Strictly speaking, upgrading from Windows for Workgroups (WfW) to Windows NT Server is not an installation option. But by installing Windows NT Server into the same directory in which WfW resides, the install program is smart enough to grab what information it can carry into the Windows NT environment by detecting and reading the WIN.INI and SYSTEM.INI files and converting program and group information into corresponding Windows NT Registry entries. This means, of course, that answer d is correct.

Answer a does not give the install program the implicit directive to convert the WfW .INI files and fails the "upgrade" requirement. Answer b apparently assumes that some magic import function for .INI files is available; because there isn't, this answer is incorrect. Finally, answer c provides the correct directory placement but calls the 32-bit version of the install program, which works only with Windows NT, not with WfW.

Question 51

The correct answers are a, b, and c. If users cannot log on to the machine across the network, they can't get to any partitions on that machine, whether FAT or NTFS. If a share is not defined where the confidential data resides, no user can obtain access to the data across the network. Finally, the user's share permissions must permit them at least to Read the data in that share, or they still won't be able to access it. The final element, d, is irrelevant because FAT partitions do not support file-level security—hence, they have no associated permissions.

Question 52

Because a RAS-connected client is no different from a direct-connected client, other than speed of data transfer, all standard network activities still occur over the WAN link. Therefore, all answers—a, b, c, d, and e—are correct.

Question 53

It is necessary to place user accounts in the NTGATEWAY group on the NetWare server only if workstations are accessing the NetWare server via a gateway. That is not the case in this example; therefore, answer a is incorrect. If an NT server is to act as a gateway to a NetWare server, Gateway Service For NetWare must be loaded onto a Windows NT server. Because this scenario describes an NT client accessing a NetWare server, answer b also is incorrect. Any user accessing a NetWare server directly will need a user account on that NetWare server; therefore, answer c is correct. An NT workstation running Client Service For NetWare can access a NetWare server directly by using the NWLink protocol; therefore, answer d also is correct.

Question 54

Only those computers running Windows NT Server (member servers and primary and backup domain controllers) can be configured to export files during replication; therefore, choices a and b are correct. NT workstations and Windows 95 cannot be export servers; therefore, answers c and d are incorrect.

Question 55

A print job won't print at all if the wrong protocol is in use, so answer a is incorrect. Likewise, nothing will print without the spooler; therefore, answer b is incorrect. If an incorrect printer driver has been installed, then documents may print illegibly. Therefore, choice c is correct. As in answer b, a print job won't print without proper spooling; therefore, answer d is incorrect.

Glossary Of Terms

AATP (Authorized Academic Training Program)—A program that authorizes accredited academic institutions of higher learning to offer Microsoft Certified Professional testing and training to their students. The institutions also are allowed to use the Microsoft Education course materials and Microsoft Certified Trainers.

account—*See* user account

account operators—A group built into Windows NT; users assigned to this account have the right to add, delete, and modify user accounts.

account policy—A policy that establishes how the passwords on a domain or a workstation are going to be used.

ACL (Access Control List)—A list of security identifiers contained by system objects that defines which users and groups have what level of services for an object.

ACLCONV utility—A tool used to transform O/S2 HPFS access lists to NTFS ACLs.

administrator—The person responsible for the upkeep, management, and security of a network. When capitalized, this term refers to a built-in user in Windows NT that has full control of the system.

AppleTalk—Apple Computer's networking protocols and software.

architecture— The structure of a network—how the network is set up and how its components are connected to each other.

ASCII (American Standard Code for Information Exchange)—A way of coding that translates letters, numbers, and symbols into digital form.

assessment exam—Similar to the certification exam, this type of exam gives you the opportunity to answer questions at your own pace. This type of exam also utilizes the same tools as the certification exam.

ATEC (Authorized Technical Education Center)—The location where you can take a Microsoft Official Curriculum course taught by Microsoft Certified Trainers.

Auto Frame Type Detection—A setting of the NWLink protocol that detects the frame type being used on the network.

AUTOEXEC.BAT—A DOS batch file launched when a computer is started or booted.

backup browsers—The machines on an NT network that maintain a duplicate list of the resources and act in a similar way within the Browser Service, as does the BDC within domain control.

basevideo—A command line parameter switch used on the BOOT.INI file, basevideo forces NT to boot using 16-color VGA video at 640×480. This setting appears by default on the ARC name line identified by [VGA mode].

BDC (Backup Domain Controller)—A backup server that protects the integrity and availability of the SAM database. BDCs are not able to make changes or modifications, but they can use the database to authenticate users.

beta exam—A trial exam that is given to participants at a Sylvan Prometric testing center before the development of the Microsoft Certified Professional certification exam is finalized. The final exam questions are selected based on the results of the beta exam. For example, if all beta exam participants get an answer correct or wrong, that question generally will not appear in the final version.

BIOS (Basic Input/Output System)—A system that houses the buffers used to transfer information from a program to the hardware devices receiving the information.

blue screen—The screen that appears when a GPF occurs under NT. This is a test display of the stop message error. Many details are included on this screen, such as the location of the error, type of error, and whether or not a memory dump is created.

blueprint survey—A part of the development process of the Microsoft Certification Exam, in which data is gathered from qualified job function experts. The blueprint survey helps decide the importance, required competence, and weighting for each individual exam objective.

boot disk—A hard drive or floppy drive that has bootstrap files on it. The bootstrap files enable an operating system to launch.

boot menu—The text menu that appears immediately after the hardware test on a Windows NT machine. It lists all the known operating systems present. The OS listed first will be booted by default when the timeout period expires, unless an alternate OS is manually selected.

BOOT.INI—One of the files placed on the system partition. This file contains the location of the system files for each OS installed on the machine. The locations are listed using ARC names.

BOOTSECT.DOS—The file containing DOS boot sector data; this file appears in the system partition only on a multiboot machine that numbers DOS, Windows, Windows 95, or some other near-DOS equivalent among the list of boot options in BOOT.INI.

break mirror—The first step in repairing a mirrored set. This is accomplished in the Disk Administrator utility, using the Break Mirror option in the Fault Tolerance drop-down menu.

cache—A specified area of high-speed memory used to contain data that is going to be, or recently has been, accessed.

CDFS (Compact Disk File System)—A special read-only file system supported by both Windows 95 and Windows NT 3.51 and higher, including 4. CDFS permits easy access to CDs in these operating systems.

Chart view—In Performance Monitor, this is the view that allows users to peruse realtime data in a line graph or histogram form.

client—A network user or a computer on a network used to access resources hosted by other machines on the network.

command line—A DOS prompt that accepts DOS-based commands.

computername—The name of a computer on a LAN that is specific to an individual workstation or server.

CONFIG.POL—In the NETLOGON share, this is the file where all policies are stored.

Control Panel—In Windows, this is the area where you modify settings such as fonts, screen color, SCSI hardware, and printers.

CPU (Central Processing Unit)—The brains of your computer—the area where all functions are performed.

CSNW (Client Service For NetWare)—Designed for Windows NT workstations that require a direct link to NetWare servers, CSNW lets Windows NT machines link up to and browse NetWare resources alongside Microsoft Windows Network resources.

cut score—On the Microsoft Certified Professional exam, the lowest score a person can receive and still pass.

database—A collection of information arranged and stored so that data can be accessed quickly and accurately.

default—A setting that is factory set and used until the user specifies otherwise.

deltree—A DOS application that deletes a directory tree and its contents.

DHCP (Dynamic Host Configuration Protocol)—A service that enables the assignment of dynamic TCP/IP network addresses, based on a specified pool of available addresses.

Dial-Up Networking—A utility, found in the RAS Phonebook|Programs| Accessories folder of the Start menu, that controls the dial-out capabilities of RAS.

directory replication—A service designed to disseminate often-used and regularly updated data (such as User profiles, logon scripts, and System policies) to multiple computers to speed file access and improve reliability.

disk administrator—An administration application in the Administrative Tools group that lets an administrator create and delete stripe sets and various disk partitions, change the assignment of drive letters, and display facts about partition size and setup.

disk controller—A piece of hardware that controls how data is written and retrieved from the computer's disk drive.

disk duplexing—A fault tolerance method used by Windows NT that employs a duplicate physical and logical drive on a separate hard disk where the drive is connected to the system via a separate controller. If the original drive or controller fails, the system continues to operate using the duplexed drive.

disk mirroring—A fault tolerance method used by Windows NT that creates an exact duplicate of one physical and logical storage device on a separate physical storage device, both attached to the same controller.

disk partition—A portion of a hard disk that acts like a physically separate unit.

disk striping—A fault tolerance method used by Windows NT that stores data across multiple physical storage devices.

Display Properties—A dialog box that allows you to modify certain properties of your desktop—the background, the screen saver, settings, and more.

DLC (Data Link Control)—A protocol used to interoperate with IBM mainframes and provide connectivity to network attached print devices.

DLLs (Dynamic Link Libraries)—Small executable program routines or device drivers stored in separate files. DLLs are loaded by the OS when called upon by a process or hardware device.

DMA (Direct Memory Addresses)—A method used by hardware adapters to get and store data from a system's RAM without involving the CPU.

DMP file—A memory dump file with the extension .DMP.

DNS (Domain Name Service)—An NT service used to resolve host names into IP addresses.

domain—A group of computers and peripheral devices sharing a common security database.

domain controller—A computer that authenticates domain logons and manages the Security Accounts Manager (SAM) database.

domain database—A database maintained by a PDC or BDC that stores three types of information: user accounts, computer accounts, and group accounts. Each user account requires 1 KB, each computer account requires 5 KB, and each group account requires 4 KB.

domain guest—A group whose members are given the minimal level of user access to all domain resources. The Guest account is automatically a member of this group.

domain model—A network setup definition used by Microsoft to describe and define organizational schemes for networks. In theory, the domain model can scale up to handle any size of network.

DOS (Disk Operating System)—Software that regulates the way a computer reacts with its floppy disks or hard disks.

driver—Software that bonds a peripheral device to the operating system.

encryption—A method of coding data in which a person has to have a decoding key to decipher the information.

ERD (Emergency Repair Disk)—A miniature first aid kit for NT. This single floppy contains all the files needed to repair the system partition and many boot partition-related problems.

ESDI (Enhanced Small Device Interface)—A pre-IDE type storage device that is low-level formatted with various values of sector per track.

Ethernet—The most widely used type of LAN; developed by Xerox.

Event log—An option in the Event Viewer in the Administrative Tools group that lets you view all of the events that have taken place on a particular computer.

Event Viewer—The application in Windows NT that displays all of the log files and lets you modify them.

Everyone—A default group that cannot be deleted or renamed and that lists each user within a domain as a member.

Exabytes—One billion Gigabytes.

Exam Preparation Guides—Guides that provide information specific to the material covered on Microsoft Certified Professional exams to help students prepare for the exam.

Exam Study Guide—Short for Microsoft Certified Professional Program Exam Study Guide, this contains information about the topics covered on more than one of the Microsoft Certified Professional exams.

FAT (File Allocation Table)—A table originally used by the DOS file system to hold information about the properties, location, and size of files being stored on a disk.

fault tolerance—The ability of a computer to work continuously, even when there is system failure.

FDISK command—A DOS command that is used to partition a hard disk.

firewall—A barrier—made of software and/or hardware—between two networks, permitting only authorized communication to pass.

firmware—A type of software that becomes part of the hardware function after it has been saved into a programmable read-only memory chip (PROM).

FPNW (File And Print Services For NetWare)—An NT service that makes resources from a Windows NT Server available to NetWare clients without requiring additional software or configuration changes.

FQDN (Fully Qualified Domain Name)—The complete site name of an Internet computer system.

frames—The segments created by the access method used when packets are being sent across a network.

FTP (File Transfer Protocol)—A protocol that transfers files to and from a local hard drive to an FTP server located on another TCP/IP-based network (such as the Internet).

Full Control—In NT Server, a level of permission that gives the person to whom it is assigned all of the general permissions, as well as the authority to change permissions.

gateway—The service performed by a computer that converts the protocols between different types of networks or computers.

GDI (Graphics Device Interface)—A component that provides network applications with a system for presenting graphical information. The GDI works as a translator between an application's print request and the device driver interface (DDI), ensuring that the job is rendered accurately.

global groups—Groups that apply to all computers within a network. A global group needs to be defined only once for each domain. Global groups may only have users as members.

Gopher service—An Internet service that provides text-only information over the Internet. A Gopher service is most suited to large documents with little or no formatting or images.

GPF (General Protection Fault)—In Windows 3.x, this is an error that occurs when two or more programs are assigned to the same area of memory. In Windows NT, this appears as a blue screen.

graphics—Pictures and images created in a computer.

groups—Collections of users defined with a common name and level of resource permissions.

GSNW (Gateway Service For NetWare)—An NT service that lets Windows NT servers map a drive to a NetWare server. GSNW provides access to NetWare server resources for Windows NT workstations (via a gateway).

GUI (Graphical User Interface)—A computer setup that uses graphics, windows, and a trackball or mouse as the method of interaction with the computer.

HAL (Hardware Abstraction Layer)—In the NT operating system, the HAL creates a bridge between the Windows NT operating system and a computer's CPU.

hard drive—Also called the hard disk, the hard drive is the permanent storage area for data.

hardware—The physical components of a computer system.

HCL (Hardware Compatibility List)—A list that comes with NT Server; this list indicates what hardware is compatible with the software. The most updated version of this list can be found on the Microsoft Web site or on the TechNet CD.

hive—A section of the Windows NT Registry.

HPFS (High Performance File System)—The first PC-compatible file system that supported LFNs. Like FAT, HPFS maintains a directory structure, but it adds automatic sorting of the directory and includes support for special attributes to better accommodate multiple naming conventions and file-level security. HPFS is no longer supported under Windows NT 4.

HTML (Hypertext Markup Language)—Based on SGML, HTML is the markup language used to create Web pages.

HTTP (HyperText Transfer Protocol)—The World Wide Web protocol that allows for the transfer of HTML documents over the Internet or intranets and responds to actions (such as a user clicking on hypertext links).

IDE (Integrated Device Electronics)—A type of storage device interface in which the electronics required to operate the drive are stored on the drive itself, thus eliminating the need for a separate controller card.

IEEE (Institute of Electrical and Electronic Engineers)—A group of technical professionals that sponsors technical conferences worldwide, publishes over 25 percent of the world's technical papers, and contributes significantly to the establishment of technical standards.

IIS (Internet Information Server)—Web server software by Microsoft; included and implemented with Windows NT Server.

INI files—Files that contain all of the startup information essential to launching a program or operating system.

Input/Output System—A system that requires input into an input device (such as a keyboard) and outputs.

Internet—The collection of TCP/IP-based networks around the world.

intranet—An internal, private network that uses the same protocols and standards as the Internet.

IP address—Four sets of numbers, separated by decimal points, that represent the numeric address of a computer attached to a TCP/IP network, such as the Internet.

IPC (InterProcess Communications)—Within an operating system, this is the service that facilitates the exchange of data between applications.

IPX/SPX (Internetwork Packet Exchange/Sequenced Packet Exchange)—Novell's NetWare protocol, reinvented by Microsoft and implemented in Windows NT under the name NWLink. It is fully compatible with Novell's version and in many cases is a better implementation than the original.

IRQ (Interrupt Request)—On a PC, IRQ is a hardware interrupt.

ISDN (Integrated Services Digital Network)—A form of digital communication that has a bandwidth of 128 Kbps.

ISP (Internet Service Provider)—An organization that charges a fee for providing your Internet connection and other related services.

job function expert—A person with extensive knowledge about a particular job function and the software products/technologies related to that job. Typically, a job function expert is currently performing the job, has recently performed the job, or is training people to do this job.

kernel—The essential part of an operating system; provides basic OS services.

kernel debugger—An NT application that records NT's activity during bootup and when a stop error occurs.

LAN (Local Area Network)—A network confined to a single building or geographic area and comprised of servers, workstations, peripheral devices, a network operating system, and a communications link.

LAN Manager—A network operating system product developed by Microsoft, deployed as a server application under OS/2.

Last Known Good Configuration (LKGC)—A recording made by NT of all the Registry settings that existed the last time a user successfully logged on to the server.

leased line—A communication line leased from a communications provider, such as an ISP or a telephone company.

LFN (Long File Names)—File names of up to 256 characters.

LMHOSTS—The predecessor to WINS, LMHOSTS is a static list of NetBIOS names mapped to IP addresses.

local group—A group of users on a single workstation; when the group is set up, the users are given privileges and rights. Local groups may contain users or global groups.

lockout—In Windows NT security, lockout is a feature used to prevent compromised accounts from being used.

logical partitions—The multiple segments of a physical hard drive. Each segment can be used independently of the others, including belonging to separate volumes and hosting different file systems. Most logical partitions have a drive letter assigned to them and can be referred to by an ARC name.

logical printers—The software component used by NT to direct print jobs from applications to a print server. A physical printer can be serviced by numerous logical printers.

logoff—The process by which a user quits a computer system.

logon—The process by which a user gains access or signs on to a computer system.

MAKEDISK.BAT—A utility located in the \Support\Hqtool directory that creates a bootable DOS floppy to run NTHQ (NT Hardware Qualifier) upon bootup.

Master Boot Record (MBR)—A BIOS bootstrap routine—used by low-level, hardware-based system code stored in Read-Only Memory (ROM)—to initiate the boot sequence on a PC. This in turn calls a bootstrap loader, which then commences to load the machine's designated operating system.

master browser—A computer on an NT network that maintains the main list of all available resources within a domain (including links to external domains).

MCI (multiple-choice item)—An item (within a series of items) that is the answer to a question (single-response MCI) or one of the answers to a question (multiple-response MCI).

MCP (Microsoft Certified Professional)—An individual who has taken and passed at least one certification exam and has earned one or more of the following certifications: Microsoft Certified Trainer, Microsoft Certified Solution Developer, Microsoft Certified Systems Engineer, or Microsoft Certified Product Specialist.

MCPS (Microsoft Certified Product Specialist)—An individual who has passed at least one of the Microsoft operating system exams.

MCSD (Microsoft Certified Solution Developer)—An individual who is qualified to create and develop solutions for businesses using the Microsoft development tools, technologies, and platforms.

MCSE (Microsoft Certified Systems Engineer)—An individual who is an expert on Windows NT and the Microsoft BackOffice integrated family of server software. This individual also can plan, implement, maintain, and support information systems associated with these products.

MCT (Microsoft Certified Trainer)—An individual who is qualified by Microsoft to teach Microsoft Education courses at sites authorized by Microsoft.

Microsoft certification exam—A test created by Microsoft to verify a test taker's mastery of a software product, technology, or computing topic.

Microsoft Certified Professional Certification Update—A newsletter for Microsoft Certified Professional candidates and Microsoft Certified Professionals.

Microsoft official curriculum—Microsoft education courses that support the certification exam process and are created by the Microsoft product groups.

Microsoft Roadmap to Education and Certification—An application, based on Microsoft Windows, that will take you through the process of deciding what your certification goals are and inform you of the best way to achieve them.

Microsoft Sales Fax Service—A service through which you can obtain Exam Preparation Guides, fact sheets, and additional information about the Microsoft Certified Professional Program.

Microsoft Solution Provider—An organization, not directly related to Microsoft, that provides integration, consulting, technical support, and other services related to Microsoft products.

Microsoft TechNet Technical Information Network—A service provided by Microsoft that provides helpful information via a monthly CD-ROM disk. TechNet is the primary source of technical information for people who support and/or educate end users, create automated solutions, or administer networks and/or databases.

Microsoft's NWLink—Microsoft's implementation of the Internetwork Packet eXchange/Sequenced Packet eXchange (IPX/SPX) protocols.

migration tool—An application that converts a hardware or software technology from one form to another. The NetWare migration tool converts users and groups to NT equivalents.

mirror set—A pair of disks that have been duplicated through the Windows NT disk mirroring fault tolerance method.

modem applet—An application for installing and maintaining a modem.

MOLI (Microsoft Online Institute)—An organization that makes training materials, online forums and user groups, and online classes available.

motherboard—The main circuit board in a computer system.

MRI (multiple-rating item)—An item that gives you a task and a proposed solution. Every time the task is set, an alternate solution is given and the candidate must choose the answer that gives the best results produced by one solution.

MS Exchange—An enterprise-wide messaging and mail system, developed by Microsoft.

MSDN (Microsoft Developer Network)—The official source for Software Development Kits (SDKs), Device Driver Kits (DDKs), operating systems, and programming information associated with creating applications for Microsoft Windows and Windows NT.

MULTI—The designation in an ARC name of the type of hard drive; the other option is SCSI.

multicast—The transmission of a message to several recipients simultaneously.

multichannel—Having more than a single inbound or outbound communications port, link, or connection.

multilink PPP—An NT network protocol that allows you to combine the bandwidth of multiple physical links, which increases the total bandwidth that could be used for a RAS connection.

multiple master domain model—A domain model that has two or more master domains; they must trust each other via two-way trust relationships. Centralized administration of user accounts also must be provided.

multitasking—Running more than one computer application on a system at a time.

NDA (nondisclosure agreement)—A legal agreement signed both by Microsoft and by a vendor, rendering certain rights and limitations.

NetBEUI—A simple network layer transport protocol developed to support NetBIOS networks.

NetBIOS—Originally developed by IBM in the 1980s, this protocol provides the underlying communication mechanism for some basic NT functions, such as browsing and interprocess communications between network servers.

NETLOGON—An administrative share created and used within domain controllers for authenticating users logging on to the enterprise domain.

NetWare—A popular network operating system developed by Novell.

Network Client Administrator—Located in the Administrative Tools Start menu, this is used to create a boot disk or a set or startup disks for DOS workstations.

Network Filing System—A popular distributed file system on Unix networks.

Network Neighborhood—Within Explorer or My Computer, this is the area in which you access other computers on the network.

NIC (Network Interface Card)—An adapter card used to connect a computer to a network.

No Access permission—A level of permission assigned to users or groups, restricting them from accessing the designated area.

nodebug—A BOOT.INI switch that informs you that debugging information is being used.

NTCONFIG.POL—The file that defines a system policy as the default policy.

NTFS (New Technology File System)—A naming file system used in Windows NT.

NTGATEWAY—The suggested default name of the group account for GSNW.

NTHQ (NT Hardware Qualifier) disk—The disk that checks a computer against a built-in version of the HCL (except on machines with hardware newer than August 1996, which the software may not recognize).

NTLDR file—The executable program, launched by the boot files, that loads the NT kernel. The name is a shortened version of NT Loader.

NTOSKRNL.EXE—The executable file for the Windows NT operating system that includes all the basic capabilities and components necessary to establish a working runtime environment. This file resides in the \Winnt_root\system32 directory on the boot partition.

null-modem cable—An RS-232 cable used to enable two computers within close proximity to communicate without using a modem.

NWLink—Microsoft's "clean room" implementation of Novell's IPX/SPX protocol suite for NetWare networks.

operating system (OS)—A software program that controls the operations on a computer system.

OSLOADER.EXE—The OS loader program for RISC computers. This program provides all of the services and information provided by NTDETECT.COM, BOOTSEC.DOS, NTDETECT.COM, and NTLDR on PCs. This file resides wherever the nonvolatile RAM location data indicates.

/OX—The parameter switch used on WINNT.EXE or WINNT32.EXE to force setup floppy creation. If /OX appears as the only parameter, it will simply build a set of installation disks for Windows NT.

pagefile—The file used by the virtual memory manager to store segments or pages of memory temporarily to hard disk.

PAP (Password Authentication Protocol)—A clear-text authentication protocol.

parity—Redundant segments of data used to provide fault tolerance to information. Within NT, this term is most commonly used when discussing stripe sets with parity. Also, a disk storage configuration where additional data is stored so that, in the event of a single drive failure, all data can be reconstructed.

partition—A portion of memory or a portion of a hard disk.

password—A word used by an individual to gain access to a particular system.

PDC (Primary Domain Controller)—The central storage and management server for the SAM database.

Per Seat—A licensing mode that allows users to connect to as many servers as they want without requiring a separate license for each connection.

Performance Monitor—A graphical application that lets you set, graph, log, and report alerts.

peripheral device—A hardware device connected to a computer.

permissions—A level of access assigned to files or folders. Permissions determine who has access rights to those files or folders.

PGP (Pretty Good Privacy)—An encryption program that is not native to Windows NT.

phonebook entry—A collection of settings used by a RAS to establish a connection with a remote dial-up server. A phonebook entry contains details such as phone number, name, password, protocol settings, and encryption type.

physical disk—The hardware component that adds additional storage space. A physical disk must be partitioned and formatted with a file system before data can be stored on it.

PING—A TCP/IP command used to verify the existence and connection to remote hosts over a network.

policies—A set of specifications or limitations that restrict the environment of a user. NT has three policies: account, user rights, and audit.

POSIX—An operating system type that complies with the IEEE Std 1003.1 standard. NT supports only POSIX.1.

potential browser—A computer with the ability to participate in the support of the list of resources for a domain. A potential browser will be elected to a position of backup or master browser by the browser service automatically, as needed.

PPP (Point-to-Point Protocol)—An industry-standard protocol used to establish network-protocol-supporting links over telephone lines using modems.

PPTP (Point-to-Point Tunneling Protocol)—A protocol that enables "tunneling" of IPX, NetBEUI, or TCP/IP inside PPP packets in such a way as to establish a secure link between a client and server over the Internet.

print device—The physical hardware device that produces printed output.

print driver—The software component that enables communication between the operating system and the physical printing device.

print job—A document or image sent from a client to a printer. A print job is typically coded in Windows EMF or the RAW language of the printer.

Print Operators—A default group that has full control over all printers within a domain.

print queue—The list of print jobs waiting to be sent to the printer for processing. The print queue can be viewed by opening the printer folder for any individual logical printer.

print server—The computer that hosts the spool file for a printer and/or that physically is attached to the printer.

printer—Typically refers to the logical printer (software component) within the NT environment, as opposed to the physical printing device.

printer pool—A collection of identical printers served by a single logical printer.

printing device—The hardware device that creates marks on paper in the pattern dictated by the driver software.

priorities—The designation of the importance of a process to gain processing time.

process tracking—A type Audit event that records process activities, such as handle duplication, indirect object access, and process termination.

processor time—A counter in the Performance Monitor that shows you how busy the processor is.

protocol—In networking, a set of rules that defines how information is transmitted over a network.

RAID (Redundant Array of Inexpensive Disks)—A standardized method for categorizing fault tolerance storage systems. Windows NT implements Level 0, Level 1, and Level 5 RAID through software, not hardware.

RAS (Remote Access Service)—A Windows NT service that provides network communication for remote clients over telecommunication lines. RAS connections are different from standard direct network connections only in relation to speed.

RDISK—The second segment of an ARC name used with the initial segment of MULTI to indicate the ordinal number of the physical storage device.

read access—The ability to view and open a file or document.

Registry—The hierarchical database that serves as a repository for hardware, software, and OS configuration information.

replication—A service of NT that automatically distributes files and directories from one server to multiple servers and workstations on the network.

replicator group—The default group whose members have permissions to access the replication service and directories. This group is used exclusively by the Directory Replication service and the user account created for the service.

resource kit—The additional documentation and software utilities distributed by Microsoft to provide information and instruction on the proper operation and modification of its software products.

Rights—Settings that define the ability of a user to access a computer or a domain.

RIP (Routing Internet Protocol)—A protocol that enables communication between routers on a network to facilitate the exchange of routing tables.

RISC (Reduced Instruction Set Computer)—A set of processor instructions that speeds up processing by using simple computer instructions. Also, a type of computer platform.

router—A device or a software implementation that enables interoperability and communication across networks.

RPC (Remote Procedure Call) Configuration—A programming interface that allows software applications running on separate computers on different networks to use each other's services.

RSA (Rivest-Shamir-Adleman)—An encryption technology that uses a public/private key pair.

SAM (Security Accounts Manager)—The security database of NT, the SAM maintains a record of all users, groups, and permissions within a domain. The SAM is stored on the PDC and is duplicated on the BDCs.

SAP (Service Advertising Protocol)—An IPX service that broadcasts the services and addresses on a network.

SCSI (Small Computer System Interface)—A standard interface, defined by ANSI, that provides for high-speed connections to devices such as hard drives, scanners, and printers.

security—A manner of protecting data by restricting access to authorized users.

Server Manager—The NT administration utility where computer accounts are managed.

Server Operators—The default group whose members can manage domain servers.

Service Pack—A patch or fix distributed by Microsoft after the final release of a product to repair errors, bugs, and security breaches.

share—A network construct that enables remote users to access resources located throughout a network.

share-level permissions—The setting of user/group access on a network share. The permissions of a network share must be met by users before access to the object is granted.

SLIP (Serial Line Internet Protocol)—An older industry standard for RAS communication links. It is included with NT only for establishing connections with Unix systems that do not support the newer PPP standard.

SMTP (Simple Mail Transfer Protocol)—An Internet protocol used to distribute email from one mail server to another over a TCP/IP network.

SNA (Systems Network Architecture)—A widely used network architecture developed by IBM.

SNMP (Simple Network Management Protocol)—A protocol used to monitor remote hosts over a TCP/IP network.

spooler—A software component of the print system that stores print jobs on a hard drive while the jobs wait in the print queue.

SQL Server—A Microsoft product that supports a network-enabled relational database system.

Stand-Alone server—Also called a "member server," this is a server in a workgroup or a domain environment that does not participate in domain control or user authentication; therefore, it must rely on other domain controllers to service its domain logons.

stripe set—A hard disk construct in which segments of data are written in sequence across multiple drives.

subnet—A portion or segment of a TCP/IP network.

System log—The log, viewed through Event Viewer, in which general system information and errors are recorded.

System Policy Editor—The administrative tool used to create and modify system policies for computers, groups, and users.

take ownership—The command that allows you to grab Full Control authority over an object.

tape drives—Devices, used for backing up data, that employ metal film cassettes for storage.

TAPI (Telephony Application Programming Interface)—An interface and API that defines how applications can interact with data/fax/voice devices and calls.

Task Manager—A utility with which applications and processes can be viewed, stopped, and started. Task Manager also offers CPU and memory status information.

TCP/IP—The most widely used protocol in networking today, because it is the most flexible of the transport protocols and is able to span wide areas.

Telnet—A terminal emulation utility used to interact with remote computers.

Token Ring—A network topology in which the computers are arranged in a ring and a token is used to pass the privilege of communicating over the network.

trust—A link between two domains that enables pass-through authentication, so that users from one domain can access the resources of another. A trust is a one-way relationship only.

two-way trust—A link between two domains established by the creation of two one-way trusts.

UDP (User Datagram Protocol)—A TCP component that transmits data through a connectionless service. This type of transmission does not guarantee the delivery or sequencing of sent packets.

UNC (Universal Naming Convention)—A standardized naming method for networks taking the form of \\servername\sharename.

Unicode character set—An ANSI standard for encoding characters and letters shared between different languages' character sets and keyboards.

Unix—An interactive time-sharing operating system developed in 1969 by a hacker to play games. This system developed into the most widely used industrial-strength computer operating system in the world, and ultimately supported the birth of the Internet.

UPS (Uninterruptible Power Supply)—A semi-intelligent, rechargeable battery system that protects a computer from power failures and fluctuations.

user account—The collection of information—such as name, password, group memberships, access privileges, and user rights—stored by NT about a specific network user. User accounts are managed through the User Manager For Domains utility.

User Manager For Domains—The NT administration utility controlling account management, group membership, and security policies for a domain.

user name—The human-friendly name of a user account. The user name is one of the two data items used to log on to NT. NT does not recognize an account by the user name, but rather by the SID.

user profile—The collection of desktop and environmental settings that define the work area of the local computer.

user rights—Settings that define the ability of a user to access a computer or a domain.

users group—Another term for group.

VFAT (Virtual File Allocation Table)—This file system is currently supported by Windows 95, Windows NT 3.51, and Windows NT 4; VFAT provides 32-bit Protected Mode access for file manipulation.

VGA (Video Graphics Array)—A PC display standard of 640×480 pixels, 16 colors, and a 4:3 aspect ratio.

volume set—A disk construct comprised of one or more logical partitions formatted with a single file system.

VPN (Virtual Private Network)—A WAN, provided by a common communications carrier, that works like a private network; however, the backbone of the network is shared with all of the customers in a public network.

WAN (Wide Area Network)—A network that spans geographically distant segments. Often a distance of two or more miles is used to define a WAN. Microsoft, however, considers that any RAS connection establishes a WAN.

Windows NT Workstation—A Microsoft OS product that is a client version of the NT system. It is the same as NT Server, but without the ability to host multiple services and resources for a network.

WINS (Windows Internet Name Service)—A Windows network service used to resolve NetBIOS names to IP addresses.

workgroup—A collection of networked computers that participate in a peer-to-peer relationship.

World Wide Web—An information distribution system hosted on TCP/IP networks. The Web supports text, graphics, and multimedia. The IIS component of NT is a Web server that can distribute Web documents.

write permissions—The ability to create or modify files and directories.

XCOPY—A command-line utility used to copy files and subdirectories while maintaining the directory tree structure.

Index

Order Practice Tests from the
Authors of the *Exam Cram* Series

LANWrights offers diskette copies of practice tests for these MCSE exams:

70-058 Networking Essentials
70-063 Windows 95
70-067 NT Server 4
70-068 NT Server 4 in the Enterprise

70-073 NT Workstation 4
70-059 TCP/IP for NT 4
TBD Exchange Server 5.5*
TBD   IIS 4*

*available Q2/98

Each diskette includes the following:

√ Two practice exams consisting of 50-60 questions, designed to help you prepare for the certification test. One test automates the test that appears in each *Exam Cram* book; the other is new material.

√ Feedback on answers, to help you prepare more thoroughly.

√ Access to the LANWrights Question Exchange, an online set of threaded discussion forums aimed at the topics for each of these books, where you can ask for help and get answers within 72 hours.

Note: These tests are written in HTML and use Java and JavaScript tools, so you must use Navigator 3.02 or Internet Explorer 3.02 or higher.

Fees for practice exam diskettes:

$25 for single diskette
$45 for any two
$65 for any three
$85 for any four

$100 for any five
$115 for any six
$135 for all eight
All amounts are US$

To order, please send a check or money order drawn on a U.S. bank. Please include complete delivery information with your order: Name, Company, Street Address, City, State, Postal Code, Country. Send all orders to LANWrights Exams, P.O. Box 26261, Austin, TX, USA 78755-0261. For orders from Mexico or Canada, please add US$5; for orders outside North America, please add US$10. For expedited delivery, online orders, or other information, please visit www.lanw.com/examcram/order.htm.

Ordering information:

To complete your order for the Practice MCSE Certification Tests, we will need the following ship-to information:

Name

Company

Street Address

City, State

ZIP/Postal Code

Country

Send a request (you can use this page if you wish) and a check or money order drawn on a U.S. bank in $US to:

LANWrights Exam Orders
PO Box 26261
Austin, TX 78755-0261 USA

For orders from Mexico or Canada, add US$5 to your order fee; for orders from locations outside the United States, add US$10 to your fee. All orders will be shipped as soon as funds clear, and will be sent via the U.S. Postal Service, unless other arrangements are made.

For more information, including telephone orders, processing of purchase orders, licensing of practice tests, or expedited shipment, please visit the LANWrights Exam Cram Web page at: **http://www.lanw.com/examcram/order.htm.**

If you would like to receive news about new LANWrights books and products, please provide your email address.

If you have any comments or questions, feel free to email us at **examcram@lanw.com. Thanks for your order!**